GENDER AND CULTURE
A SERIES OF COLUMBIA UNIVERSITY PRESS
Edited by Carolyn G. Heilbrun and Nancy K. Miller

PLOTTING WOMEN

GENDER AND CULTURE

Carolyn G. Heilbrun and Nancy K. Miller, EDITORS

Frida Kahlo, *Self-Portrait with Cropped Hair*.

PLOTTING WOMEN

GENDER AND REPRESENTATION IN MEXICO

Jean Franco

COLUMBIA UNIVERSITY PRESS

NEW YORK

Frida Kahlo, *Self-Portrait with Cropped Hair*
(1940; oil on canvas, 15 3/4″ × 11″),
is reproduced courtesy of Collection, The Museum of Modern Art, New York;
gift of Edgar Kaufman, Jr.
Photograph © 1988 The Museum of Modern Art, New York.

Frida Kahlo, *Moses*
(1944; oil on masonite; 24″ × 30″)
is reproduced courtesy of Marilyn O. Lubetkin.

Stills from Luis Buñuel's *Los olvidados* (1949) are reproduced
courtesy of The Museum of Modern Art/Film Stills Archive.

COLUMBIA UNIVERSITY PRESS
New York
Copyright © 1989 Columbia University Press
All rights reserved

LIBRARY OF CONGRESS CATALOGING-IN-PUBLICATION DATA
Franco, Jean.
Plotting women: gender and representation in Mexico/Jean Franco.
p. cm.—(Gender and culture)
Bibliography: p.
Includes index.
ISBN 0-231-06422-5
ISBN 0-231-06423-3 (pbk.)
1. Mexican literature—Women authors—History and criticism.
2. Women and literature—Mexico—History.
3. Women—Mexico—Intellectual life.
4. Mexico—Civilization.
I. Title. II. Series.
PQ7133.F73 1989
88-23451
860'.9'9287—dc19
CIP

Casebound editions of Columbia University Press books are Smyth-sewn
and are printed on permanent and durable acid-free paper
PRINTED IN THE UNITED STATES OF AMERICA
c 10 9 8 7 6 5 4 3 2 1
p 10 9 8 7 6

*To the memory of Alaíde Foppa, Fantina, Angel Rama,
Joseph Sommers, Marta Traba, and Paco Urondo*

CONTENTS

ACKNOWLEDGMENTS

The origins of *Plotting Women* go back to a project on writing and orally transmitted culture for which I was given a Guggenheim grant. I wish to thank the Guggenheim Foundation for their help on a project whose final version was so widely different from the original proposal. I owe thanks to Kathleen Myers for generously letting me see her dissertation, "Becoming a Nun," to Ruth Lewis for permission to use the Oscar Lewis archives, and to the Archivo General de la Nación in Mexico, which is one of the most congenial of places to study. I thank all those who read the manuscript and offered suggestions—Emilee Bergman, Mary Louise Pratt, Nancy Miller, Beatriz Sarlo, Josefina Ludmer, Kathleen Newman. Elena Urrutia and members of the research seminar on women at the Colegio de México were invariably willing to discuss their ideas with me. Francine Masiello and Tununa Mercado gave me shelter when I needed it. Cynthia Steele and Electa Arenal were generous with material. Special thanks are due to Carlos Monsivais for making *Enamorada* available and for countless helpful suggestions, and to Marilyn O. Lubetkin for permission to use the reproduction of *Moses* by Frida Kahlo.

INTRODUCTION

Plotting Women is about struggles for interpretive power, struggles waged not on the high plane of theory but very often at the margins of canonical genres—in letters and life stories. The scenario, Mexico, seems ex-centric, off center as far as the normative power of the metropolitan nations is concerned. Yet inasmuch as these metaphors—center/periphery, norm/exception, metropolitan/Third World—demonstrate the persistence of hierarchical thinking, a shift of perspective becomes all the more imperative. Indeed, it can be argued that the gendering of subjects in a society such as Mexico challenges the often unexamined assumptions that yoke feminism with bourgeois individualism.[1] It is precisely in those societies that the conflicting claims of national, ethnic, and gender identity have to be confronted. And it is precisely Third World women who have insisted not only that there are differences *between* women but also that there are circumstances in which women's emancipation is bound up with the fate of the larger community.[2]

Although I originally intended *Plotting Women* to be a study of modern women writers in Latin America, I soon found myself facing questions that could not be answered by readings of contemporary texts nor by a bird's-eye view of the entire continent. In the first place, as an English woman writing about Latin America, I wanted to resist any temptation to adopt what Gayatri Spivak

calls the "information retrieval" approach to Third World literature—that is, selecting and recuperating isolated texts which can
then be used as tokens within a different cultural economy.[3] This
is one reason I take the long historical view which makes it possible to understand the different discursive positionings of Woman
within a Mexican society whose history has been marked by dis-
continuity and violence. The idea is not to focus solely on the state's
discourse on women nor to claim an alternative tradition of feminine writing, but rather to trace those moments when dissident
subjects appear in the social text and when the struggle for interpretive power erupts. Just as contemporary critics of Renaissance literature have attempted to reconstruct the dynamic interaction of subjects, domains of discourse, and political constraints
which are no longer part of the modern reader's repertoire, so this
study attempts to constitute a common ground for a feminist understanding of Mexican culture.[4] Indeed, one of the contentions
of *Plotting Women* is that the intervention of modern feminism in
the sphere of public debate demands critical reflection on the differences between cultures and on the diverse configurations of the
struggle for interpretive power.

There are other reasons that make it imperative to include Third
World culture in feminist scholarship. For in studying the very different articulations of gender and subjectivity in societies formed
by conquest and colonization, we confront a problem which has
seldom been posed in modern theories of ideology—that is, the
violent incorporation of a population into "forms of life" which
they can never perceive as organic or natural.[5]

Clearly it is not continuity that is my prime concern but rather
the violent transitions from Aztec empire to colonial New Spain
(a colony that covered the immense area from California to Panama), from colonized New Spain to Independent Mexico, and from
revolutionary Mexico fighting for its autonomy to an increasingly
crisis-ridden society that has undergone violent modernization.
Religion, nationalism, and finally modernization thus constitute
the broad master narratives and symbolic systems that not only
cemented society but plotted women differentially into the social
text. Yet there was always violence involved in the shifts from one
discourse to another—the religious mission of New Spain came
in the wake of conquest and subjugation, and nineteenth- and
twentieth-century nationalism involved civil war and revolution.

Plotting Women begins with the first of these master narratives—that of religion—at its most powerful moment, in seven-

teenth-century New Spain when colonial society was already well established, when the small elite of the white ruling class seemed firmly in control in Mexico City. We have to remember that the conquerors came from a society preoccupied with purity of blood. Having "cleansed" itself by expelling the Jews as it would later expel the Moors, Spain found itself faced with the vast problem of the subjection and conversion of the racially heterogeneous New World. The problem was all the greater in that the indigenous inhabitants, the imported black slaves, and those of mixed blood outnumbered the Spaniards and criollos (the white population born in Mexico). Though the Spaniards attempted to keep the Indian villages separate from the rest of society and decrees forbade Spaniards or castes to reside in Indian villages, nevertheless the mestizo population steadily increased throughout the colonial period. In Mexico City, there was a substantial black population, which caused one seventeenth-century traveler to observe that "Mexico may have one hundred thousand inhabitants, but the majority are blacks and mulattoes."[6]

Within this heterogeneous society, white women were at once privileged and devalued. "If you are to send any merchandise, let it be women, which is the biggest business in this country," wrote a judge to a friend in Seville in 1529.[7] Yet upper-class women at least had the option of entering the convent where they could, on occasion, pursue learning and practice their own form of piety. Under these circumstances the struggle for interpretive power crystallized around certain positions which are by no means irrelevant to contemporary feminist debate, for they center on the question of rationality. This familiar struggle, however, takes on unfamiliar aspects in colonial society given the polemics around the rationality of other marginalized members of society—the indigenous and the black slaves.[8]

In order to secure the purity of boundaries, the Church privileged two locations—the pulpit and the confessional—and two genres of discourse—the sermon and confession—through which a celibate male was authorized to warn, harangue, interrogate, educate, and interpolate the population. This hierarchy debarred all women of whatever color or class from preaching and hence from the centers of learning. In this, Mexico was no different from other Catholic countries. The "natural" weakness of women was the ideological pin that rotated the axis of power, enabling what mattered (what involved continuity and identity) and therefore lay in the male public domain to be separated from the ephemeral and the formless. But in other respects criollo (Hispanic) women lived the ideology of their inferiority in a very different manner from their European counterparts. As members of a minority in a country in which the white elite were in fear of ideological contamination from the suppressed indigenous and black races, they were subject to extreme surveillance and control, at least in urban areas. At the same time, they were dependent on black and indigenous servants whose magic practices they often adopted. Blacks, mulattas, and indigenous women (and men) were perceived to be the dangerous guardians of the erotic arts, all the more perilous since, as servants and slaves, they penetrated the heart of the home.

It was the convent, not the home, however, which produced a distinct form of feminine culture.[9] It was here in the seventeenth century that mysticism became accepted as a form of knowledge in which women were especially adept. Mysticism was a knowledge that bypassed book learning and whose claims to truth had to be judged in part by its emotive effects—levitation, rapture, groans, and sighs. And since feeling was outside textuality, its assessment presented problems. By subordinating women on the grounds of their lesser rationality and relegating them to the domain of feeling, the clergy unwittingly created a space for female empowerment. Celibate women, weakened by fasting, in perpetual pain from the hair shirt and from self-flagellation, prostrated before the glittering images in the Church, living a daily life of dulling routine (the perpetual prayers), found their lives transfigured by moments of extraordinary illumination and by the bizarre behavior of their ungovernable bodies. So it was that visionary women had to be closely watched, their behavior classified and recorded.

The notes, records, and life histories of mystical nuns represent a singular kind of fantasy literature, a literature that was able to gather into itself all the material of dream, vision, and fantasy that had been excluded as "fictional." Novels were prohibited in the New World (which does not mean that they were not read) for fear that their fictions might mislead the indigenous, but there is plenty of evidence to show that the life stories of mystical nuns, especially the paradigmatic story of Saint Theresa of Avila, provided an imaginary repertoire, a language and a structure of behavior much as the Romantic or Gothic novel did in Protestant Europe. Women who were not written as protagonists into the epic narrative of Reconquest and Conquest imagined themselves as heroines; they enjoyed escape fantasies that nearly always involved getting away from their families to go and live as hermits in the desert or to die as martyrs in the land of the infidels. The fact that nuns were encouraged to cut family ties completely and subject themselves to the Church not only intensified their imaginary life but allowed them to plot themselves into a narrative in which self-effacing heroines and the feminized figure of Christ displaced the epic hero and the militant clergy. It should be stressed, however, that mysticism is essentially outside writing, and even outside the spoken word.

If I dwell at length on mysticism, it is because it has been considered the space of the feminine in some contemporary theory, particularly in the French theories that hold that the place of the woman is that which cannot be present in discourse. The problem is, as the example of seventeenth- and eighteenth-century Mexican mystics clearly reveals, that in accepting silence and self-obliteration, the mystics legitimized the institution's separation of male rationality from female feeling and the exclusion of women from the public domains of discourse.

This explains why any attempt made by women to move into the sphere of rationality was met by such hostility—as was the case with Sor Juana Inés de la Cruz. Sor Juana skillfully used every space afforded by courtly and religious discourse. For her, literature became a game of masks that allowed her to assume any identity, to change genders or to become neuter. The freedom, however, was precarious, since at any moment the Church could intervene to censor and control writing. The importance of Sor Juana is that she defended the rationality of women and was able to do so because the slippage between her devalued status as a woman and her empowerment by writing led her to understand gender difference as a social construction, and interpretation as a rationalization of male interests. This is why she separates "true" knowledge from its instrumental use—a major insight, all the more remarkable for the fact that she came to it on her own. In contrast to this masculine rationalization, she counterposed the feminine figure of the Virgin who gave birth to the Word, thus making a woman the matrix of Christian reason.[10] This makes all the more tragic the story of her final years—her capitulation to the clergy, her sacrifice of her books and musical instruments, her renunciation of learning in favor of good works—all of which can be seen as a defeat—and one that was a defeat for all colonial women. Sor Juana could not found a school. She had no disciples. Yet, as

I shall argue, her defense of reason as distinct from patriarchal rationalization was potentially a far more productive path for women than that of the mystic.

Yet it is the mystic and the Virgin in her maternal role that have been priviliged by the French critics Luce Irigaray and Julia Kristeva as female forms of empowerment. Mysticism, says Irigaray, was the "only place in the history of the West in which woman speaks and acts so publicly."[11] The mystic's babble puts her outside common sense and rationality, outside labor value. "She is torn apart in pain, fear, cries, tears, and blood that go beyond any other feeling. Words begin to fail her. She senses something *remains to be said* that resists all speech, that can at best be stammered out." Kristeva, on the other hand, is more interested in the Virgin Mother. She comments that it is "frequently suggested that the flourishing of feminism in the Protestant countries is due, among other things, to the fact that women there are allowed great initiative in social life and ritual. But one wonders if it is not also due to Protestantism's *lacking* some necessary element of the Maternal which in Catholicism has been elaborated with the utmost sophistication by the Jesuits (and which makes Catholicism very difficult to analyze)."[12] Both critics valorize forms of subjectivity that are radically different from bourgeois individualism. On the other hand, in decontextualizing mystical experience and the Virgin Mother in order to align them with the antirational and anti-authoritarian arguments of contemporary criticism, they ignore the very aspects of mysticism that allow it to be successfully recuperated by patriarchy.[13] More importantly, they reject the possibility, so forcefully defended by Sor Juana, of forms of reason that are not mere rationalizations of male authority.

There were other less visible struggles, however, especially those of subaltern women who were driven into that "discontinuous and illegitimate knowledge" which, according to Foucault, constantly comes up against the "claims of a unitary body of theory which would filter, hierarchize and order them in the name of some true knowledge and some arbitrary idea of what constitutes a science and its objects."[14] Here the contested boundaries were between truth and fiction, knowledge and superstition, and it was again writing that policed those boundaries at the other side of which were the motley beliefs of orally transmitted culture. Popular performances and storytelling belonged not to the controlled discursive domains of Palace or Church but to the street life of the cities.[15] Despite the Church's attempts to enclose women in the home, in convents, or in *recogimientos*—that is, houses that took in "marginal women"—prostitutes, women who were separated from their husbands, and orphans—there was still a floating population of unattached women who had to fend for themselves somehow.[16] Some of these were regarded as particularly dangerous by the Church because they directly challenged the power of the clergy and were therefore stigmatized by the Inquisition as "deluded." These women prophesied in public, went into trances, and claimed to have mystical experiences. Unlike those mystical nuns whom the Church encouraged, however, the "deluded" woman was outside the surveillance of the convent, often unmarried, and often eager for publicity. These women used their bodies in virtuoso fashion. They suckled the Child Jesus, regressed into infantile behavior, spoke baby language, and had to be fed as if they were infants; they daubed themselves in menstrual blood, thus *publicly* expressing women's sexuality and even appropriating exclusively male terrains such as the pulpit (see chapter 3).

It is clear that all these struggles—over the claims of intuitive and unverifiable knowledge, over women's right to rationality, over the regulation of women's public behavior—took on their particular character because of the Church's mapping of knowledge and gender under the particular stresses of the colonial situation. With Independence and the secularization of society that occurred in the mid-nineteenth century, when convents were destroyed and the religious orders dispersed, Catholicism ceased to be hegemonic, although it remained an integral and important "life-form," especially for women. At the same time, with the new hegemonic discourse of nationalism, the sites of struggle fundamentally changed. A secular intelligentsia—whose base was the press and the publishing houses—were to become the main force in defining the nation and its future.

Women had played a major role in the Independence movement and this, together with the intense interest of the new intelligentsia in the education of women and children and the proliferation of newspapers and journals for the discussion of ideas, would seem to open the way for the full participation, at least of upper-class women, in cultural and political life. But it was not so. A bleak wind seems to have shriveled up nineteenth-century women's writing—the bleak wind of nationalism. In order to account for this we have to look at woman's place within the signifying system of nationalism that came to be embedded in discursive formations, in educational and judicial institutions, in the spatialization and conduct of everyday life. Nationalism demanded new kinds of subjects invested with authority to define the true and the real. Yet the secular intelligentsia who emerged with Independence were a literary intelligentsia whose primary locus of power was in the periodical press from which base they harangued those who were still infants (i.e., *in-fans*, "without speech"). Because of their inability to develop scientific thought (an obstacle that has nothing to do with their capabilities and everything to do with the dependence of Latin America on the industrialized countries), this secular intelligentsia of necessity concentrated on areas of knowledge that did not require professional training[17]—that is, on culture in the widest sense of the word. What differentiated the Latin American intelligentsia from their European counterparts was that they had to think what others had done, while acting as the vanguard in their own countries. And if they were the vanguard, someone had to be the rearguard—and not only uneducated blacks and the indigenous but also fanatical and superstitious women.

Woman (as opposed to women), however, played an ambiguous role in the construction of national identity. The cosmic Virgin of Guadalupe—a Virgin who is not represented as a mother but rather as the woman of the Apocalypse, crushing the serpent and in possession of the heavens from which she protects her chosen people—was the symbolic icon of criollo nationalism.[18] Yet, in constructing a new nationalism founded on their racial heritage, the intelligentsia were confronted with miscegenation and hence with the impossibility of establishing any pure boundary on the basis of race. The alternative was to convert the racially heterogeneous into the homogeneously modern nation, and since this could not be based on racial homogeneity, then it had to be achieved by a modern education that would mold the different races into one race. At the same time a mythic scapegoat was found for Mexico's dependent status within the modern world in the person of La Malinche, the mistress and interpreter of Cortés.

"It is one of the mysteries of fate," Ignacio Ramírez would say in 1886, *that all nations owe their fall and ignominy to a woman.*"[19] The story of female treachery is particularly necessary in the nationalist epic, especially the epic which has its origin in a conquest and a defeat. Fortunately there was a historical person to fit the bill—Doña Marina, known to the indigenous peoples as Malintzín or La Malinche. As in the cult of the Virgin Mary, the scarcity of textual evidence is no drawback to the growth of myth. What is certain is that she was a much-exchanged woman, born in Nahuatl-speaking territory, given to merchants who took her to Tabasco where she learned Maya and where she was given as a gift (along with other women) to Cortés. She became Cortés' mistress and interpreter, bore him a son, and continued to act as interpreter after being exchanged yet again and given in marriage to one of his captains. In the narrative of the conquest she is the hero's "helper" and takes her place as such in the chronicle written by Bernal Díaz de Castillo; to the indigenous she became identified with the magical power of the Spaniards. The indigenous painted her into the codices (illustrated manuscripts relating the story of the Conquest) as a translator through whose transparent body words like droplets pass from Cortés' mouth into the ears of Moctezuma. She is the medium for conquest. The scarcity of documentation enabled her to become a literary function (the "helper" of the hero story), the medium-translator (traitor) of conquest and the flawed origin (mother) of a nation who would make her the symbol of the schizophrenic split between the European and the indigenous. Writing in 1950, Octavio Paz, in his *The Labyrinth of Solitude,* located the "Mexican disease" precisely in this ambiguous subjectivity of the sons of the Malinche who were shamed by her rape (conquest) and thus forced to reject the feminine in themselves as the devalued, the passive, the mauled and battered, as *la chingada,* the violated, the one who has been screwed over, fucked, and yet is herself the betrayer.[20]

The constitution of Mexican nationalism was a long process that had its roots in the criollo nationalism before Independence and that received a new impetus with the Mexican Revolution of 1910–1917, a revolution in which the peasantry played a major role. The postrevolutionary society was at first dynamized by populist nationalism, whose rhetoric tended to obscure the real nature of the Mexican state as an instrument of capitalist modernization. Between 1917 and 1953, when women were finally given the national vote, the issue of women's emancipation was part of a major campaign against the obscurantism of the Church, and some revolutionary leaders supported emancipation because they saw women's religious "fanaticism" as an obstacle to revolutionary ideology. Supporters of women's emancipation included men like Venustiano Carranza, the first president of postrevolutionary Mexico, and the

governors of Yucatán, General Salvador Alvarado and Felipe
Carrillo Puerto. The latter gave women the right to vote in Yucatán and promoted feminist associations which fought drug abuse
and advocated birth control. Carrillo Puerto believed in free love
and defined marriage as a "voluntary union based on love, for the
purpose of founding a home," and advocated dissolution of marriage when either party wanted out.[21] Yet radical positions on free
love and birth control not only failed to mobilize Mexican women
but did not prevent them from flocking to support Catholic resistance to the militant secular state. When President Calles closed
religious schools in 1926 and ordered priests to register with civil
authorities, women participated in the boycott organized by the
Church and took part in the riots that ensued. When armed conflict broke out (the Cristero movement), Feminine Brigades were
formed. Women hid the man who attempted to kill General Obregón
in November 1927, and when José de León Toral assassinated him
in 1928, Madre María Concepción Acevedo was condemned to
twenty years in the Islas Marías fortress as the intellectual author
of the assassination.[22] On the other hand, women participated as
maestras in the formation of the new societies and were active in
the literacy campaigns. During the presidency of Lázaro Cárdenas
(1934–1940), an official women's organization, the FUPDM (Frente
Único Pro Derechos de la Mujer), was founded.

Even so, official ideology would once again turn to the idealized
patriarchal family which the mass media and cinema were now
able to represent and transmit to a population that literature had
never reached. It should be stressed, however, that the gulf between representations of the family especially in mass culture and
real practices was considerable. And it was this that once again
involved women in bitter struggles for the space in which to record
their story.

Because of the scope of this struggle, the political aspects of which
have been documented by others, I have concentrated on certain
symptomatic situations, and on two women in particular who interrupt the discourse of Messianic nationalism by revealing the
mortal female body that sustains the male hero. The examples are
disparate, however. Antonieta Rivas Mercado, companion of the
Messianic leader José Vasconcelos, puts a bullet into the text and
commits an "inexplicable" suicide. Frida Kahlo uses her mutilated
body to contest a system of representation that still identified
Woman with nature. But the struggle also occurs, though perhaps

less dramatically, within the literary institution and particularly within the genre privileged as the allegory of national formation— the novel. Women writers such as Rosario Castellanos and Elena Garro who attempted to plot women as protagonists in this allegory could not but confront the fact that national identity was essentially masculine identity.

By the time Castellanos and Garro began writing, however, new and powerful forces were at work in Mexico—on the one hand, modernization, which involved the migration of large segments of the population into the cities and across the frontier into the United States; and on the other hand, the growth of a culture industry— particularly cinema and popular literature—which, though at first appropriated by nationalism, was also instrumental in its destabilization.[23]

Plotting Women closes with two essays that focus on different aspects of this situation. The first is an examination of films and ethnographic narrative that capture the moment of transition when new social subjects—delinquents, the lumpen who resist modernizing nationalism—appear on the scene. The second charts the emergence of modern feminism in the arena of public debate. Mexican feminism of the seventies was a middle-class movement, but one which took as its premise the need for alliances with the subaltern classes. This alliance is reflected particularly in the writing of Elena Poniatowska, which I discuss in the final chapter. At the same time, the critique of official nationalism, particularly after 1968, opened a space for women's writing of which they took full advantage; first, to tell their own side of the story of the family romance and, second, to show the articulation of patriarchy and nationalism. Since this is an ongoing process, I confine my discussion to those contemporary texts which intervene in the discussion over feminism's contestatory power within postindustrial society.

It should be clear by this time that *Plotting Women* owes much to Foucault's theories of discourse and to writings such as those of Stallybrass and White (following Mikhail Bakhtin) which deal with the politics and poetics of transgression.[24] But though Foucault's theories help us think of those large unifying bodies of institutionalized knowledge, they do not account for the way that this is inflected by gender representation, nor do they account for particular modes of resistance. Thus, although Foucault's ideas are highly suggestive in discussing the broad process of exclusion and discrimination that occurs within discursive formations and in identifying the domains of discourse and institutional practices that support those formations,[25] there is something missing in his theory which I can best identify by introducing the word "experience"—or, better perhaps, Raymond Williams' "structures of feeling" or Habermas' "life forms."[26] Indeed, Foucault uses experience to account for being able to recognize "something cracked, dully jarring, or dysfunctional in things I saw, in institutions with which I dealt, in my relations with others" and that led him to embark on his work as if it were autobiography.[27] Dissidence generally occurs as a clash of discourses, which is not an abstract dialectic but a lived "noncoincidence." Before the emergence of the feminist movement it was generally experienced by women in serialized fashion, that is, as singular experiences.[28]

Feminist theory has, of course, been centrally preoccupied with questions of subjectivity and dissidence, though over the last decade there has been a marked divergence between what is broadly defined as Anglo-American criticism, with its emphasis on female authorship and its preference for realism,[29] and French theory, with its critique of the unitary subject, identity, and authorship. I do not wish to revive the debate between Anglo-American feminism and French criticism, since this has been exhaustively discussed by Michèle Barrett, Toril Moi, and Alice Jardine,[30] and in any case it is not to my purpose. Rather I wish to emphasize its aftermath, especially as reflected in the collection of essays edited by Teresa de Lauretis, *Feminist Studies: Critical Studies,* in which several contributors, including de Lauretis herself, attempt to formulate new ways of empowering women that do not necessarily assume unitary subjects or the traps of authoritarian attitudes. De Lauretis in particular has tried to ground feminism both as a politics working for change and as an enabling theory.[31] It is precisely the contradictory claims between life practices and textuality, political power and the virtues of marginality, that mark this present and as yet uncrystallized stage in feminist theory.

Yet the specificity of Latin American feminism still remains outside this debate. This specificity surely consists in the entirely original concept of feminist "intellectuals"—that is, of women who become the organic intellectuals of the emergent movements. Among these one would count the Mothers of the Plaza de Mayo and of the Chilean women's movement, and the Guatemalan Rigoberta Menchú.[32] What distinguishes these women from either Anglo-

American or French critics is that they have found ways of aligning gender politics with other forms of struggle without subordinating gender issues and without sacrificing politics.

The essays included in *Plotting Women* belong, perhaps, to the prehistory of this process, for they center on the solitary struggle of isolated women. Again and again, in the course of writing, I was struck by the gulf between the longevity and power of institutions and the fragile life story of marginality. Yet, though the women I speak of are singular and lonely, their actions do not stop with themselves. The lowly Ana de Aramburu charges menstrual blood with symbolic power; Sor Juana multiplies herself until she has as many "I"s as a peacock's tail. Antonieta Rivas Mercado's gun explodes at the very center of Western culture, the Cathedral of Notre Dame de Paris; Frida Kahlo's mutilated body trespasses on the place of the classical nude; and Elena Poniatowska's heroine, Jesusa, seeks an anonymous death in the traitor's spot outside the city walls.

Though lonely, these actions and interventions cannot be considered trivial or isolated. But plotting is an activity that depends on the predictability of the opponent, on secrecy and surprise. In Borges' short story "Tlon, Uqbar, Orbis Tertius," a group of philosophers create a hoax by inventing an imaginary planet complete with language, history, and science. Is not this the way the master narratives of patriarchy have worked?—as inventions which nevertheless powerfully controlled interpretation. Women have long recognized the imaginary nature of the master narrative. Without the power to change the story or to enter into dialogue, they have resorted to subterfuge, digression, disguise, or deathly interruption. The situations described in this book can therefore be described as pre-feminist insofar as feminism presupposes that women are already participants in the public sphere of debate. This makes it all the more important to trace the hidden connections and continuities, the apparently isolated challenges and disruptions of the social narrative which testify to a history of struggle and disruption, though not necessarily of defeat. For in that struggle new social selves are constituted, from the mystical nun to the *ilusa,* from the bohemian woman to the writer.

Rather than attempting to write the history of women and writing in Mexico, I have tried in *Plotting Women* to discover those incandescent moments when different configurations of gender and knowledge are briefly illuminated. Writing of the Mashpee Indians, James Clifford comments, "The Mashpee were trapped by stories that could be told about them." These stories, he goes on to say, are always defined by "technological progress, national and international cultural relations. Are there other possible stories?"[33] This is precisely what *Plotting Women* is intended to suggest: other possible plots, sometimes thwarted, but always recurrent—as they will be, as long as master narratives persist.

PART I

THE RELIGIOUS NARRATIVE

WRITERS IN SPITE OF THEMSELVES: THE MYSTICAL NUNS OF SEVENTEENTH-CENTURY MEXICO

He ordered me to write all the time giving me only an hour of sleep at night; and only that so that I might sleep and all the rest of the time, I had to spend writing. I obeyed him in this and wrote day and night.[1]

In seventeenth-century New Spain, mystical nuns, enraptured by the voice of God and visions of Heaven, were often forced by their confessors to write down these blissful communications. They were not unnaturally reluctant to reproduce in plodding prose their soaring escape from self. Writing gave them no pleasure, for it was only a pale form of recollection carried out as an unpleasant task in the hangover deadness that followed the rapture. Often they showed little interest in their notes or the notes that others made of their behavior. They had no property rights over the records, which were often spirited away by confessors to reappear many years later as the raw material of a biography written by a priest. If all this has a familiar ring, it is because the marginalized have always been used as grist for the mill of writing.[2] Someone is always there—a priest, a psychologist, a sociologist—ready to put halting, disjointed, or apparently irrational babble to productive use.[3]

The motives of the clergy in using this "raw material" were hardly new and certainly no mystery. Not only did they believe that it was important to replenish the store of edifying examples in the fight against heresy, but many were confident that God could not have given such material wealth to the Indies if he had not intended it to be matched by a spiritual bonanza. In the preface to his life of María de Jesús Tomelín, Father Diego de Lemus wrote that New Spain had not only enriched the monarchy with tribute in the form of metals "but had enriched (Spain) with the gold of celestial examples." Don Diego de Victoria Salazar seized on the same metaphor. God had pronounced his *fecit* when he placed mines and treasures in the New World. Now came the *dixit,* for he had placed "this Virgin there in order to communicate His inner speech to her spirit."[4] The priest clearly implies that the woman, like the silver hoarded in the ground, must be mined and made productive, and this task has properly been conferred upon the clergy.

How did this sexual division between raw material and production come about? There were, of course, male mystics—for instance, Don Pedro de Arellano y Sosa who, despite his considerable size, levitated during mass.[5] Yet expressions of religious fervor were commonest among nuns whose potentially disruptive raptures were carefully watched by confessors who had the power to interpret, record, or destroy evidence. Further, in New Spain, where the novel was an impossible genre, "mysticism" was a language of the self and the body that women could speak and, if they were fortunate, could legitimately speak. By reserving scholastic theology and disputation to the clergy, the Church ceded the terrain of feeling to women who, though they were not forbidden to learn, in practice were hindered from doing so in myriad ways; even their reading was controlled.[6] They were not expected to know much Latin, which was the language of the scholar, nor were they allowed to participate in disputation, which was the way learning was refined and propagated. They could not speak on learned matters in public, since they were not allowed to preach. Under these circumstances, it is not surprising that many women bypassed rationality to enter into mystical communion with God, converse directly with the Saints and the Virgin, and obey the dictates of inner voices. These mystical nuns of New Spain did not produce the great literature of Saint John of the Cross or Saint Theresa of Avila; yet the rough vernacular language that often rips through the sanitized prose of hagiography opens up a space beyond the boundaries of the rational, a space of potentially transgressive feminine desire.

But mysticism was also a risky road to take, one that sometimes ended in the secret prisons of the Inquisition,[7] for even clergy who were sympathetic to mystical knowledge—for instance, the Jesuit Miguel Godínez, author of a *Treatise of Mystical Theology*—were wary of "external manifestations" of religious fervor and aspirations to sainthood, especially when they attracted attention. Mysticism was too close to the practices of the heretical *alumbrados* whose satanic pride was fueled by their intoxicating visions.[8] The humility and obedience of mystical nuns were thus constantly put to the test by the confessor and any demonstration of an unhealthy desire for publicity suppressed. Antonio Núñez de Miranda advised all nuns to go about their common tasks without seeking to draw attention to themselves by excessive mortification. Their religious observance should be silent, as was appropriate, for unlike men who were used to arguing their business and were therefore able to formulate prayer in speech, "women had no such skill and were best suited to contemplation."[9]

Yet the more the Church felt its hold over reason threatened by the new scientific thought emerging in Europe, the more it began to look to religious sentiment to revive its flagging spirituality. Even the great princes of the Church like the Archbishop of Mexico, Antonio Aguiar y Seijas, practiced severe forms of self-mortification—fastings, flagellations, the wearing of the hair shirt.[10] The other side of this austerity was considerable "wickedness"—if we are to believe Thomas Gage, who in the early seventeenth century describes the gallants in the coaches, accompanied by trains of blackamoor slaves "in brave and gallant liveries, heavy with gold and silver lace, with silk stockings on their black legs, and roses on their feet, and swords by their sides."[11] Yet an astonishing percentage of the criollo population elected celibacy either by entering a convent or the priesthood—a percentage that defies functional theories of social formation, since this voluntary confinement diminished the number of "white" births. What the enclosure of women ensured was ideological purity, for there were no independent domains of discourse outside the palace and the church, a limitation that affected men as well as women. The difference was that men had authority and the freedom to occupy public space whereas women had not. And this, in turn, helps to explain why the mystical journey that took women out of their enclosure, at least in the imagination, held such attractions for them.

Despite the reservations of some members of the clergy and the potentially transgressive aspects of mysticism, it had strong defenders who claimed that it constituted a higher and more immediate form of knowledge than scholastic theology. Even so, the defenders found it hard to account for the fact that it was a gift more commonly bestowed on women than on men. Miguel Godínez would argue that it was God's way of compensating women and, as they are "not suitable for the priesthood or for apostolic preaching, he honors them in this manner with visions, raptures, and revelations."[12]

The mystic's life tended to be one of constant sensation, however. Not only did God communicate secrets to her but she was transported to distant places (a holy parallel to the flight of witches); she saw visions and hallucinated. When her gratification was at its height she lost all sense of self and of boundaries. Nor did she feel any need to communicate this "melting" to others except when God instructed her to do so. Only external signs—deep sighs, a trancelike state, and bodily marks—revealed to the outside world what was happening. Was this a peculiarly feminine *jouissance* which, as Luce Irigaray maintains, also feminized the men who participated in it?[13] If it was, its subversive potential had in seventeenth-century New Spain become locked into the system. This "feminine" power so threatening to masculine authority could actually be made to energize the Church.

The central figure in all this was the confessor. The confessional, which had grown in importance after the Counter-Reformation of the sixteenth century, was the axis of the Church's power and extended into every aspect of life, even into private thoughts. The confessor was far more than the mediator between the nun and the institutionalized church; he was, in the words of Núñez de Miranda, a "Celestial Oracle" who monopolized "the cure of souls" rather as psychoanalytic societies aspire to do in modern times. Núñez de Miranda expressly warned that nuns should not have recourse to "any other for the governance of the soul, except when ordered otherwise or in case of clear and very serious necessity and obligation."[14] The confessor thus sat firmly in the center of the web that the mystics spun out of mysterious and fragmented surges of feeling, and constituted a veritable panopticon from which every wayward thought was scrutinized. It was he who determined the difference between the clever mimicry of deluded women possessed by the devil and the real thing. He had tried and tested rules at his disposal and practice in close reading of speech and actions.

In the "Opinion" printed at the beginning of Sebastián Santander y Torres' life of María de San Joseph, doctor don Luis de la Peña, examiner of the Inquisition, explained how he determined the holiness of visions. They must not contain anything contrary to the Scriptures, must not contain anything intrinsically evil, must not include novelties never preached by the Church, and so on. The personality of those who had visions was also taken into account. They should not be "frenetic or furious," should be in good bodily shape, and should be silent rather than loquacious. They should not be too old, since in this case the visions might result from senility. The revelations of women were the most dangerous "since women are not only weaker and more susceptible, but are humid, crass, and viscose by nature, and because of this temperament are not only subject to lunatic impressions, but are easily overcome by passions of hatred, love, happiness, and sadness."[15]

Writing was an important instrument in this scrutiny, and there was little in the way of unusual behavior that did not go undocumented by the Church. When María de San Joseph entered the convent of Santa Mónica in Puebla de los Angeles in 1687, her bizarre conduct quickly caught the attention of the Bishop of Puebla, Manuel Fernández de Santa Cruz, who ordered her to write down everything she experienced, "for like a good Shepherd, he wished to know thoroughly the pastures and roads along which this Sheep walked, for it is not easy to bring back the one that goes astray or is lost, if the Shepherd is not an Argos to observe her movements."[16]

Paradoxically, however, the confessional may have encouraged the very transgressions it was designed to control because of the manner in which it regulated subjectivity and because of its insistence on the sexual subject. Certainly when dealing with converted members of the indigenous population, the confessors submitted penitents to a veritable "technology" of sex which must have changed their entire sense of awareness of their own bodies.[17] The listing of carnal sins in confession made the person confessing hypersensitive to every bodily sensation. Fingers became charged with eroticism and one nun could not clasp her own hands for fear of the libidinal discharge this might release.[18] The baroque art of the convents (the art favored by the Jesuit order) was an added stimulus to the imagination. It dramatized both suffering and rapture. Churches were incredibly sumptuous. "The roofs and beams are in many of them all daubed with gold. Many altars have sundry marble pillars, and others are decorated with brazil-wood stays standing one above the other with tabernacles for several saints richly wrought with golden colors, so that twenty thousand ducats is a common price of many of them. These cause admiration in the common sort of people, and admiration brings on daily adoration in them to those glorious spectacles and images of saints."[19] It is little wonder that the mystic's eyes, fixed on the dramatic soaring forms, should close in rapture in order to internalize these vivid representations of gaping wounds, thrusting bodies, and ecstatic eyes. The borderline between rapture and sexual deviation was, however, sometimes blurred. María de San Joseph, who later became a nun in the convent of Santa Mónica, Puebla, for years practiced her own self-mortification and fasting with the help of the maids in her own home. One of her sisters accused her of indecent intimacies and had her servant dismissed, revealing how conscious people were that religious devotions could degenerate into "disgraceful" practices.[20]

But the mystics took other risks. For by privileging a purely subjective experience for which there was often no external evidence, they tended to put themselves outside clerical control. Michel de Certeau has argued that the mystical speech act originated in a willing subject, one who must want and actively seeks the experience. The "I will" of mystical desire constitutes a performative speech act that is felicitous only when the "I" is absorbed into the will of the Other, i.e., of God. "The performative consists in establishing a place (for the subject) and the autonomy of an inwardness (mystical by definition, escaping the labyrinth of social control) rather than establishing a dialogical convention." The "I" in this discourse has no institutional authority beyond that of subjective experience: "Deprived of the legitimacy that would be provided by a social authority (hierarchical, professorial, etc.) the author presents him(her)self in the name of that which speaks through him (or her); the Real (in mystical discourse) or the Word (in prophetic discourse)." Such discourse is not derived from authoritative sources, "although it frequently manifests the same spirit."[21] In this case, the mystic is, strictly speaking, a medium whose awareness of self occurs in moments of deprivation and emptiness from which she longs to escape. There are therefore problems in trying to lay claims to mysticism as a particularly "feminine" language—at least for feminists who are interested in consciousness.

It is primarily the French feminist Luce Irigaray who has celebrated mystical discourse because it subverts the symbolic and because it is outside the logic of the linguistic system: "She [the mystic] is cut to the quick within this shimmering underground fabric that she had always been herself, though she did not know it. And she will never know it or herself *clearly* as she takes fire, in a sweet confusion whose source cannot at first be apprehended. She is torn apart in pain, fear, cries, tears, and blood that go beyond any other feeling."[22] There is no speech for this. "All the words are weak, worn out, unfit to translate anything sensibly." These women, who evade the boundaries of self and identity, Irigaray calls *mystériques*—

which is a neat play on mysticism, the mystery of the dark continent and the masculine designation of this as hysterical speech.

Even so, the assertion that the mystérique has subversive power requires careful examination, for in many ways the mystical nuns were behaving in the way that women were expected to behave. It is not that their speech was essentially feminine but rather that it was *strategically* so. They traded on the unverifiability of their experience and the clergy's conviction that female knowledge was a way of feeling and experiencing rather than abstract thought. María de Jesús Tomelín, for instance, claimed to have seen heaven and purgatory, and there was nobody who could contradict her claim since the journey took place during a trance. This direct access to the supernatural gave the mystical nun the kind of irrefutable authority of the investigative journalist who can always say "I was there." But it was *writing* that finally brought the mystic down from her rapture and back into the web of rationality. Indeed, writing served several purposes at once—it allowed more than one confessor to examine the mystic, ensuring that any new knowledge retrieved in her conversations with God was recorded, and it framed the experience as a case history designed as far as the clergy were concerned, for information retrieval.

The genre adopted for this purpose was often the life story, which had the advantage (for the confessors) of contextualizing these surges of rapture and organizing them as a conversion story. Life stories enabled confessors to judge whether they were dealing with a woman who had been specially singled out over a long period of time to receive God's favors, or whether they were dealing with isolated instances of "delusions." These life stories, often reluctantly recorded or dictated, always using the same old metaphors of fire and thirst, of wounds and blood, are texts in which women experience their surges of feeling as a gift of God, but which the clergy rewrite as didactic texts that illustrate the cardinal virtues.

In order to understand both the production and the control of mystical nuns in New Spain, I shall concentrate on two especially interesting cases—María de Jesús Tomelín (1574–1637) of the convent of Conception of the Virgin Mary in Puebla, whose experiences were recorded by a sister nun, Sor Agustina; and María de San Joseph (1656–1736), an (Augustinian) Recolite nun in the convent of Santa Mónica in Puebla, who wrote and rewrote her life story in lively and homely vernacular. It is now a valuable documentary source since it provides many details of her life before becoming a nun.[23]

Both women had a difficult relationship with members of their family before they were accepted into a religious order. María de Jesús Tomelín's father was so enraged by her rejection of marriage that he attacked her at knife point—no doubt because he was losing a potentially valuable commodity.[24] Though María de San Joseph's vocation was determined from the moment when a lightning bolt struck quite near her when she was playing in the patio, killing one of the farm animals, it took years for her to be accepted into a convent. She was self-taught as a mystic, since for her first thirty years she lived on the family hacienda where it was difficult even to go to confession. Here she invented her own form of self-mortification, using the *cilicios* (hair cloth) for her waist; her sister Leonor taught her how to weave pig hair to wear on her legs and arms. With some satisfaction, she notes how these punishing garments turned her hands black, and how they cut into her skin and sheltered fleas: "I felt them running like ants in the wounds that had been made around my waist, and they almost ate up the bones of my ribs. In the morning there were stinking pools in the place that I had slept and that had come from these stinking wounds."[25] She wore rough clothes and existed on a diet of herbs and tortillas. Her fasting and self-mortification and her shorn head made her look so emaciated that the abbess of Santa Clara refused to take her as a novice because she appeared to be suffering from some illness. Hearing that the Bishop of Puebla, Manuel Fernández de Santa Cruz, was about to found a college for poor and virtuous girls dedicated to Santa Mónica, she repeatedly tried to gain admission and was brutally treated by the bishop (whom we will meet again as he reprimands Sor Juana). In a loud voice from the confessional box he told her stop bothering him, a rebuke that she accepted with exemplary humility.[26] She was finally admitted to the college, which was later made into a Convent of Recoletas (Augustianian), and she eventually became one of the founders of a daughter convent in Oaxaca.

For both these women, rejection of their earthly families was the essential prelude to the mystical life. Even as a child, María de Jesús Tomelín had recognized the Virgin as her true mother.[27] María de San Joseph, though greatly attached to her family, sternly rooted out filial affection.[28] Rather like Britain's empire builders whose public school education trained them to live in remote parts of the world, these women broke affective ties with the family in order to free themselves for their true vocation. They would now live as much as possible in the imagination, in an unreal world, one in which words and silence both were charged with extraordinary intensity. Curiously, and as I show in the final chapter of the book, this same anxiety for separation from the family occurs in modern writing.

Once in the convent, however, the nuns' difficulties only increased, for here they were under the vigilant eyes of other nuns and the confessors. The more "favors" they received, the more the vigilance increased. María de Jesús Tomelín's superior prevented her from taking communion one day, whereupon the Host leapt out of the chalice and flew to the back of the church where María de Jesús was sitting. The convent vicar, Don Antonio de Servantes Carvajal, "seeing that our Lord communicated many secrets and particular favors to the venerable Mother judged convenient that some memory of them should be kept, for whatever Our Lord might decide in the future."[29] From then on she was constantly watched and was personally examined by the expert on mystical knowledge, Miguel de Godínez.[30] Her friend, Agustina de Santa Teresa, was made to write down everything she said, although she suffered torments because of her ambiguous role as the confessor's spy and the faithful servant of María de Jesús. Not surprisingly, she encountered a writing block as soon as she tried to fulfill her duties in accordance with Godínez' instructions. "She erased and tore it up, [her writing] since it appeared that she was not attaining the accuracy she desired."[31] Recognizing that Agustina must have been afraid of incriminating her, María de Jesús assured her that whatever she wrote would be guided by God, saying:

> We are both obeying a command; you that of the Prelates that you show me nothing, and I am obeying the will of God who wished to record the marvels that his infinite goodness has worked in me and is still working in me, the vilest of creatures; so you may proceed from this point onward without fear, since it is God's will that I discover the mercies he has bestowed unto me to you so that you may write them down.[32]

Even so, writing was a continuous source of anxiety. In one of María de Jesús Tomelín's visions, she saw Agustina poised over hell, as if writing was closely associated in her mind with damnation. It was God himself who explained to her that Agustina "is writing for the honor and glory of God, and of the most Holy Mary." This did not altogether calm María de Jesús who then received Our Lord's assurance that, in spite of hell, "this has to be my work which is above everything; and she has to write for the sake of my honor and glory, the love and the sincerity with which I communicate to souls through the intercession of my most Holy Mother must be recorded."[33] On another occasion she saw a black veil covering her writing, the meaning of which was disclosed to her by the Patriarch Saint Joseph. The veil signified that people will attempt "to cover up these writings, but they will not be able to because the Lord will defend them."[34] The vision proved to be prophetic, for a new chaplain, Don Gutierre Bernardo de Queiros, who had decided to have Agustina's notes burned, revoked the order. To the very moment of death, however, María de Jesús was concerned about the fate of the written records, for just before dying she had a vision of Christ sealing the writing and assuring her "I seal the book in which your words are written. I am the seal."[35]

María de San Joseph underwent an even more difficult apprenticeship, since she did not even have the help of another nun but was forced to write constantly on the orders of the convent confessor, who, in turn, was pressured by the Bishop of Puebla, Fernández de Santa Cruz. The latter seems to have been expecting some extraordinary revelation. He urged the confessor to "hurry her, so that she tells the rest of what will happen in the twenty years of the century, because it is not possible that she does not have more; and when she mentions instances of temptation or other interior labors and spiritual assistance from God she should remember to relate them."[36] The Bishop himself sometimes listened to her confessions, "examining her very slowly until he was satisfied," and he gave strict orders that her papers should be carefully preserved.

The obligation to write was a veritable torture for María de San Joseph, especially when confessors treated her in a highhanded manner. For instance, Father Dionisio sometimes made her write all the time, with very little rest, and at other times prevented her from writing and reading altogether. She also showed constant anxiety as to the ultimate destination of what she had written.[37] Fortunately, as in the case of María de Jesús Tomelín, God was able to bring her reassurance, by revealing that writing was a necessary self-mortification, for otherwise she would "feel too much relief and comfort and she was not born to rest in this life."[38] He urges her to go on with her unpleasant task and "to tell [the confessor] to look after the papers that you write, because they are to serve as an example and will be of great profit to souls."[39] On one occasion God's voice came from the altar, reassuring her that "it is all mine and nothing is yours, and if you doubt it, see whether you alone could have made a single step and done what you have done."[40]

Relieved of the responsibility of authorship, María de San Joseph became a prolific writer, leaving twelve volumes of writing, much of it written for her different confessors. And as the confessors were the first readers, the writing betrays the struggle for truthful relation of experience that the act of confession demands but that writing seemed to make even more difficult. For one of them, Fray Plácido de Olmedo, who was her confessor between 1702 and 1709, María de San Joseph wrote a much fuller version of her life, evidently in the hope that it would be useful for other nuns. Apart from her own life story, her works include descriptions of the foundation of the convent in Oaxaca, relations of the virtues of her confessors, her visions, stories of everyday life in the convent, and her work as the instructor of novices. The horror of writing that she had felt at the beginning was completely overcome at the end of her life because, as she wrote, "I felt Our Lord at my side."[41]

The biographies that were later written on the basis of these notes and records turn the extraordinary experiences they record into hagiography.[42] This means that the life is first told chronologically and then broken down and recomposed into sets of anecdotes or examples that illustrate the virtues of poverty, chastity, and obedience. The culminating point of the story is the "good death," usually accompanied by extraordinary signs and miracles. That the composition of such hagiographies illustrates the unequal power of men and women hardly needs comment. In the first place, it was the confessors who controlled the notes and records, deciding not only whether the nuns should continue to write but whether or not the manuscripts should be preserved.[43] The women's experience then became "raw material" which the male author felt free to exploit without fully acknowledging the source. Sor María de Jesús' amanuensis, Agustina de Santa Teresa, for instance, was quoted in extenso by the male biographers, but she was never recognized as an author in her own right. Father Lemus condescendingly observes that "they would have been more to the point had she been more orderly and selective, but since she wrote in order to preserve the records and not to communicate them, she noted things as they occurred without linking the events [sin trabazón *en los sucesos.*]"[44] In other words, Agustina had failed to write a proper narrative. By the time Félix de Santa María wrote his biography of Sor María de Jesús in the eighteenth century, Agustina is mentioned primarily as a disciple and friend of the mystic rather than as her amanuensis.[45]

A similar devaluation of female writing occurred in the case of María de San Joseph. Among the numerous presentations and "approvals" of the published version of Santander y Torres' funeral oration on her death, the Bishop of Antequera praised the deceased for having provided such admirable material for the learned rhetoric of the orator. And, in his "approval" of the publication, Father Miguel de Artoche, assessor of the Holy Office of the Inquisition, observes that the nun's virtues would not have shone so brightly had not the orator publicized them "by lending them the dazzling splendor of his lips."[46] Little wonder that in writing the biography on the basis of her notes, Santander y Torres felt the need to correct María de San Joseph's rude prose and deck it out with erudite references and sententiousness. The difference between the nun's language and that of her biographer is striking, illustrating the gulf between "high" language and lowly vernacular. María de San Joseph wrote in homely language and used her own idiosyncratic spelling. She also went into concrete details of her daily life and life in the convent, remembering, for instance, the time that her sister had been frightened by the devil in the form of a black man and the maid had "put the candle out in her fright."[47]

Clearly Santander y Torres is not interested in such details. He does not record the names of her family members and quotes María de San Joseph directly only on rare occasions. Otherwise he transforms her everyday language into the approved abstract language of hagiography. Confessors and biographers of "mystical" nuns thus acted as publishers, examiners, and editors of material to which the women writers could not claim authorship. In addition to providing raw material for biography, the notes offered clerics valuable insights, placing in their hands a powerful and secret literature, which, if properly used, could enhance their own authority. Even lascivious scenes could serve the faith when properly editorialized. When María de San Joseph writes of being tempted by the devil in the guise of a handsome young man who tries to rape her, Santander y Torres exclaims, "What must her body have suffered being so tightly embraced and pinned down by the arms of the Demon!"[48] Santander y Torres writes a heroic version of what

María de Joseph tells as a very different tale—that of the welling up of subversive thoughts (her insecurity about her vocation and all kinds of lascivious images) which could conveniently be attributed to the devil.[49]

The torment and obstacles the nuns relate reveal, however, that they were well aware of the danger of their words, since they constantly deny authorship. It was only by disappearing as authors and becoming mediums for the voice of God (or targets of the devil) that these women were able to speak of their experiences at all, though this did not always exempt them from the petty jealousies and entrapment in the web of intrigue that were intrinsic ingredients of convent life. More important, this self-effacement and their constant professions of obedience whenever they appeared to be trespassing on alien territory were the preconditions for their flights of the imagination. When they returned with messages from God or the Virgin, they still had to resort to considerable hedging before conveying these messages and "secrets" so that their mystical knowledge should not be seen as undermining in any way the authority of the clergy. María de San Joseph, for instance, ostentatiously abstains from interpretating visions unless she has received clear directions from God, and she believes (in sharp contrast to Sor Juana Inés de la Cruz) that obedience to God and the confessor is a guarantee against error.[50] Her professions of obedience certainly helped to authorize a form of knowledge that bypassed the authority of the confessor.

Yet knowledge it was. According to Santander y Torres, "it is when God gives to the understanding a very sudden intelligence, and to the will a most intense fervor; which he does not give nor communicate except to those souls who are already purged and pure."[51] Women could thus "know" without going through the painful process of book learning. Theological mysteries like transubstantiation presented no problem. For instance, Sor María Magdalena de Lorravaquio Muñoz (1576–1636), a nun who had lived in the same Hieronomite convent that would later house Sor Juana Inés de la Cruz, saw the Holy Trinity in a shell, and, although the three persons were not very distinct,

> in divinity I saw and knew them and in this interior vision my heart seemed to burn in an ardent love and desire to love God by offering my heart to each person of the Holy Trinity, and as I was asking each one to communicate their grace and love in order to love them in return, this vision disappeared, and

once I had returned from this state I was left with many affects
from loving God and with a profound knowledge of my sins.[52]

What is this knowledge? Not an intellectual understanding of
dogma, but a bodily sensation, a burning, the effect of which is
the permanent sense of desire and guilt. Transported in dreams
and visions beyond the narrow confines of the cell, the mystic flew
across time and space, beheld the future, and was allowed to penetrate the secrets of purgatory and of heaven itself, before returning like a homing pigeon to her cell. This flight was the feminine
equivalent of the heroic journey of self-transformation, with the
difference that it met no obstacles and was less a narrative than
an epiphany. The epiphany, however, tended to make the mystic
mute and secretive, for the gap between her feelings and the standard language of mystical experience—metaphors of fire and water,
of burning, melting, of thirst and drinking, which came to her from
Saint Theresa and Saint John of the Cross—was by the seventeenth century fixed and conventional.[53] The hubbub of inner voices
must have seemed out of tune with any available language, for it
left the nuns speechless. When Miguel de Godínez tried to get María
de Jesús to speak of her spiritual life, it was as if she had been
gagged and could not find words for the marvelous works of God.
María de San Joseph was for years unable to confess properly and
could answer her confessor only in monosyllables. She explained
this—and her inability to walk to the choir—as demonic torment.[54] She claimed that the devil prevented her from reciting the
rosary or reading the breviary,[55] and she constantly feared that
speech would be misinterpreted. One of her demonic visions clearly
reveals her self-doubt. She had been chosen as one of the founders
of a daughter-convent in Oaxaca and was immediately tormented
by a sense of her own unworthiness which she externalized as a
horde of demons who exclaimed:

> Oh what a great day we are going to have, when the Bishop
> and the Confessor, realizing your mischief, pronounces you a
> hypocrite, intriguer, and possessed by the devil. Then they will
> put you in a prison, separated from the others and will give
> you the reward that your Revelations merit. There you will
> receive just payment for your Prophecies in fasting and dis-
> cipline.[56]

Such hallucinations were dramatizations of inner speech and offer a clear indication that the nuns themselves were aware that

their experiences were close to sinful delusion and perhaps could not be distinguished from it. One way of resolving the problem was to portray a self split between conflicting (and devilish) spontaneous speech and the will to virtue:

> I can swear that for each virtue that I offered and wished to exercise, I have a Demon who contradicts me and of that I have no doubt. And they force me to say so many and such terrible blasphemies against our Lord that it can only be attributed to the dreadful iniquity of the one who forces me to say them with such violence that I press my teeth together with all my strength because it appears, according to what I feel that my tongue pronounces them of its own accord.[57]

It is in passages such as these that the mystic's mask of effacement slips. Those turbulent desires cannot always be channeled toward God. The words that come spontaneously to the lips are obscene, forbidden, so that she must struggle with the demon to prevent herself from being his ventriloquist as well as God's.

But this also permitted women to speak explicitly of sexuality. María de San Joseph, for instance, graphically describes a vision of demons whose gestures made her body burn. When this troop of demons stopped tormenting her, others came and celebrated the fact that their companions had secured such a triumph and had forced her "to consent and enjoy temptations and impure representations."[58] The devil can thus be put to good use, since he enables María de San Joseph to describe her sexual pleasure while absolving her from responsibility.

The mystical nuns' fears of what they were seeing and doing (backed by terror of the Holy Office of the Inquisition) was thus quite close to the surface. Often, as we have seen, they were reassured only by hearing inner voices, although sometimes their own words took on comforting physical properties. María de Joseph, for instance, saw her words transformed into beams of light,

> with each word that I pronounced a shining light like a star came out of my mouth; I saw this rise upward until it entered Heaven and arrived at the Throne of His Divine Majesty. There it stopped and in this way I saw all my words that I was saying going upward until I ceased praying Vespers.[59]

It was only by *seeing* words reach their proper destination that their purity could be guaranteed. But even more bizarre was the rapture in which her entire body and all its articulations and mus-

cles turned into tongues voicing the "Our Father" and "Ave María"
in chorus and during which she experienced such ecstasy that she
felt that she was in Glory.[60]

For María de San Joseph as for María de Jesús there was a twi-
light zone between inner speech and private conversation, a zone
that was secretive and mysterious. Like the automatic writing of
the surrealists, speech and demonic visions seemed to well up from
dark recesses, taking control of the body, independent of the mind.
Yet the nuns' struggle usually took place in silence and solitude.
They were ridiculed by others nuns and were frequently ill from
fasting and from other afflictions. But they were comforted by
knowing that they had been singled out by God. Paradoxically, in
attempting to annihilate the self, the mystic stood out from the
crowd. For instance, when God grants María de San Joseph a special favor, He tells her, "This and much more I shall give you and
now make your heart bigger to receive the mercies that I am going
to give you." She continues, "then I saw and felt that Our Lord
entered my heart in the form of a fiery flame in such a manner
that he seemed to have united with me and to have become one
with me."[61] Each mystic believed herself to be the unique bride of
God, chosen above all others to receive special gifts and mercies.

Because their knowledge bypassed book learning and was supposedly unmediated, one of their favorite metaphors was that of
drinking. Through the mouth (or the soul's mouth), divine love
and mystical knowledge were imbibed directly without need of
words. María de San Joseph in particular seems to have felt an
intense need to return to this primary form of satisfaction. On one
occasion she describes the "lips of my soul penetrating the Wound
of my Lord and I drank fully his warm blood."[62] The lips are constantly sucking in like those of a greedy child. Our Lord often
invited María de San Joseph to drink him. Thus he told her, "Dear
daughter of my heart and of my María, rest in me or in thyself;
since you thus participate in my sorrows and my bitterness, then
it is right that you participate in my pleasures and glories. Drink,
daughter, fill your mouth from the river of my sweetness and love:
rest in my arms since you are so weary."[63] Whether we call this
jouissance or something else, it is a strange form of self-forgetfulness, one which seems to restore that childlike state of dependency
on the mother as the source of all good, a state before traumatic
separation and a state that is increasingly valorized in modern criticism. Drinking Christ's blood is also a significant reversal of
women's weakness—menstruation. For imbibing pure and holy

blood which gives them eternal life is the reverse of ejecting impure blood in the all-too-human menstrual cycle.

All was not comfort, however. María de San Joseph described being spiritually transported to Christ's side and placing her lips onto his wounds: "What I felt here, I cannot find words to explain: because I felt His Majesty incorporating me into his pain and suffering."[64] The mystic thus fastened on the apertures in the Holy Body in a gesture that is not only erotic but is also a negation of phallocentrism. Her relationship with Christ was essentially an erotic relationship beginning with arousal, stimulated by obsessive fascination with the wounds and openings on the body. Hence it is a fascination with the grotesque rather than the classical body, constituting a carnivalesque inversion of the ideal.

Mystical language is obviously a language of desire, without necessarily implying sublimated sexuality. On the contrary, it seems to focus precisely on those parts of the body least associated with male sexuality. As in profane love, it was the heart that was the symbolic home of joy and suffering. María de San Joseph felt such a burning in the heart that she asked the Lord to relieve the pain of ecstasy, whereupon he obligingly raised two of her ribs so that her heart would have more room.[65] Among the seventeenth-century mystics of New Spain, the heart acquired an existence independent of the rest of the body. María de Jesús' heart left her breast altogether and sang the praises of the Lord in a choir of angels. Our Lord's heart was equally versatile. He once appeared to her as a beautiful body with a heart in place of a head and with a gold key which had a cross imprinted on it. He told her, "this is your heart."[66]

This erotic vocabulary, which has been banalized in popular music where hearts are regularly lost, simply underlines once again the limited language available for affective life. Religion and sexuality jostle one another for possession of language. What is not often recognized, however, is that if mysticism pillaged the courtly love tradition, Romanticism, in turn, deployed strategies long familiar to mystical nuns whose object of desire was always imaginary. And even more recently, philosophers such as Bataille, seeking to subvert a capitalist economy based on exchange find in mystical experience an alternative libidinal economy.[67]

Yet in other respects, the seventeenth-century nuns of New Spain were culture bound; since they were members of a small white population who often felt themselves beleaguered by an indigenous and mulatto population, it is not surprising that their erotic vocabulary should reflect the racial preferences of the time. Beauty and goodness were always blond. In one of María de San Joseph's visions, "the hair [of an emissary from the Virgin] was fine like golden thread, his eyes were very beautiful, his color whiter than snow, his cheeks rosy, and he was wearing scarlet ribbons."[68] Devils, except when disguised as attractive gallants, were often dark or mulatto.[69]

Further, because of the dangerous nature of these visions, the mystic often covered herself by confirming the status quo. She would reel up loose fantasies and bring them firmly back into the dominant ideology. This is strikingly illustrated by a miraculous journey in which María de Jesús Tomelín was transported in a vision through heaven, hell, and purgatory, and then back to heaven again. Under the guidance of her guardian angel she was first transported to a meadow (part of the geography of bliss from the Middle Ages onward). She was then shown the Virgin's heavenly throne, the souls of members of the religious orders, Jesuit saints and martyrs, and some living persons, among them her confessor, for whom she was given a special message. On the return journey, she flew over "wild peaks, sinister caverns, sharp summits, and deep darknesses" until she finally came to an immense burning wasteland full of demons. She passed over this in a great fright for demons called out, "Seize that nun, bring her, wound and torture her." Hands came out of the dark precipice and tried to seize her. From this place, the angels took her to remote "lands of infidels" and places of great luxury and pleasure, "fine groves and agreeable fruit."

Even as she watched, however, the inhabitants were changed from men into animals, and she was able to observe the large number of demons waiting to carry the inhabitants into eternal flames. Finally she reached Christian lands where many people had become ugly because of their sins, but here even the sinners were bathed in clear and resplendent light "which especially surrounded those lands inhabited by Catholics; but that light only surrounded Christian territories and not those countries or climates of the pagans." She flew over purgatory where she saw one of her slaves who had recently died, before returning to the Virgin and our Lord who told her that she had been able to make the journey thanks to the intercession of the Virgin and promised her that she would receive a tunic of light when she went to Heaven. She asked her guardian angel for the meaning of a vision of a place of heavenly delight in which she had seen the nuns of her convent. The angel replied that it was "the narrow space of the cloisters where the nuns of your monastery follow the road of perfection by observing exactly and punctually the precepts of their spouse, and sovereign, Christ, and also the obligations and vows of religion, always punctual in serving God, mortifying themselves in their passions and exercising virtues."[70]

What is interesting about the journey, which one commentator has compared to Dante's *Divine Comedy*,[71] is the contrast between the heady flight of the imagination which transports the immobile nun to distant and supernatural realms and the disappointing closure which confirms María de Jesús's vocation and enclosure in the convent. This is not Sor Juana's dream nor is it the scientific fantasy of a Kepler. Rather it is a dream of mobility that can only take place within the tightly policed borders that every detail of the dream reinforces. The convent is the only safe place on earth.

It is true that if such visions had not confirmed dogma, they would no doubt have been lost to posterity or confined to the archives of the Inquisition. The initial strategy that had enabled María de Jesús to seize control over her words by instructing Agustina how to write—her boldness in communicating messages from God—is not merely attenuated by the male power over writing; her very ecstasies regenerate that power.

This is the ambiguity of the *mystérique* whose transgression may even strengthen the system. Just as modern mass culture uses the seductive power of mythic narrative, so the Church of New Spain admitted into its order the powerful forces that could not altogether be contained within the narrative of fall and redemption. In fixing their gaze on the androgynous and mutilated body of Christ, in placing their mouths over the body's apertures, the mystical nuns appeared to bypass speech and deny the boundaries of gender. But in considering writing as an unnecessary supplement best controlled by the confessor (often, it is true, because there was no alternative), their religious experiences were caught up in the dominant discourse. Indeed, even their raptures, their body language, and their imagery were, by the seventeenth century, a commonplace, forms of behavior that had been unconsciously learned from the lives of women saints and from the oral lore of religiosity.

The mystérique is not entirely effaced, however; her flight and rapture enter into the imaginary repertoire despite all the attempts to sanitize her experiences or, worse, to stigmatize them as the heretical journeys of witches or *ilusas*. Her solitary rapture became part of the repertoire of contemporary novelists, a feature of "magical realism." A character like García Márquez' Remedios la Bella in *One Hundred Years of Solitude* is wafted into the ether on the end of a sheet, like a nun being transported to Heaven. But, in the seventeenth century, such raptures took nuns momentarily out of reach of hierarchical authority. They were important as expressions of female piety. At the same time they confirmed and even reproduced the identification of women with the irrational.[72]

2

SOR JUANA EXPLORES SPACE

The previous chapter described how the grotesque, emaciated body of the mystic, her potentially transgressive feelings and rough language were converted into "legitimate language." Potentially a threat to clerical power, the mystical nuns of New Spain ceded discursive space and did not trespass on male preserves such as the pulpit, the body politic, and publication. Sor Juana Inés de la Cruz, on the other hand, not only trespassed, at least symbolically, on clerical terrain but directly defied the clergy's feminization of ignorance. From a contemporary vantage point, she is thus easily cast in the role of the individual challenging social and literary conventions, although it is doubtful whether modern notions of individuality are applicable to her. The "individual" often fades at crucial moments in Sor Juana's poetry or reappears with unexpected vehemence to mark a distance from the joyless writing of the mystical nuns whose goal was ultimate silence. The irony was that in refusing this "feminine" convention of silence, Sor Juana found herself transformed into a fairground freak, something of a New World marvel who was constantly on show, exhibited, as she herself recognized, as a "rare bird" because she was a woman who wrote on religious matters and a nun who wrote profane poetry.[1]

Both religious and secular authorities saw political advantage in her celebrity. Lima had its Santa Rosa, who was canonized during Sor Juana's lifetime. Mexico had its Virgin of Guadalupe, whose cult was just beginning to flourish in the seventeenth century.[2] In the minds of some clerics at least, Sor Juana was targeted as the New World Saint Theresa, a role she herself persistently rejected. Even so, her renunciation of writing in her final years and her exemplary death provided material for a satisfying conversion story which, according to one commentator, caused even greater astonishment than her "wit, writing, and talents."[3] She was also used as a secular symbol (although this probably caused her less distress than being a candidate for sainthood) by patrons who were anxious to exhibit the spiritual wealth of the New World. Her first collection of poetry, published in Madrid in 1689, bore the title *Inundación Castálida* (i.e., a veritable inundation of the Castalian spring), suggesting an abundant, overflowing talent. On the title page, her poems were described as "the outpourings of the Tenth Muse and Unique Poetess," which "in different meters, idioms, and styles, fertilize various subjects with elegant, subtle, clear, ingenious, and useful verses, offering examples, entertainment, and surprise."[4] This language, worthy of a modern publicity campaign, played on the expectations of peninsular readers for whom everything that came from the New World was disproportionate. In the third edition of her poems, published in Barcelona, a prefatory essay by Father Tineo de Morales refers to her work as a New World "treasure brought by the waves to the Spanish shore," saying that it could only have been produced by someone out of the ordinary, an *Ave rara* "which would only be found in the New World since in the Old, even though they repeat the proverb 'rara Avis en terris,' I doubt very much whether, till now, one has been seen."

Sor Juana was, in fact, singled out from an early age. To begin with she was illegitimate, a fact she did her best to overlook, and one which was unknown to her first biographer, Father Calleja, and was only brought to light in this century.[5] Sor Juana rapidly overcame this inauspicious beginning, however. At an early age she was transported from her native village of Nepantla to Mexico City where she became a protégée of the viceroy's wife, the Countess of Mancera, the Laura of her early poems. In 1669 she entered the convent of Santa Paula of the Hieronomite order, as she explained, to "bury my understanding along with my name," but also because of her absolute rejection of marriage.[6] She did not succeed in burying her name, however, for her fame and notoriety grew. Her conflicts with the clergy, her defense of women's right to learn, her renunciation of profane writing two years before her death, perhaps under pressure from the Church—all these well-known aspects of her life and work have provided a wealth of possible narratives, some of which are even now being transposed to the stage and screen. These contemporary stories have tended to represent Sor Juana as a heroine pitted against a villainous Church, depicting her as a woman fighting a male institution, an artist forced into conformity by official ideology, a woman whose talents were held in check by sexual repression.[7]

The problem with such narratives is that they impose a false unity on a corpus of writing in which the "author's" ownership of writing is always in question and in which publication was beyond the control of the individual. In addition, the discontinuous nature of literary production, the different conventions of the genres in which Sor Juana wrote, and the inevitable distancing of the empirical "I" from the "I" that frames the utterance make any attempt to trace the "radiography" of her soul a hazardous prospect. Indeed, the corpus of Sor Juana's work is formed by a number of discrete and often very different interventions in the "language games" of her time. This Wittgensteinian term is singularly appropriate for Sor Juana's "moves" within different genres.[8] At the same time, these games are played according to rules and within symbolic systems that are located within institutions. We therefore need a concept such as "discursive practice" or "discursive domain" to account for the stabilization of discourse and the deployment of particular symbolic constellations to maintain power.[9] The resourcefulness of Sor Juana in finding ways to destabilize such constellations, especially when they involved the "natural" association of women with ignorance and men with learning, is extraordinary, ranging from the camouflage of allegory, the disguise of parody, mimicry of what was accepted as feminine discourse (obeisance, self-denigration), to anonymity—and the reverse—the foregrounding of a gendered author.

How can we grasp these different interventions without turning them once again into an exemplary "master narrative"? In the first place, it is important to situate the genres in which these different tactics are employed within two broad discursive domains in which the symbolic repertoires of the society of New Spain were at work. In colonial New Spain the domains of discourse were constituted around the viceregal court and the Church, which were never entirely separate since courtly relations were apt to be transcoded into the religious—Sor Juana describes herself as "sacrificing" at

the altar of the divine Countess of Paredes—and the religious was
transcoded into the courtly as, for instance, in her discussions of
Christ's "courtly" behavior—his finesse (or *fineza*).[10] If I refer to
"domains of discourse" rather than the more familiar Foucauldian
term "discursive practices," it is because I wish to stress not only
institutional affiliations but the symbolic importance that attaches
to certain spaces—in this case, the palace and the convent—and
the allegorical "bodies" (personified courtly virtues or personified
theological virtues) with which they were associated.[11] In England
and in France at this time, new domains of discourse had come
into being around the marketplace and the printing shop. Literature was gradually emerging as one such domain independent of
court and Church. In New Spain, on the contrary, there was as
yet no possibility of a literature that was not closely bound to courtly
or religious patronage.

THE PALACE AS A DOMAIN OF DISCOURSE

The seventeenth-century viceregal court was instrumental in
socializing children and adolescents and setting standards of
decorum and behavior. For women, it was a relatively free space
between the father-dominated parental home and the husband-
dominated marriage. This intermediate stage of court life provided
the model for the theatrical space of Sor Juana's two secular
plays, *Los empeños de una casa* (The Pledges of a House) and
Amor es más laberinto (Love is a Greater Labyrinth).[12] Although
these plays faithfully reflect the conventions of Spanish Golden
Age theater, nevertheless, as is often the case in Sor Juana's work,
they mimic the convention to the point where its arbitrariness becomes visible.

In Golden Age Spanish drama it is male honor that is the predominant concern; in Sor Juana's theater, the predominant concern is the confusion and misrecognition brought about by the necessity of choice. The house becomes a space of disguise,
transvestism, play, and riddles before the final decision when all
will be resolved by matrimony. Yet this space of uncertainty is
always one of distress and dislocation both in her plays and in
many of her poems, perhaps because to be without an "estate" in
colonial New Spain was to be exposed, to be a nonperson.[13] More-

over, the choice for criollo women lay between two highly controlled states—matrimony and the convent—so it is not surprising that in her plays and in many of her sonnets a choice between equally balanced alternatives (and often equally undesirable alternatives) can only be made by an arbitrary act of will.[14]

A deconstructive reading of Sor Juana's moments of indecision would seem to be indicated, especially as the leap into decision is nearly always represented as mortal (like that of Phaeton). It was the palace, however, that provided her with a model both for the theatrical space of "plotting" and "designing" and on a more abstract level for the playful mimicry of choice, although the language and practices of courtly behavior disguised the crude practicalities behind the exchange of women. The values of which her poetry and theater speak are, in consequence, distinctly foreign to our understanding of psychology and often do violence to that understanding. Freud's oedipal theater transposed the struggle for tribal succession into the heart of the modern bourgeois family. The aristocratic values that compete in Sor Juana's *loas* (sketches performed before religious and secular plays) include *merecimiento, obsequio, fortuna, fineza, acaso*—deserving, graciousness, fortune, finesse, and chance—notions as alien to us as sibling rivalry, fear of castration, and sublimation would have been to the seventeenth century.[15] Not only did these values permeate Sor Juana's writing, but in her poetry she used court genres such as games, riddles, amorous contests, dances; and she often referred to court rituals, carefully observing conventions of hierarchy and distance and appropriate homage. Yet even the fact that women might have enjoyed a fleeting superiority at court, the ability to choose (even if only in play) and to refuse, could hardly compensate for the harsh realities of the marriage market and the Church's subordination of women in a hierarchy that made the pursuit of truth and knowledge a masculine occupation.

THE RELIGIOUS DOMAIN

Sor Juana was to give many reasons for entering the convent, but all of them add up to the fact that the cell was preferable to marriage, learning a higher goal than bearing children. She contrived to enter the convent without relinquishing her connections to the court, but she would find a substantially different grid within this domain of discourse, one that defined learning as masculine and mystical knowledge (or hysteria) as feminine. This separation was reinforced by the institutional rules of the Church. Women could not preach or administer the sacraments and therefore there was no imperative for them to learn. Writing by women, even by holy women, was treated with suspicion. A fanciful biography of the Virgin written by the Spanish nun María de Agreda was published with a long *apologia* by a Father Samaniego who felt obliged to cite precedents for this unusual female authorship, and this despite the fact that María de Agreda had attempted to deny any authorship by claiming that the biography had been dictated to her by the Virgin.[16] It was not even thought necessary for nuns to read sacred texts, although one Mexican authority, Father Juan Díaz de Arce, had in the sixteenth century suggested that learning was desirable in members of the religious orders and was necessary in parents for the pious instruction of their children.[17] But the Jesuit confessor Antonio Núñez de Miranda, who more than anyone had wanted to save Sor Juana (and the males who were attracted to her) by having her enter a convent, believed that nuns should know only enough to help them understand the offices.[18]

Saint Paul's injunction that women should be silent in church was interpreted in many ways, most of them unfavorable to women.[19] Its narrowest interpretation was simply that they should not preach, but there were many who interpreted it as meaning that women should not speak on religious matters or read sacred books. Confessors both encouraged and tightly controlled the writing of nuns, often confiscating and hiding their notes on mystical experience. Nuns were naturally enough influenced by this control and many held writing in suspicion. Sor Juana mentioned a superior who thought writing to be "a thing for the Inquisition."[20] Other nuns criticized Sor Juana's handwriting because it resembled that of a man and was therefore an indication of her transgression of boundaries.[21]

THE NEUTER

Sor Juana's relationship to these domains of discourse—court and Church—was not, however, overtly transgressive. She did not practice a carnivalesque inversion of low and high, nor offer a grotesque body in defiance of the classical body of the state, nor did she cross those boundaries of signification which would have meant falling into heresy or the babble of the *ilusas* (see chapter 3). In fact, in one respect, she followed no consistent path at all but rather, opportunistically, took advantage of the moves that were open to her within the patronage of court and Church. In these interventions she sometimes drew attention to the fact that she was a woman; at other times she deployed an impersonal subject or adopted a male persona.[22] Further, living in a convent did not prevent her from engaging in activities that belonged to the public sphere. For instance, in 1680 she was commissioned by the cathedral authorities to design a triumphal arch for the viceroy's entry into Mexico City, and in her explanation of the allegorical paintings, she took care to draw attention to the fact that the arch was designed by a woman. She appropriated the space of disputation in her refutation (known as the *Carta Atenagórica*), of a sermon by Father Vieira, emphasizing the fact that the opponent's position was occupied by a woman (OC, 4:435). In her plays she borrowed the discourse of students and mimicked black, indigenous, and regional speech, thus acquiring a symbolic mobility that enabled her to change her gender, class, and race. Sor Juana's "voices" are multiple and sometimes they fade into the convention itself—into the sacred language of the Bible in parts of her religious play *El Divino Narciso* (The Divine Narcissus), and in her religious exercises.[23] Nevertheless each of these different positions of enunciation constitutes a move within a particular set of rules and frequently it is a destabilizing move—either because the enunciating and gendered voice mimics the conventions to the point of parody, or because it takes gender differentiation out of the rules of the game, thus untying the apparently natural association of the male with power.

These various interventions nevertheless suggest something more than opportunism. They suggest a problem around the constitution of women's subjectivity and around constituting woman as an authoring subject, especially when the authoring was in the domain of religion. Because certain discourses, for instance the sermon, were authorized only when spoken by qualified subjects, Sor Juana was constantly forced to seek alternative forms of authorization (for instance, obedience to the command of a superior) or to deploy disguises. The fictionalization of the "I" and the system of representation that worked through allegorical "characters" were necessary masks.

Both mimicry and allegory are forms of concealment, the first being, according to Luce Irigaray, typically a woman's ploy, an attempt

> to try and recover the place of exploitation by discourse, without allowing *herself* to be simply reduced to it. It means to resubmit herself . . . to ideas about herself that are elaborated in/by a masculine logic, but so as to make "visible," by an effect of playful repetition, what was supposed to remain invisible: the cover-up of a possible operation of the feminine in language. It also means "to unveil" the fact that if women are such good mimics, it is because they are not simply reabsorbed in this function. *They also remain elsewhere.*[24]

Yet, as I have already suggested, Sor Juana was not interested in the feminine in language so long as that feminine was a mystical babble, just as she was not interested in simply inverting power relations. Her procedure can perhaps be described as an *écart*, a sidestepping that produced a new kind of subject.

One of her instruments was allegory, although allegory itself serves a double function in her work, being intended both to make visible matters of faith which otherwise would be too abstract and to conceal certain themes from the vulgar as the Egyptians had done, out of reverence for the gods and so as not to vulgarize their mystery to common and ignorant people.[25] More importantly, allegory allowed apparently disparate discourses to be linked by the operation of the intellect while admitting their disparity.[26] In her dramatic works personified abstractions often "resolve" problematic ideological areas—such as the use of force during the Conquest and the conversion of the indigenous—or elucidate difficult matters of dogma.[27]

The ingenious and often strained comparison between pagan mythology and Christian plot is exemplified in the religious play *El Divino Narciso,* which transposes the story of the passion and the transubstantiation of Christ in the Host into the myth of Narcissus and Echo. Yet it could not have escaped Sor Juana's notice that the allegorical procedures of concealing matters that the reader must decipher through the play of resemblance was not unlike the role that she assigned to the creator of all things. For instance, in her *Respuesta a Sor Filotea de la Cruz* (Response to Sor Filotea), she demonstrates that very different disciplines are in reality interconnected. Knowledge consists of revealing the "variations and hidden links—which their Author put in this universal chain—in such a manner that apparently they correspond and are linked with admirable unity and harmony. . . . Everything comes from God who is at once the center and the circumference from whom comes and to whom goes all created lines."[28]

Like Athanasius Kircher, a Jesuit philosopher whom she greatly admired,[29] Sor Juana found the world to be a "marvelous compendium of analogies," a labyrinth "through which the philosopher guided as if by Ariadne's thread can be admitted without danger into the penetration of created nature." Because the soul cannot have access to unmediated knowledge of the divine, it must "take the indirect route, allowing itself to be guided by the indications furnished in the symbolic language of things."[30] Knowledge meant assembling and ordering elements, according to the laws of *convenientia, aemulatio,* analogy and sympathy, of a virtually inexhaustible yet replete universe.[31] The poetics that corresponded to this philosophy was "ingenuity," a metaphoric yoking of incompatible elements which allowed the poet to reveal not only his wit but also the intricate concatenations that were God's signature on apparently discrete phenomena.[32] Such a poetics also implied the heretical notion that the poet was god-like. Hence the need to find digressive paths that avoided both the babble of the possessed mystic and demiurgic creativity.

DIGRESSION AND TRANSGRESSION

This poetics, whose classic formulation is to be found in the Spanish theorist Baltasar Gracián, suggests an author made in the likeness of God, a position that would certainly have been a difficult one for a woman to assume. The nearest Sor Juana comes to "authoring" in this sense is in her allegorical poem *Primero Sueño,* a poem that according to her *Respuesta a Sor Filotea* was the only work she had not written on command or outside the patronage system. Although the poem alludes to and imitates the style of the *Soledades* of the Spanish poet Luis Góngora, and although contemporaries recognized this affiliation, Sor Juana breaks with this "father" in significant ways. In Góngora's poem, the protagonist is a male pilgrim. Sor Juana's poem is motivated by an ungendered soul that is not superior to creation but subject to its laws.[33] Whereas Góngora's poem liberates literature by putting religion in parentheses, Sor Juana's poem, written under greater constraints, has to dissimulate the secular process of production, representing the work as the involuntary (and God-given) effect of fantasy. This dissimulation and simulation point precisely to Sor Juana's problem of authorship, her attempt to establish a "neuter."

Sor Juana frequently claimed that as a nun she was no longer a woman, that "souls ignore distance and sex," that her body is "neutral or abstract in so far as it is the repository of the Soul,"[34] but it is in this long philosophical poem that she makes her most serious attempt to speak in the space of the neutral subject she calls "soul." This soul does not correspond to an unconscious, nor is it permanently separated from body and time, but rather it is a function of abstract thought, which can only occur when mind is freed from "self." In Protestant England, John Milton would describe a similar process of abstraction:

> What Worlds, or what vast regions hold
> The Immortal mind that hath foresook
> Her mansion in this fleshly nook.[35]

For Sor Juana's soul this liberation is fleeting. The soul momentarily feels the delirum of space—"joyful yet suspended, suspended and proud"—but must beat a "cowardly" retreat before the fearful prospect of equalling God.

The *Primero Sueño* is usually read as the flight of this soul that has been released from its bodily impediments by sleep, its attempt to attain absolute knowledge of the world through intuitive panoptic ("Platonic") vision and, when this fails, its attempt to attain the same end by orderly progression through the Aristotelian categories. The second search is halted because the soul cannot understand the simplest phenomenon of nature although its will to knowledge persists. With daylight and the awakening of the self, the shadowy inner world of disembodied fantasy dissolves in the "more certain" light of day.

This admittedly schematic summary suggests a disparity between the will to knowledge that is all too close to Satanic pride and the safer road that allows celebration of creation without transgression. It is, however, a mistake to insist too much on the poem's narrative cohesion. For it is possible that the "story" of the poem is not a story at all, that it is like the villa of Triste-le-Roy in Borges' story "Death and the Compass," whose interior seems immense because of mirrors which incessantly reflect its symmetrical rooms.

Like the villa of Triste-le-Roy, Sor Juana's poem is obsessively symmetrical. The progressive onset of night at the beginning of the poem is mirrored in reverse at the end when night disappears and the sun comes out. At the same time the troping is differently nuanced as the soul enters the field of light or darkness. Light and dark alternatively reveal and conceal images. Neither light nor dark have a stable, Manichean set of connotations. Though night brings out the forces of transgression, it also allows fantasy (like a lighthouse) to illuminate the mind. At the end of the poem this source of powerful illumination gives way to another image—that of a magic lantern on which shadows flicker in an unsatisfactory reflection of reality. Thus light sometimes signifies illumination but at other times confusion and bedazzlement. Night brings out transgression but also represents the secrecy necessary in any approach to the sacred.

Light and dark, revelation and secrecy, enlightenment and confusion, melancholy and joy suggest a binary system. Yet the poem also has its triadic patterns—first the pyramid of darkness that rises from the earth, then the rising of the Moon identified as the triform goddess (as Luna related to heaven, Diana related to earth, and Persephone related to the underworld). The three-sided pyramids of Memphis are analogies of the structure of the soul divided into understanding, intellect, and spirit. The cosmos is divided into heaven, earth, and water, and living creatures into the angelic, the animal, and man, who links the heavenly and the earthy spheres; all significance depends on the Trinity and the union of God with his created world through the passion and the Eucharist. Finally there is also a four-fold pattern consisting of the four laws of resemblance—analogy, sympathy, contiguity, and emulation— that knits together a heterogeneous archive that includes the wonders of the ancient world, natural phenomena like Mount Olympus, the animal and vegetable worlds, optics, pharmaceutics, geometry and logic, the Platonic and the Aristotelian, the Incarnation, pagan mythology, the body and its humors, and so on.

The reader, like the protagonist of "Death and the Compass," easily gets lost in the play of symmetries, especially as the soul's flight is continually halted by long digressions, metaphorical paraphrase, and hyperbaton (transgression) which shifts the syntactical flow. These digressions form plots within a plot, setting up contrasts and similarities across the grain of the diegesis. Digression also permits the poem to wander into the byways of knowledge, commenting on the sympathies and antipathies of Galeno's science, the great chain of being, the diversity of languages that resulted from the punishment of those who built the Tower of Babel, and the multiple significances of the pyramids of Memphis. I want to trace just one of these digressive clusters—a group of mythological figures, three of whom appear at the beginning of the poem and three at the end.[36]

Although Sor Juana's esoteric references help to separate the "incompetent" reader from those who can penetrate the darker purposes of allegory, they also allow her to smuggle into the poem two opposing views of poetics—a poetics based on transgression of the sacred, which is therefore to be avoided, and an ethical humanistic poetics. Both are presented in the guise of mythological figures, the first group being associated with darkness and the latter group with light. At the beginning of the poem, as night falls and the moon appears, the birds of night emerge as allegories of this negative poetics. The first is Nictimene, who was transformed into an owl after committing the sin of incest and who now drinks the oil from the votive lamps dedicated to Minerva, goddess of wisdom. The oil in these votive lamps has been produced by the arduous labor of others. Sor Juana suggests that one form of transgression is to steal the knowledge/labor of others or to feed on the divine oil without having labored for it—an emphasis that might well escape the attention of ignorant clergy and witless mystics who are guilty precisely of this sin. With Nictimine emerge the daughters of Minyas, transformed into bats as a punishment for weaving stories instead of respecting the cult of Bacchus, thus underlining the point that art and knowledge are not simply diversions. Finally appears Ascalaphus, also transformed into an owl. Ascalaphus had informed on Persephone when she ate pomegranate seeds; he thus prevented her from returning to her mother Ceres and forced her to spend six months of the year in Hades. Ascalaphus' information had allowed death to triumph over life.

The metamorphosized transgressors not only appear as subjects of lengthy paraphrase but are also rhetorical "emphases." In classical rhetoric, "emphasis" is somewhat akin to dramatic irony, and depends on dividing the public, as I have already indicated, into those who are expected to understand and those who cannot. To "emphasize" a phrase means that the speaker is hiding the meaning from one group of listeners and underlining it for another. It is thus an ideal trope to be used by a poet who wishes to separate her public into those who will pick up the clue and those who will not. The former could be expected to understand that the birds are linked by a common crime of sacrilege, not only against God but against true art, which must not be stolen or used merely for entertainment or for malicious purposes.

Since the poem is symmetrically constructed, the reader now expects to find this negative poetics balanced by a positive one. And indeed there are three mythological figures poised at the threshold of daylight: Arethusa, Venus, and Phaeton. Unlike the night figures whose diegetic function is merely descriptive, these three illustrate the limitations of the human mind. The stream, Arethusa, and Venus—represented in the poem by her emblem, a rose—are intended to show that even the simplest things are beyond human understanding. Phaeton, who had tried to drive the sun's chariot, illustrates the daring and dangers of the will to knowledge. Yet because all three figures appear in prolix digressions that introduce secondary matter apparently irrelevant to the main argument, they indicate something beyond a purely diegetic function. They are *écarts,* opportunities to digress from the masculinist assertion of truth and from mystical knowledge.

Let me illustrate this with the example of the stream, which metaphorically and literally digresses. The passage is followed by my rough translation:

> quien de la fuente no alcanzó risueña
> el ignorado modo
> con que el curso dirige cristalino
> deteniendo en ambages su camino
> —los horrorosos senos
> de Plutón, las cavernas pavorosas
> del abismo tremendo,
> las campanas hermosas,
> los Elíseos amenos
> tálamo ya de su triforme esposa,
> clara pesquisidora registrando
> (útil curiosidad, aunque prolija,
> que de su no cobrada bella hija
> noticia cierta dió a la rubia Diosa,
> cuando montes y selvas trastornando,
> cuando prados y bosques inquiriendo,
> su vida iba buscando
> y del dolor su vida iba perdiendo)—;

The one [i.e., Sor Juana's mind] who could not discover the secret methods by which the smiling stream directs its crystalline path, its progress slowed by its digressions—into the horrid breast of Pluto, the fearful caverns of that terrible abyss, across the beautiful meadow, the pleasant Elysian field, the marriage bed of his three-formed spouse—a pure observant seeker [i.e., the stream that is also the nymph Arethusa] whose useful—if impertinent—curiosity brought certain news of her beautiful sequestered daughter to the fair Goddess [Ceres] who, combing mountains and wilderness, seeking in meadows and woods, searched for her life [her daughter] while losing life through sorrow . . .

Arethusa's story allows Sor Juana to mine a rich vein of allusion. This nymph had been transformed into a stream by Diana when her virtue was threatened by the river god Alpheus, who then tried to mingle his waters with hers. Diana comes to the rescue by opening a secret passage under the earth and sea where the waters disappeared before rising again in Syracuse. In the course of her journey Arethusa penetrates the realm of Pluto, where she meets the sequestered Persephone; returning to the surface, she communicates this news to Ceres (the Magna Mater also identified with Isis, and hence with the Egyptian god of silence, Harpocrites, who had appeared at the beginning of the poem to warn of the need for secrecy).[37]

But the myth is also a poetics. Chaste Arethusa (like chaste Sor Juana) uses digression to cross boundaries (between the earth and the underworld), enabling nature to be redeemed through Persephone's resurrection.

Critics have rarely commented on this "digression" which (neutral soul notwithstanding) introduces a feminine form of creative redemption. It is especially forceful when compared with the hedging around the other two mythological figures of this part of the poem—Venus and Phaeton—both of whom have to be separated from their "bad" associations—Venus from feminine vanity and Phaeton from hubris—before they can stand for the positive virtues of style and poetic ambition.[38]

Phaeton's mortal leap is, however, significant in another respect; it counterbalances the example of Arethusa and allows Sor Juana to comment on a favorite figure of *culterano* poetry whose pure aesthetics she wished to combat in favor of an ethical vision. Phaeton, who had tried to prove himself the legitimate son of his father, Apollo, god of knowledge and poetry, by guiding the sun's chariot and whose daring had nearly brought about the destruction of the world, was a figure for poetic ambition. A Spanish poem on the subject by the ill-fated Count Villamediana (who was assassinated) was regarded by Góngora and others as something of a manifesto of *culterano* poetics. Daring, in Villamediana's view, overcomes death and wrests secular immortality for the poet who is prepared to take the risk.[39]

But though Sor Juana lavishes praise on Phaeton, she is also aware of the dangers of the myth. Significantly, her attempt to control meaning leads her to introduce the first person pronoun—the only place in the poem except for the last line where there is an "I." The "heroic boy" and "proud driver of the blazing chariot," whose spirit was fired by "rare, lofty if unhappy ambition," is presented not only as a deterrant but as exemplary. "Neither the watery tomb nor the lightning rod will change the intention of that arrogant soul who scorns such warnings and steadfastly immortalizes his name in his own destruction." It is just at this point that Sor Juana uses the first person pronoun as an emphasis. "Once Phaeton had trodden the open paths to daring; there is no punishment enough to prevent a second attempt (the second ambition, *I say*)." This innocuous "I say" has the effect of introducing a subjectivity that has been occluded in the rest of the poem and only reemerges at the end. Why the need for such emphasis? Perhaps because she had turned to the dangerous subject of secular immortality. The author's emphasis draws attention to herself as the subject behind the soul's flight, the master mechanic who had modeled a world of resemblances and disguised it as a landscape of ruins.

Sor Juana takes care, however, to emphasize that Phaeton's example does not apply to everyone and warns that punishment for daring should never be made public and that authorities should even pretend ignorance of it so that it will not be publicized. This curious and tortuous caveat suggests that Sor Juana wished to salvage the will to knowledge while recognizing the dangerous lure of secular immortality. Classical myth is useful for camouflaging her ambition, but it is also treacherous because polysemous. The correct reading (that no threat can divert the noble soul's ambition) can only be guaranteed by authorial intervention. The poem uses the ungendered soul to mask the subtle distinction between legitimate and illegitimate ambitions, between aspirations to be godlike and the dynamic, intrepid will necessary to acquire knowledge, while at the same time juxtaposing this daring with Arethusa's ethical curiosity. The inquiring soul is not so much neutral as a combination of feminine and masculine.

The paradox of Sor Juana's exploration of space is that it must appear to be undertaken in sleep, although it is written by an author who is awake and who, like God in her universe, fabricates an intricate labyrinth that conceals and reveals. Her sleep is not a dark night of the soul but the translation of the self into the realm of abstraction. Her exploration ends "naturally" with the coming of dawn and an awakening consciousness of the body and of time.[40] Far from being disappointed, the sleeper awakes to a joyful world. The sun, "restoring to the exterior senses their complete operations and illuminating the World with a more certain light," replaces the shadows. The gendered "I" that now awakens is the author of the poem who is left only with the memory of a flight of fantasy. But that memory will reshape and celebrate a luminous Utopian landscape, a chiaroscuro in which light falls on a redeemed nature whose meaning is given by the Incarnation. It is as if, in Walter Benjamin's words, Sor Juana's subjectivity, "like an angel falling in the depths . . . is brought back by allegories, and is held fast in heaven in God, by *ponderación misteriosa*."[41]

Sor Juana uses allegory not to camouflage heretical leanings but to provide a Utopian space for a knowledge and a poetics that can "digress" from rigid gender hierarchies. Both knowledge and poetics are purposive efforts to connect the seemingly discrete elements of the archive. The breakdown of allegory, those moments in the poem when the poet has to intervene in order to ensure a correct reading, reveals the fact that its Utopian space where knowledge and poetry meet is always susceptible to destruction by tendentious readings. It is precisely the overt presence of this controlling hand that signals the fragility of the space that it sets out to protect.

TRESPASSING IN THE PULPIT

Though in *Primero Sueño* Sor Juana explores authorship, ambition, and ethics under the guise of a neutral subject, in poems written without the camouflage of allegory she fell back on the age-old tactics of feigned humility. She always maintained that she wrote only out of obedience to her superiors whether lay or ecclesiastic. In the introductory poem of the verses published under the patronage of the Countess of Paredes, the speaker refuses to claim ownership of the poems, which by right belonged to the countess as her feudal superior.[42] She often employed the common female tactic of protesting her inferiority the better to show her superiority. When the Cathedral commissioned her to design the arch for the entry into Mexico of the Marqués de la Laguna in 1680, she stressed the fact that her patrons were perhaps relying on the fact that "her lack of learning and her soft nature" would be "more effective in soliciting favors."[43] This retreat into womanhood is, of course, a rhetorical stratagem intended to highlight the learned and witty text, "Neptuno Alegórico" (The Allegorical Neptune), that follows. She proclaims that "this is written by an ignorant woman," but that declaration only serves to foreground every erudite reference and every Latin quotation.

But what was playful to the palace verged on insolence when used in writing on religious matters—on truth as opposed to fiction—for when the slave, protesting her humility and unworthiness, outwits the master, the latter is forced into a dangerous acknowledgement of defeat that puts hierarchical authority at risk.

Three crucial texts document the long-standing struggle over interpretation between Sor Juana and the institutionalized power represented by confessors, bishops, and archbishops. The first is a letter, probably written in 1682, in which she dismisses the powerful Jesuit confessor Antonio Núñez de Miranda because he had complained that her writing was a public scandal; the second, her criticism of the Jesuit orator Father Vieira, which Father Manuel Fernández de Santa Cruz, Bishop of Puebla, published without her knowledge in 1690 using the pseudonym Sor Filotea, and giving it the title *Carta Atenagórica* (Letter Worthy of Athene); the third, her *Respuesta a Sor Filotea,* written three months after the publication of the *Carta Atenagórica* and intended for the Bishop's private perusal.

The letter to Father Núñez de Miranda is a recent discovery and is not completely authenticated.[44] The *Respuesta a Sor Filotea* was sent privately to the Bishop of Puebla and was published posthumously in 1700. All these documents belong to a genre that occupies an ambiguous place between secrecy and publicity—the letter. The letter generally addresses a single reader known to the sender, is assumed to be a private document (although there are public letters), and is an interpersonal act of communication which often, though not always, depends on mutual trust. What is significant about Sor Juana's three letters is that they play on the personal relationship between Sor Juana and the recipient in order to attack the institution that he represents.

As Michel de Certeau points out, all institutions establish their criterion of the real and "the story which speaks in the name of the real is injunctive. It 'signifies' in the way a command is issued."[45] In each of the three instances, an institutional command was issued that left only two choices—refusal or a gesture of obedience.

In the first instance, Sor Juana rejected Núñez de Miranda's condemnation of her poetry as a "public scandal" on the grounds that he did not know what he was talking about. He had urged her, as others did, to try to become a saint. She argues, however, that there are different paths to salvation, that "Saint Anthony is saved by his holy ignorance (but) Saint Augustine goes by another path and neither of them err." Since Núñez de Miranda's Christian name was Anthony, the statement identifies him with the ignorant and she herself with the wise, thus inverting the "natural" association of men with wisdom and women with ignorance. She asserts that "saints can only be made by the grace and help of God" and not by threats and, in a bold gesture, she dismisses him as her confessor. Her letter is a communication that breaks off communication.

There is no need to dwell on the seriousness of her action, which was a desperate attempt to create a space for writing where she could escape being categorized as a holy ignorant. The fact that she recalled Núñez de Miranda as her confessor toward the end of her life shows that she had understood the risk. This did not prevent her from returning to the theme of clerical hubris in the *Carta Atenagórica* and the *Respuesta a Sor Filotea*.

In the *Carta Atenagórica* Sor Juana trespasses knowingly on a male monopoly—the sermon. The sermon she undertook to refute was delivered by the Jesuit Father Antonio Vieira before the Portuguese court in Lisbon in 1650. It was published in Portuguese and later translated into Spanish. The subject was Christ's demonstrations of love (*finezas*).[46] Vieira was more than a Jesuit orator. He had a Messianic vision of the world and believed that a fifth empire (which was the last empire before the Apocalypse) was destined to be realized in Portugal. His sermons often alluded indirectly to the human preparation for this great event. But Sor Juana, who had a sharp sense of humor, was probably particularly diverted by a sermon delivered on Maundy Thursday, the day on which the powerful stooped to wash the feet of the poor, since far from demonstrating humility Father Vieira showed pride in his intellectual superiority by refuting the Church Fathers. Vieira, no doubt, did not see the irony in this, being perhaps more concerned with the political point he was making, for he advised "all those present who hate one another" to pardon their enemies.[47]

Sor Juana seems to have entertained herself and others by refuting the sermon verbally in the convent *locutorio*, a room in which nuns received visitors (often clergy and members of the religious orders) and talked to them from behind the protection of a wooden bar. Her skilled refutation caused the Bishop of Puebla, Manuel Fernández de Santa Cruz, to request that she write down the arguments, which she accordingly did, though she also took care to frame them as a private communication to the Bishop, which she believed would remove any suspicion that she was trying to trespass on clerical terrain.

In the letter to the Bishop that prefaces and concludes her refutation, she emphasizes the fact that she is a woman acting in an anomalous role. In the opening paragraphs of the letter she asserts that she has undertaken this task only out of obedience, assuring the Bishop that to engage in polemic is alien to her nature. She also insists on the privacy of the letter and her confidence in a sympathetic reading which will excuse what "in another's eyes might appear to be outrageous pride and even more coming from a sex so discredited in letters according to the common opinion of the world." At the end of the letter, again emphasizing her devalued female status, she suggests that God has used her as an instrument to humble Vieira. Describing the refutation of Vieira as a task worthy of Hercules and therefore seemingly impossible for a woman, she asserts that "it is no light punishment for one who thought that no man would dare to answer him to see that an ignorant woman for whom this kind of attack (so alien and so remote for one of her sex) dares to do so; yet the use of arms was alien to Judith and the exercise of justice to Deborah." At one stroke Sor Juana establishes a tradition of women who had acted like men when the occasion demanded it, and at the same time she implies that women are less likely to suffer from the sin of pride.

The main matter of the refutation is no less emphatic. She defends the Fathers of the Church from whom Vieira had differed, thus emphasizing her own orthodoxy while trespassing on the male terrain of disputation. Her argument is two-fold. Vieira's male pride had led him into a voluntaristic and erroneous interpretation of the writings of the Church Fathers and of the passion of Christ to the point that he believes "that his wit can outdo that of the Fathers and does not believe that anyone can equal him." Second, in a coda to the refutation, she obeys a promise to the Bishop by giving her own opinion of God's greatest "finesse," arguing that the greatest demonstration of God's love is that he withholds demonstrations of love "because of our ingratitude, even though it is easier for him to be bountiful" (p. 436). And she concludes, "Let us think and ponder on this beauty of Divine Love in which to reward is a demonstration of love, to punish is a demonstration of love, and not to demonstrate his love is the greatest demonstration of love" (p. 437).

Sor Juana was not only making a theological point but was addressing herself to a bishop who was constantly promising those nuns in his spiritual garden that God would reward them for their spirituality. In contrast, Sor Juana argues that, by withholding favors, God not only allows us to avoid the overwhelming responsibility they bring but allows human beings to show their active correspondence without seeking immediate rewards. Placed in the context of a society and a bishop for whom women were at best passive instruments of divine will, the coda calls for an active subject, a subject able to realize human potentiality. Sor Juana ends the letter by reiterating the private nature of the document: "since this paper is so private that I only write because you asked for it and so that you may see it, I subject it entirely to the correction of our Mother Church and detest and count as nothing and as unspoken all that may depart from your common sense and that of the Holy Fathers."

The ending of the *Carta Atenagórica* is thus paradoxical. She had created a space of "decontrolled" intellectual motivation in which human will is the active element. Yet she insists on her "subjection" to an institution regulated not by God but by the "common sense" of human prelates who, like Father Vieira, might err because of their pride. The implication is that obedience may be exacted by an irrational human agent and that freedom is the true indication of the divine within the human.

The third and most crucial letter, the *Respuesta a Sor Filotea*, was provoked by the breach of the trust that was implicit in the last lines of the *Carta*. The Bishop of Puebla published the *Carta Atenagórica* without seeking Sor Juana's consent. From a modern point of view this seems an outrageous action, but, as we have already seen, bishops and confessors believed they had the right to control the writing of nuns. It was unusual, however, even in seventeenth-century New Spain, for the Bishop to have added to the publication a public admonition signed "Sor Filotea," for though books were generally prefaced by letters from Church authorities, these were usually in the form of statements that the material did not transgress Catholic doctrine or in the form of adulatory prefaces and apologia. Sor Filotea had been the pseudonym of Fernández de Santa Cruz' favorite saint, Saint Frances de Sales.[48] It is quite probable that he thought that he was doing Sor Juana a favor by abandoning the authority of his position and reprimanding her as a friend and equal (hence the transvestite disguise of Sor Filotea). Yet he was unable to avoid the tone of priestly authority, smugly complaining to a nun who had written subtle and beautiful verse for countless Church festivals that "it is a pity that such a great understanding should be so attached to the tawdry information of this world, that it does not desire to understand what is happening in Heaven." Since "her understanding had sunk to the ground, perhaps it should delve deeper and find out what goes on in Hell." He accompanied this crude deterrant with an even cruder promise that, if she obeyed, she would soon "burn and be sweetly wounded with love of God," a God who had showered her with so many favors that she ought, indeed, to become saintly rather than dwelling on "negative benefits" (as she had done in her refutation of Father Vieira).

The publication of the *Carta Atenagórica* proved to Sor Juana (if any proof were needed) that there was no private space, nowhere outside the domain of discourse of the church and court. To write was to write within an institution. The only possible response was parody and mimicry. Throughout the reply, therefore, Sor Juana addresses the Bishop as if he were Sor Filotea, while showing that his words are loaded with an institutional authority that no woman could possibly have. In semiotic terms we have the opposition and its negation:

male	female
not male	not female

Yet this simple schema of difference does not show the inequalities that accrue when male may represent an entire institution while female is never more than an individual. Even as transvestite the Bishop still wields male authority under female guise. He had not become "not male" by exercising this fictional disguise. Sor Juana, on the other hand, could mimic a male voice but would never be invested with real power.[49] In addressing the Bishop as "mi señora" while insisting on his "pastoral suggestions" and his high authority and intelligence, Sor Juana foregrounds the fact that Sor Filotea is, indeed, a rara avis—the impossible woman, the one who wields authority. If Sor Filotea is a woman and intelligent, then there is no reason why women should not be priests. If Sor Filotea is a woman and not as intelligent as a priest, then what right has she to admonish Sor Juana?

Professing to write to Sor Filotea with "homely familiarity" and "less (fear of) authority, since treating you as a nun, as a sister, made me forget the distance from your very illustrious person which were I to see you without the veil, would not have happened," Sor Juana plays a game of abolishing the hierarchical difference and then restoring it again by using phrases such as "your pastoral suggestion," thus playing the transvestite game in such a way that the unequal power relationship is exposed. The transparent fiction of the pseudonym "Sor Filotea" is turned into a double-edged weapon, permitting an exaggerated deference to the recipient who is supposed to be a powerless woman and thus exposing the real power relations behind the egalitarian mask.

The most blatant manifestation of institutional power is the power to publish, a power that, in the opening lines of the *Respuesta*, she insists has left her dumb because the Bishop's magnanimous gesture in "giving her scribbles to the press" exceeds her capacity for expressing gratitude. But even silence, as she goes on to show, is polysemous. There is the silence of those who, like herself, are overwhelmed by gratitude and the silence of those who, like Saint Paul, are in possession of esoteric knowledge which should not be divulged to the masses. And there is a third kind of silence, that of the Bishop himself who had published her letter without telling her (in other words, there is the silence of treachery). This careful distinction between silences is important, for it places the Bishop's silence not in the category of knowledge but in that of betrayal. Even in silence we must understand the difference between divine knowledge and instrumental behavior.

It was relatively easy for Sor Juana to score debating points against the Bishop—by arguing, for instance, that reading sacred texts was not necessarily a sign of virtue, as was shown by the fact that young boys were not allowed to read *The Song of Songs* in case "the sweetness of those bridal poems might lead them to transform their sense into carnal affects." Art does not run the same risk of misuse as the Scriptures since "a heresy against art is not punished by the Holy Office but by the wise with laughter and by the critics with censure" (p. 444).

There is no doubt that Sor Juana enjoyed scoring these points, and at least one eminent critic has marveled at the ingenious way in which she articulates the different levels of the *Respuesta* around four highly charged terms—"speaking," "knowing," "not speaking," and "not knowing," and all possible permutations of these.[50] It is, however, as important to attend to the disarticulations, the places in the text where coherence cannot be maintained, the intrusion of other texts (especially hagiography), and the fluctuations between the extremes of a representative "I" (all women) and a singular and exceptional "I." It is precisely these disarticulations (and the inarticulate because impossible to articulate) that constantly point to the authority when there was no institutionalized basis for that authority, nothing which authorized a woman to speak on religious matters.

This led to an interesting paradox—the very same woman who tried to establish the space of knowledge as "neutral" is now forced to fall back on her own experience as a woman in order to explain her obsession with learning. It is this section of the *Respuesta* in which Sor Juana describes her persistent attempts to learn, the inconveniences caused by her fame, and her obstinacy in continuing her studies when deprived of books that have led many to conclude this to be a feminist text. Yet, in writing her intellectual life story, she must also have been aware of those prior texts from which she so clearly deviated—the life stories of mystical nuns. She attempts to affiliate herself with tradition of learned women—women like Deborah, who acted as a judge, and women like Esther, who pleaded a successful cause. She mentions Nicostrata, inventor of Latin letters, and Aspasia Milesia, who was teacher to Pericles, and the astrologer Hipasia; and among Christian women, Saint Gertrude, Saint Paula, the learned wife of Saint Jerome, and her daughters, Blesila and Eustoquio. She mentions Queen Isabel of Spain and, among her contemporaries, Queen Christina of Sweden and the Duchess of Aveyro, protectress of the Jesuit missions in America. Significantly missing from this list, however, are mystical nuns, except for Saint Theresa, who is mentioned as a writer, not as a mystic (p. 467). Sor Juana's arguments in favor of allowing women to study and older women to teach sacred texts were not original but were drawn from Father Juan Díaz de Arce's *Compendium Operis de studioso sacrorum Bibliorum,* in which he had concluded that there was nothing that need prevent women from studying, writing, and teaching in private.[51] But though there is "nothing to prevent" women from studying, Sor Juana knew from experience that there was *someone* to prevent them—that is, confessors who pressed them to mortify the flesh and who praised the ignorant. To counteract these individuals, Sor Juana used a weapon she knew to be doubled-edged—the authority of her own individual talent.

In seventeenth-century America, women who stood out from the mass were generally saints or *beatas*.[52] Sor Juana must certainly have been familiar with their writing since her own convent had housed Sor María Magdalena de Lorravaquio Muñoz. This saintly nun was destined for the holy life, according to her own account, almost from birth: "By the divine grace and Mercy of God who took care of my soul from my most tender years, since I had the use of reason and knew how to use it, I had great desires for loving and knowing God and to employ myself only in this, and with these desires I tried to avoid the games and play normal at that age."[53] It is precisely this kind of text that Sor Juana now sets out to displace by imitating it to the point of parody, so that she can replace it by a new kind of singularity—that of the woman of learning.

The structure of hagiography demands the referential—the exemplary life story which is often then broken down into illustrations of the theological virtues of humility, poverty, obedience, and chastity. By the seventeenth century such texts followed a routine pattern in which the biographer insists on the subject's early vocation for saintliness and the obstacles that she has to overcome.[54] In like manner, Sor Juana describes a God-given and inexplicable talent which meets not with the demonic mockery that so often plagued the mystics but with man-made obstacles such as lack of books and teachers and a hostile environment in the convent where she was sometimes forbidden to read. Despite these obstacles, her "black inclination" had prevailed; she had learned to read without her mother's knowledge or consent by accompanying an older sister to the *amiga* (the name given to women who taught small children). She had imposed penances on herself if she failed to accomplish a particular task. After entering the convent she had been hindered not only by the rules of convent life but by her solitude and the lack of teachers. Mimicking the mystics, she describes how she had prayed to God to relieve her of the burden of her talent and had asked Him to leave her only with sufficient understanding to fulfill her religious duties, "since according to some people any greater understanding is excess in a woman and there are even some who maintain it to be harmful"—a clear reference to her former confessor, Núñez de Miranda. And just as the mystics went through gradations of prayer until they reached union with God, so Sor Juana describes a progression upward through a hierarchy of disciplines—Logic, Rhetoric, Physics, Geometry, Architecture, and Music, at the summit of which is Theology. She regards prayer and chastity, which the mystics also emphasized, as necessary for the pursuit of knowledge.

Sor Juana would claim that her desire to learn was so intense that it kept her apart from the active social life of the convent and brought her into conflict with the anti-intellectualism of some of her superiors. On one occasion, when forbidden by a superior to read, she had spent the time observing the angles of a room, a child's spinning top, and the chemistry of an egg when mixed with different substances, thus adding to her store of knowledge and leading her to state, in an often-quoted aside, that if Aristotle had cooked, he would have written more. She thus broadens the field of rationalism beyond book learning. And as the Argentine critic Josefina Ludmer concludes, "if the personal, private, and everyday are included as a starting point of other perspectives and practices, they disappear as personal, private, and domestic. Sor Juana's argument thus breaks down the very separation of private and public that is used to subjugate women."[55] However, it should be stressed that this is not the same mapping of the public and private that pertained to the bourgeois state. In Sor Juana's time exceptional women were not excluded from political power (at least as sovereigns), but women *were* excluded from truth activities. This is an important distinction. For when Sor Juana argues that she can pursue learning without books, she is not at all praising the mystics who abhorred practical life, but rather showing that the experiences that are supposedly feminine can enlarge the field of learning. In the struggle for interpretive power, women are forced to bring practical life into the realm of knowledge.

Critics have generally read these autobiographical sections of the letter as the unmediated voice of Sor Juana. But if it is autobiography, it leaves in silence many important areas of her life—her illegitimacy, her years at court, her reasons for leaving the Carmelite order which she had entered briefly in 1667. Even as a spiritual life, it has to be considered in relation to those texts against which it is written. Fray Luis Tineo de Morales clearly suggested this when he wrote his "approval" for the *Inundación Castálida*, contrasting Sor Juana with those who "baptize idiocy in the name of holiness" and use this to advance their own interests.[56]

But Sor Juana's brand of spirituality was not accessible to the majority. Again and again in the *Respuesta* she is forced to argue that she is a "special case," a "rare bird." Discussing the envy that surrounds those who perform unusual feats, she compares herself to Christ who stood out from the crowd, because he had "done singular things," and to the Roman emperors who were insulted after their triumphs.

The authority of Sor Juana's text thus derives from her own self-proclaimed expertise pitted against the institutionalized knowledge (and ignorance) of the Church. She herself was aware of the difference and the disparity. In her discussion of the interpretation of Saint Paul's injunction that women should be silent in church ("Mulieres in Ecclesia taceant"), she offers alternative interpretations—either the injunction refers specifically to the pulpit or it refers to the universal Church which embraces all the faithful: "If the first is understood (which is, in my view, its true sense because, as we see, women are not permitted to read publicly or preach in church), why reprimand them for studying privately? And if it is understood in the second sense and they wish that the prohibition of the Apostle should be universal and that women should not be permitted to write or study even in secret, how is it that the Church has permitted a Gertrude, a Theresa, a Bridget, the nun of Agreda, and many others [to write]?" This is one of the most crucial arguments of the *Respuesta* since it separates the Church and its sacred texts from the interpreters of those texts. Men are empowered by the institution, but this does not give them the license to interpret texts capriciously. To place power in the hands of one gender and to give them the monopoly of interpretation is highly dangerous, for as she shows, it is men, not women, who are responsible for the great heresies, men, not women, who use interpretation of the Scriptures against the interests of the Church itself.

Yet each time Sor Juana argues that she is a special case, she also confronts the reverse—that she is a devalued woman, subject to arbitrary acts of male power like any other woman. Nowhere is this more evident than in the final paragraphs of the *Respuesta,* when she once again takes up Sor Filotea's treacherous act of publishing a private document and compares it to a foundling who has been given a name by the finder—the Bishop. Yet she immediately unmasks the mechanisms behind this apparently benevolent gesture. The Bishop had used her in putting the text into public circulation—a treacherous act that leads her to conclude, "if I could have foreseen the unhappy destiny into which it was born when I threw it into the Nile waters of silence like another

Moses where it was found and embraced by you, the princess—I repeat, that if I had foreseen this, I would have strangled it with the hands that brought it forth for fear that the clumsy products of my ignorance would be exposed to the light of your knowledge" (p. 471).

Even given the aggressive tone of the *Respuesta,* the metaphor of filicide and adoption is particularly violent. Sor Juana was herself the daughter of an unwed mother and had been "adopted" by the Church. She had been forced to face the unpleasant truth that in the society in which she lived, learning, like people, could be illegitimate; literary productions were offspring, sometimes born against the mother's will as a result of rape, seduction, or obligation, and often "aborted."[57] Knowledge was legitimized, as were children, by being institutionally baptized. Literary offspring that were not thus fathered were orphans like the *Carta Atenagórica,* which, despite its unorthodox birth, was "adopted" and named without being legitimized. The reprimand signed by Sor Filotea had deliberately set the refutation apart from legitimate contenders in the great theological polemics of the time. Better, then, that it should have been killed at birth than have its destiny controlled in this way.

Sor Juana specifically refuses publication on the terms that were normally extended to women in the seventeenth century—that is, she refuses to be adopted by the father. Yet the publication of the *Respuesta* had demonstrated to her that even symbolic trespassing and symbolic Utopias were likely to be appropriated and put to institutional use. Creation for Sor Juana is precariously forged with full knowledge of the unhappy prospect of choosing between institutionality and "child murder."

THE BODY POLITIC AND THE WORLD ORDER

So far we have traced two contradictory endeavors—Sor Juana's attempt to become "neuter" and her exploitation of her singularity as a learned women. But she was also a nun living within a system of patronage that she neither resisted nor opposed. It is important to understand that Sor Juana, like other "baroque" personalities, was not a lone sniper resisting the state, but was, at times, the very voice of that state.

The center of Sor Juana's world was indeed held together by the mythical power of the divine Church and its kingdom on earth represented in the New World by the clergy and the viceregal court whose power Sor Juana did much to legitimize. It is difficult to understand this from a modern perspective, which sees the writer as the eternal dissident. Help comes from Antonio Maravall and Richard Morse, both of whom have pointed out how different a place the individual occupied in Hispanic society, where adaption to the system took precedence over the expression of individual principles, if, indeed, it is possible to speak of individual principles in this context.[58]

It is therefore important to stress that most of Sor Juana's poems were written within the conventions of court or Church and under their patronage. She dedicated poems to a succession of viceroys— first to Antonio de Toledo, Marqués de Mancera (1664–1773), who was viceroy when she arrived at court in 1665. She became a special favorite of his wife. She dedicated poems to other viceroys, to Fray Payo Enríquez de Rivera (1673–1680); to Tomás Antonio de la Cerda y Aragón, Count of Paredes, Marqués de la Laguna (1680– 1686), whose wife, the Lysi and Filis of her poetry, became an important patron; and to the ineffectual Count of Galve (1688– 1696). Church patronage was equally crucial. It was the Cathedral that commissioned the triumphal arch she designed for the entry of the Marqués de la Laguna, and scarcely a year passed when she did not contribute *villancicos* (carols) to be sung during mass on the great feast days. Great religious empires like that of Spain in the New World were cemented, according to Benedict Anderson, by the sacred language the appropriation of which made the lettered the "strategic strata in a cosmological hierarchy of which the apex was divine."[59] Far from feeling restive within this system, Sor Juana often portrayed it as an ideal "body politic" in which the poet's role is that of celebrant and occasionally humble and respectful counselor. The apparently conventional gesture of kissing the feet of those in power (literally or symbolically) ensured the proper circulation of power within the system without which signification would have been impossible. Without the Countess of Paredes, she wrote, "even her discourse would have become alien."[60] I am not denying that the passion that many have detected in the poems addressed to the Countess is real nor that they are indeed love poems; but it is impossible to separate personal love from love of the body politic, and love of the body politic included the recognition of authority.

Sor Juana was quite aware that the legitimacy of the body politic depended on force. By stressing the feminine attitude to power, she is, however, able in some measure to make a political point, contrasting, for instance, her own unforced love for the countess with the torture instruments used in extracting confession.[61] Sor Juana believed in the essential benevolence of the system in which human representatives—the viceroys—symbolized a divine order, while knowingly listing its instruments of oppression—the hooks and ropes used in torture. Sor Juana loved the countess as a friend but also as an embodiment of a world order in which she stood for the feminine element, rather as the Virgin Mary symbolized the feminine within the religious order. In a poem written in an unusual ten-syllable ballad form, the countess is identified with the cosmic woman: "May the sun make pens out of its light/and the Stars compose syllables."[62] Each part of the countess' body is compared to nature or state, geography or establishment. Her eyebrows are like the weapons of the army, she is a prison, her cheeks a university, her chin is described architectonically, her throat is the source of music, her body is described as a geography, as Doric and Ionic architecture. This is not simply a celebration of a person, but a tribute to the ideal representation of an empire.

In her religious plays, Sor Juana justified the Spanish hegemony over the Americas because it had introduced the true religion. But her argument for the superiority of Christianity over paganism is typically a literary one. Christianity replaces human sacrifice with abstract symbols just as writing replaces voice. She allowed for ethnic variations within religious practices as long as these could be subsumed under the higher form of Christianity.[63] Though she believed conquest and empire necessary, she could not condone individual cruelty. She was uneasy about black peonage, and her poems written in Nahuatl suggest a respect for indigenous culture that others certainly did not share. Her sets of religious villancicos, many written in the various dialects of Mexico, suggest her ideal view of Empire as a prefiguration of the city of God in which all races would find a place.[64]

What holds together all meaning for Sor Juana is the Incarnation, that is, the redemption of the profane world by the divine. And, just as the body politic is ideally represented in the body of the Countess of Paredes, so does religion find its highest representation in the Virgin Mary. In furthering the doctrine of the Immaculate Conception, which was made into dogma only in the nineteenth century, Sor Juana forms part of an immense groundswell of Catholic belief—though, as Marina Warner points out, for women the Immaculate Conception was double-edged, setting the Virgin apart from the human race "because she is not stained by the Fall. And if on one plane the perfection of Mary is defined as the conquest of the natural laws of childbearing and death, then the prevailing idea of perfection denies the goodness of the created world, and of the human body."[65]

But for Sor Juana the fact that the Virgin was both perfect and human seems to reaffirm the goodness of creation:

> Who doubts that if angels could feel envy, they would envy this happiness. For my part, I can say that if it were possible to exchange the miseries of my human nature for the privileges and perfections of the angelic state, thus losing our kinship with the Most Holy Mary, I would not do so even if it were possible, because of this privilege and of what I most esteem and appreciate with all my soul—that is, belonging to her same lineage.[66]

As in *Primero Sueño,* where she celebrates both abstraction and the created world, Sor Juana is fascinated by that moment of transition from flesh to spirit which is the work of intellect. That is why the Virgin Mary must be a scholar and why she accepts the idea propagated by María de Agreda that God had shown the Virgin all the secrets of the cosmos.[67] Her own version of Mariolotry characteristically modified but did not transgress dogma by stressing the intellectual role of the Virgin and the learned saints such as Saint Catherine of Alexandria. The Virgin is a "Sovereign Doctor of the Divine Schools who teaches wisdom to all the angels."[68] Original sin is even described as felicitous because it was redeemed through the Incarnation and the necessary intervention of Mary, without whom Incarnation would have been impossible.[69] She describes Mary as the clock which is harmonized with Glory, as the divine Book, "a clean book, without corrections or errata," and as divine Minerva. The female body lacerated, grotesque, and emaciated in mystical practice is in Sor Juana's poetry and religious writing made into the perfect body, the temple of God—to the point where she can write, "His August Majesty could not fit in the greatness of the Heavens, yet he fitted into the generous cloister of the virginal womb."[70] As in her praise poems to the countess, Sor Juana's celebration of the Virgin allows her to envisage female power and intellect. She describes Mary as the mother of the Word. When this is taken literally, it means that the female body is the matrix that gives birth to the logos. The womb is not only the sullied and impure repository of original sin but the source of redemption without which there would be niether life nor meaning.

MORE WORLDS

But this leads us back once again to representation and how, in that already replete world, other spaces can be found without undermining the very raison d'être of the Spanish empire. One solution is proposed in Sor Juana's religious play *El Cetro de José* (Joseph's Scepter) and as usual, it depends on allegory. In the *loa* that introduces the play, Science/Knowledge claims "rhetorical license to fabricate rational beings [*entes de razón*] and to make the invisible a possible representable object" (*OC,* 3:204). In the *loa* that introduces *El mártir del sacramento, San Hermenegildo* (The Martyr of the Sacraments, Saint Hermenegildo), she shows how this works. A group of students are discussing Christ's greatest "finesse," on which subject Saint Thomas and Saint Augustine hold opposing views. One of the students suggests a "magic" way out of the aporia—the magic consisting of producing a play within a play whose protagonists are Hercules and Christopher Columbus. Hercules boasts that his pillars encircle the world. Columbus shows that there are "more worlds" beyond the pillars (*OC,* 3:106). The example is an interesting one, for it shows that the discovery of the New World opened up a space which altered old certainties. The implication is that the method for solving dilemmas is not disputation (in the hands of the priests) but exploration (like that of the digressive stream Arethusa). The play *San Hermenegildo,* however, illustrates another form of representation, one which equally fascinated Sor Juana, but which was the more orthodox aspect of her thinking. The play culminates with a representation of the Sacrament for which Saint Hermenegildo had been martyred. His martyr's blood becomes the purple that colors the robes of the Spanish monarchs. Thus an abstract idea is incarnated in Saint Hermenegildo in the stage representation, and his martyrdom, in turn, is converted into a personified symbol. This conversion of person into symbol and symbol into person is a form of representation that implies the class division between those who need personal symbols and those who understand abstractions.

Sor Juana had the misfortune to live in dark times, times of food riots and floods, of teetering authority in which inevitably the establishment grew more rigid. Critics speak of the period as one in which there was a "crisis of colonial authority."[71] Certainly the food riots of 1892, in which Indians demonstrated and openly insulted Spaniards in the streets, spread the "great fear" which was to be revived at intervals—notably during the wars of Independence and in the "caste wars" of the nineteenth century. Critics usually interpret the final years, when Sor Juana gave away her musical instruments and books and engaged in good works, as a defeat, as evidence of her "silencing." Certainly it meant that the power struggle was over for her.

Marina Warner has stated that Catholicism on the one hand "affirms the beauty and goodness of the natural world and insists that man's purpose is to cultivate fully his God-given gifts on earth; but on the other it endorses the most pessimistic world-denying self-sacrifice as the state of the elect and accords virginity, the symbol of renunciation, the highest accolade."[72] Sor Juana's inclination was toward celebration of Creation, but might she not also have desired a resolution to her conflicts? And found in the Virgin one road toward that resolution? We should not forget that in the final months of her life she reiterated her devotion to the Immaculate Conception, signed a vow in her own blood promising to abandon her profane activities and embark on the road to perfection (a final recognition of Saint Theresa?), wrote a document asking pardon for her sins, and wrote a statement in the convent's Book of Professions in which she renewed her monastic vows and which she signed "I, the worst in the world, Sor Juana," all of which indicate a clear determination (OC 4:516–523). Whether she acted under constraint we shall never know. Probably not. For within her system of belief, there was only one "Ave raris" and that was the Virgin. All other phoenixes were bound to be too frequent.

3

THE POWER OF THE SPIDER WOMAN: THE DELUDED WOMAN AND THE INQUISITION

One class of women offered a real challenge to colonial society—those denounced to the Holy Office as *ilusas*, that is, as deluded women. The ilusas were a threat to society for several reasons—they often defied or eluded the control of confessors, inventing their own religious myths, and they generally lived outside the recognized "estates"—that is, they were neither enclosed in convents nor under the care of father or husband. Though colonial society did its best to hide this floating population in *recogimientos*, (that is, in special asylums), it was not always successful.[1] They were not witches and had not made pacts with the devil, so that the Church had to find other ways of disqualifying their discourse, defining it as "illusion" or deception by the devil. The ilusas shared a common language with the mystical nuns, but unlike the latter they often "performed" rapture and ecstasy in public and exhibited their "grotesque" bodies, which they claimed bore the signs of God's special favor.

Margins and boundaries are always dangerous. The ilusas were socially marginal; in addition, their "incorrect" behavior made them into a living and often unconscious parody of all that was held holy. They challenged the "solidity of boundaries" for, as John Frow (following Mary Douglas) points out,

What binds [the space of a discursive system] together, more or less, is the normative authority it wields as an institution,

an authority which is more or less strictly exercised and which
is always the attempted imposition of a centralizing unity rather
than the achieved fact of such a unity. Institutional authority,
which by definition is asymmetrically distributed between
"central" and "marginal" members of the institution, is deployed in particular to maintain the purity and the solidity of
boundaries, and this involves both defining and restricting access to these practices to certified or qualified agents.[2]

Precisely because the Inquisition was founded to maintain the purity of the system, its proceedings can shed a great deal of light
on how "subalternity" is produced as well as on the points of conflict that arise when stigmatization on grounds of race are played
against stigmatization because of gender.[3]

In this chapter I propose to discuss the Inquisition trial of Ana
Rodríguez de Castro y Aramburu Moctezuma, who appeared before the Holy Office of the Inquisition in the City of Mexico on
November 21, 1801, and was later sentenced to be imprisoned in
its secret prison.[4] What makes this particular trial so interesting is
that it took place not only when society was endangered by "French"
ideas but also at a time when new domains of discourse were coming into being and when there was no longer one universally accepted interpretative framework (see chapter 4). Like the case of
Pierre Rivière, described by Foucault, the trial "is a singular clash
among various kinds of discourse, a story without heroes, villains,
or fate—a battle without a stage. The power it involves is not the
power of characters but the power of discourses devised to describe them."[5] Yet people live such conflicts "as if" they are subjects. Ana de Aramburu clearly believed that mystical discourse
would set her apart from other people, would help her overcome
her devalued status. But this time the struggle for interpretive power
takes place in more humble territory and revolves around the dominant class's interpretation of subaltern behavior.

In Ana's trial, however, there was not only a clash between "her
story" and "their story" but also between older and newer map-
pings of women's behavior. The traditional view was that delusion
was the work of the demon, but this discourse was now in com-
petition with another interpretation—that which attributed it to
hysteria. We cannot speak of anything as dramatic as an "epis-
temological break," when the entire discursive field undergoes
transformation, but we can speak of a recoding of the devalued
position in terms of physical weakness.[6] Moreover this occurs at

a period when the secular intelligentsia were already beginning to challenge the Church's power. What Aramburu's trial makes clear is that before the institutionalization of hysteria, even the most modest challenges to patriarchal authority could be met by making all women potentially sick members of society.

What we know of Ana de Aramburu comes entirely from the records of the Inquisition trial, much of which was recently transcribed and published. In the introduction to this published selection, Aramburu is described as a *pícara,* and the editors read the trial as a picaresque novel.[7] This modish reading obscures the fact that the trial is a drama or struggle over meaning waged between institutionalized male authority and informal and therefore illegitimate knowledge. On the one side, there was a rational system claiming monopoly of the truth and able to defend this monopoly, if necessary, by force. On the other was a woman who used the mystical fable and mystical performance in a bid to overcome her devalued status. To this end she made public prophecies, claimed to bear the stigmata, and vomited blood copiously. Some witnesses claimed that the blood she exhibited was menstrual blood—if so, she symbolically used the very proof of women's inferiority to enhance her own status.[8]

What is most interesting about Aramburu, however, is not her singularity but the fact that she belonged to a class of women who were systematically pursued from the sixteenth century onward, both in Spain and in Hispanic America. The similarity between their "symptoms" and their symbolic language suggests either that there was a continuous orally transmitted lore or that they mimicked and represented the double bind imposed on women by the contradictory demands of asceticism and womanhood. These women exhibited and vomited blood, simulated lactation and rapture, thus performing symbolically in public "private" events of female life—menstruation, motherhood, and orgasm. "The body," says Mary Douglas, "is a model which can stand for any bonded system. . . . All margins are dangerous . . . spittle, blood, milk, urine, feces, or tears by simply issuing forth have traversed the boundaries of the body."[9]

Ana was not living in the Middle Ages, however, or even the sixteenth century. She lived at the end of the eighteenth and the beginning of the nineteenth century when Mexico City had become dominated by a vast underclass. In this city, which then had a population of 137,000, there were 6,700 artisans, 14,000 servants, and 15,000 beggars. Only a third of the population had some kind

of fixed employment. It was a hungry city, pullulating with street
life in the midst of which rose the luxurious convents and churches.
The streets were "not only used for the circulation of people and
merchandise but were the centers of social life, a privileged space.
Here, the population worked, bargained, ate, conducted civil and
religious ceremonies, sauntered, entertained themselves and got
drunk. Here too they witnessed the daily spectacle of sex and
death."[10] It was this very heterogeneity, and above all its potential
for disorder, that aroused the fears of the elite. By the end of the
eighteenth century there was a struggle to control those very streets
through the regulation of disorderly entertainment, such as the
carnival and street entertainment. The immense care taken over
the trial of Ana de Aramburu is, in fact, only explicable if we take
into account its place in a generalized struggle for the control of
public space.

Before discussing the trial in more detail, a word should be said
about the Inquisition of New Spain, for Aramburu speaks only in
and through its records. The Inquisition had been established for-
mally in New Spain in 1569 and was at first mainly concerned with
Jews, Protestants, and the occasional Moslem, though it also concerned itself with cases of bigamy, witchcraft, obscene and sedi-
tious literature, and "delusion." It had no jurisdiction over the
indigenous peoples and, despite holding the ritualistic auto de fe,
burned relatively few heretics.[11]

But the Inquisition did not need to burn in order to be feared.
Sor Juana's writing shows that the Holy Office was a powerful
deterrent whose procedures were so well known among the population that they induced a kind of self-censorship. The accused
spent months in secret prisons without knowing who had denounced them or of what they were accused. They were forbidden
to speak of the proceedings, except during interrogation. Enor-
mous care was taken in the collection of evidence—some of it
being extracted by torture of the accused or their acquaintances—
and all evidence was written down. On being sentenced, the guilty
were stripped of their possessions and usually were forced to take
part in the auto de fe. Carrying green candles, wearing caps and
gowns painted with the burning flames of hell, they ran the gaunt-
let of crowds before whom they played out their last act of public
defiance or their humiliating recantation. Those condemned to the
stake were handed over to the civil authorities for burning. The
rest were exhibited, sometimes publicly whipped, and thereafter
returned to the secret prisons of the Inquisition where they were

denied human intercourse.[12] By the time Ana was tried, the auto de fe was no longer held nor were prisoners tortured; nevertheless the culture of fear had been so successfully inculcated in the population that the Holy Office was still an important instrument of social intimidation.

What is particularly interesting about the trials of ilusas, however, is that they seem to have begun at a time when the power of the confessional as an instrument of social control was on the decrease. Inquisitors sometimes linked the ilusas to the heretical movement of the *alumbrados* (enlightened ones), a sixteenth-century sect that had held that it was not necessary for the faithful to confess.[13] However, the ilusas of New Spain were not always heretical. Rather, they attempted to mimic the raptures and ecstasies of holy women. They either wished to be saints or to pass themselves off as saints, and their language was often similar to that of mystical nuns like Sor María de Jesús Tomelín. Where they differed from the *beata* was in their defiance of the power of the confessor and the fact that they often gave public performances in which they levitated or prophesied.[14]

The clergy defined illusion (or delusion) as a form of self-deception in spiritual matters, although there seems to have been some confusion as to whether this was voluntary or the result of ignorance—a confusion that is evident in Ana's trial.[15] In Inquisition trials deluded women were often represented as con women who used mystical raptures and language for all kinds of perverse reasons—in order to earn money or pass off unwanted pregnancies as the result of a devil's trick. For instance, in the seventeenth century the women of the Romero family, who had gathered quite an audience for their performances, were labeled false mystics. One of them, Teresa de Jesús, gave birth to an illegitimate child while awaiting trial in the secret prisons of the Inquisition,[16] thus confirming in the eyes of the Inquisitors the scandalous life she hoped to conceal by saying that the devil had done it all.

Yet to explain these women as pseudomystics detracts from more interesting aspects of the phenomenon. For in a rather different way from Sor Juana Inés de la Cruz, they struggled for discursive space in a society that denied them any. Because they had no learning, they used the only instrument they truly possessed—their bodies. By bleeding, they offered proof of their special relationship to God. They also created fantasies around motherhood. The seventeenth-century ilusa Teresa de Jesús (not to be confused with Saint Theresa) pretended to suckle an image of the Christ child.[17] Ana de

Aramburu claimed to be a virgin and adopted an orphan with whom she was said to have a strangely intimate relationship. Both women transgressed the apparently natural categories of virgin or mother by claiming to be both. In the set of oppositions:

virgin	mother
not virgin	not mother

only one woman can transgress the opposition and that is the Virgin Mary, who is unique because she is both virgin and mother.[18] Not to be a virgin and not be a mother was to be a prostitute. The only legitimate categories were virgin/not mother (nun and unmarried woman) or mother/not virgin (a married woman). Thus when Teresa de Jesús suckled the Christ child she transgressed this system of meaning in a way that gave her a place unattainable by the clergy, who could have no such corporeal relationship with Christ even in imagination. Teresa also regressed into childhood, "behaving like a baby, speaking like one, and not eating or drinking unless she was fed by someone else."[19] She thus became an *infans*, that is, one who has not yet reached the age of language, consciousness, and sin.

Ana de Aramburu came under suspicion in 1799 when she was living in Puebla but was not brought to trial until 1801 in Mexico City. Details of her life before she became notorious for her performances are sketchy. It appears that she had lived with an uncle who was a priest, had wanted to enter a convent, and no doubt had lacked the money for a dowry. When she first appeared before the Inquisition she was married but living separately from her husband, Juan Ortiz, a tailor by profession. The Inquisitors regarded this separation as highly irregular for, as they pointed out in the summary of the trial proceedings, Saint Peter had exhorted unhappily married women to remain in the care of their husbands, "because when other methods had failed to reform an erring male the wife's saintly and admirable conduct, even when she is silent, should influence him for the better" (p. 134). But Aramburu was no patient Griselda. By the turn of the century she was moving about Mexico City and Toluca, often changing her address, sometimes living with other women or on the charity of priests, sometimes scraping a living by rolling cigars or aiding the sick in return for food. But most of all she exploited a mysterious physical disability of vomiting blood, turning this into a veritable performance in which she levitated, prophesied, and claimed to bear the stigmata.[20]

On November 1, 1801, she presented herself "voluntarily" before the Holy Office, apparently having been denounced by a neighbor, but also under pressure from a veritable horde of confessors anxious to have her put away—among them Fray Lázaro de Santa Teresa, a Tolucan prior, Fray Francisco de Jesús María y Joseph, and several others, including a Fray Felipe, who had threatened to have her put in a *recogimiento* for leading young women astray ("por inquietadora de niñas doncellas"; p. 46). Her activities perturbed Father Ynfantas so much that he hounded her throughout the Inquisition proceedings, putting pressure on witnesses and ferreting her out when she tried to hide after her condemnation. Even a sympathetic priest, Licenciado Ildefonso de Esquivel y Vargas, felt the need to keep her under constant surveillance.

Ten months after her first appearance, on September 2, 1802, and after an extremely thorough questioning of confessors, friends, acquaintances, and doctors both in Mexico City and in Toluca, an order was issued for the confiscation of property and her arrest on the grounds that she was deluded, had passed herself off as a saint, had worked false miracles, and had faked divine revelations. She also claimed to bear Christ's wounds (p. 83). Thanks to the detailed dossier and careful investigation of the officers of the Inquisition, her trial offers a fascinating glimpse of life in the popular neighborhoods (the *casas de vecindad*) of Mexico City and introduces a cast of characters that includes priests, painters, traders, a starcher, and several women who lived alone. But even more interesting than this glimpse "from below" is the symbolic performance of Ana herself, which constituted both a parody of the mystical fable and a struggle for power.

In order to follow Ana de Aramburu's struggle with the Inquisition it is important to understand the chronology of the trial, which went through several stages spanning the course of a year. The following is a summary of the main episodes:

1. In November 1801, Aramburu presents herself to the Inquisitor, Antonio Bergara y Tordán, knight of the Royal and Distinguished Order of Charles III and bishop-elect of Oaxaca (this listing of rank alone suggests the unequal distribution of power). He is aided by a Juan Bautista de Arechederreta who gathers evidence and questions witnesses. Ana, in her only deposition, is questioned (as was customary) in the third person: "Does [the witness] know of anyone who has said or done anything against Our Holy Catholic Faith, or against the true

and free exercise of the Holy Office or has the witness done any such thing, etc." (p. 25). She declares that she had spoken of her infirmities (the stigmata, vomiting blood, levitation) to several people, including her two Carmelite confessors, Fray Joseph de la Expectación and Father Ildefonso Esquivel, who have denounced her. She has also spoken of her "accidents" to some lay people, among them Juan Domingo Gutiérrez, described as a starcher, and mention of whom allows her to slip in some information which was evidently intended to undermine her accusers. It appears that when Gutiérrez' wife was sick, a Carmelite friar, Fray Manuel, had come to confess her and had tried to get into bed with her. When Gutiérrez complained, Father Francisco de Jesús María had said that not even the Pope could change the confessor, so Fray Manuel continued visiting Gutiérrez' wife.

After the preliminary declaration, her confessors make declarations in person or by letter. In addition, several of her disciples are called, including Ana de la Colina, "a commercial agent," and the starcher, Juan Domingo Gutiérrez, both of whom testify in her favor. Other witnesses, for instance María de la Merced Alvarez, testify against her on the recommendation of their confessor (p. 49).

2. After examining these witnesses, Juan Bautista Arecherredeta becomes impatient, complaining that if the Holy Office were to record "all the miracles and prophecies attributed to the Aramburu, a folio volume would not be enough" (p. 48). He charges that she has

> moved from one corner of the city to the other and every single *beata* who has confessed with the same confessors as the Aramburu is a witness to her deceptions and fictions, because she had lived with all of them, and everywhere there have been raptures, prophecies, the sweating of blood, and so on, and therefore I have tried to examine only the main witnesses, but I see that day after day the scandals continue and there will be greater scandals, in my opinion, if the bold conduct of this woman is not corrected by the serious and Christian measures of the Tribunal. (p. 71)

In contrast to his severe condemnation of Ana, he "suspends judgment" on Fray Manuel's alleged attempt to seduce

Gutiérrez' wife, "because I know the misery and frivolity of men, but my concept of the accuser [Gutiérrez] is that he is a very captious and stubborn man, who, feeling to the extreme the weight of the cross of matrimony because his wife spends without the care and economy which Gutiérrez would like, tried to leave her and abandon her in a sister's house to live on a pittance" (p. 72). Whatever the merits of Ana's accusation of clerical lechery, Arecherredeta refuses to discuss them further. It is not the clergy who are on trial.

3. Between November 1801 and March 1802 Aramburu publicly claims that the Inquisitor had exonerated her. She makes various favorable prophecies intended to sway the tribunal in her favor. Certain members of the clergy, on the other hand, put pressure on witnesses, inducing them to give evidence against her.

4. A new commissioner, the careful and patient Marqués de Castañiza, is appointed. Accompanied by a notary, he witnesses one of her raptures, gathers evidence from Toluca, where Aramburu had lived for several months under the protection of a Carmelite prior, and reexamines many of the same witnesses as Arecherredeta, including Ana de Colina and Juan Domingo Gutiérrez, who have been persuaded to change their testimony (p. 98). Ana de Colina now describes her former friend as a drunkard, bad-tempered, a liar, a woman who moves house and confessors frequently, "for as soon as they pressure her (as she says), she leaves them and criticizes them as crazy, imprudent, and rogues, as she expressly said of Licenciado Esquivel and Father Fray Francisco de Jesús María and Fray Joseph de la Expectación" (p. 91). Evidence of perverse sexuality begins to accumulate. Gutiérrez accuses Ana of masturbating in public during her trances, of exposing her body, and of having been seen lasciviously embracing an orphan she had adopted (p. 104). He also produces a lampoon which had been put on the house of one Josefa Orcolaga when Aramburu lived there. She is continually described as a rogue and a cheat who has feigned sainthood, caused scandal in the neighborhood, and deceived the credulous.

5. Ana de Aramburu had already broken with her "disciple," Ana de la Colina. In May 1802, fearing that more witnesses were turning against her, she caused a scandal by in-

sulting and threatening Micaela Orcolaga and Juan Domingo
Gutiérrez, possibly when drunk.[21]

6. The Inquisition's summary of its findings, issued on August 5, 1802, finds her guilty of "delusion." She has shown no
particular devotion to support her claims to be a *beata* and
has made false prophecies. The officers of the Inquisition at-
tribute her infirmities to hysteria, for

> experience shows that according to the greater or lesser
> degree of this accident (to which the women of this king-
> dom and especially of the capital seem to be greatly prone)
> so are the number of those who seem to suffer in greater
> or lesser degree from this excess which is perhaps invol-
> untary and unnoticed and which breaks out in practices
> and words which horrify, frighten, astonish, and con-
> found those who see and know their conduct, especially
> if they do not know of this harmful and pernicious evil
> which should inspire pity and human compassion since
> otherwise they may be brought to the threshold of mad-
> ness. (p. 121)

In addition, she has sought *auras favorum,* the glitter of
applause, by staging false miracles, and, in her ignorance, has
spread inaccurate statements about the Immaculate Conception. One example cited by the Inquisitors is the conversation
Ana was supposed to have had with Our Lord during which
he proposed that they exchange hearts. The Inquisitors cast
doubts as to whether Our Lord could have spoken in such a
frivolous manner, since, according to Saint Theresa, God only
utters grave and complex judgments. Hence those conversations must be false, invented to deceive people and to give
Arambura a reputation for sainthood.

Even more serious is her attack on the power of the confessional. "It is said that this woman has no other director than
God and she only goes to the confessor to please God and
avoid people's gossip, and that from the age of six, God had
already guided her directly" (p. 116), and "she usually seeks
bland confessors and when she finds one that 'squeezes the
orange,' as she puts it, she says he is a fool" (p. 119). In their
remarks the Inquisitors point out that Our Lord has never
been known to divert souls from the teaching of those appointed as ministers of the Holy Sacrament of Penance. "As

for her prophecies, they could easily be attributed to guessing on the basis of anticipated experience, divining the effects that come from causes; this kind of power is common in women according to Aquinas." The Inquisitors conclude that either Ana has been lying for her own self-interest or her visions are true and are the work of the demon since God sends visions only in order to improve understanding. Significantly, there is no mention in the entire summary of her supposed sexual aberrations.

7. On September 2, the order for arrest is drawn up and the charges summarized—pretending to be a saint, staging false miracles, prophecies, ecstasis, raptures, devotions, celestial visions, pretending to speak to God, bearing the wounds of Our Lord, and having emissions of blood, especially from the head and heart, in which she soaks a rag so that the credulous believe her; she is accused of promising favors to those who believe and protect her and terrible punishments if they do not, of predicting the death of some subjects and claiming that some have left Purgatory thanks to her intercession, "and many other fictions, lies, and intrigues."[22]

8. A new witness, María de la Encarnación Mora, appears on September 27, 1802, that is, after the Inquisition has already passed judgment. She presents a document of some thirty-one pages, "formed with the help of her confessor, who was don Francisco Ynfantas." This same confessor had also coached Ana de la Colina into changing her testimony. But María de la Encarnación's accusations are far more serious than those made by other witnesses, for they involve sexual perversion and heresy. In her testimony María declared that she herself had been possessed by the devil between January and September of 1802. She reported that Aramburu had expressed disbelief in the efficacy of the rosary and that spiritual confession to the Holy Christ and in the presence of God was enough for salvation,

> and so she said that I should not even spend time on meditation or any other practice; on other occasions (as I have said), she said that I should pray and meditate in order to follow the dictates of my heart, and she said that she had no faith in the most Holy Mary nor in the other saints because they had not given what she had asked for and that therefore she [only had faith] in Jesus Christ.

Not only does María de la Encarnación accuse Aramburu of dragging the crucifix through excrement—one of the standard accusations made against Jews—but also of perverse sexual behaviour, including lesbianism and having unnatural relations with the orphan she had adopted.

9. This damning accusation is discounted by the Marqués de Castañiza who, in a covering letter to the Inquisitor, writes that he noted "artifice and fiction in the way of presenting herself, for on the one hand, she shows much shame and on the other boldness and frankness which are contrary to the shame that she appears to feel."[23] It also struck him as odd that María de la Encarnación should be "bedeviled" (*endemoniada*) during the time when she was apparently confessing to Father Franciso de Ynfantas. The confessor, the Marqués observes, had coached María de la Encarnación, telling her to make notes. "All that he has produced has been extracted through the interrogation and insistance of the confessor." The Marqués discovered in the confessor's interrogation "certain imprudences." He is pious and well-meaning, but

> I do not have confidence in his education or talents. He appeared to me somewhat credulous and inclined to give credit to vulgar gossip and old wives' tales. He is also of a fiery disposition and somewhat capricious, so that what with his ardent character, his small learning, and his timidity, he may have loaded his questions. And perhaps some of the things which are in the declaration [of Mora] are illusions produced by the questions themselves, rather than ideas or reports known beforehand.[24]

The Marqués is equally skeptical of various objects that Mora had produced in order to prove Aramburu's evil intentions— a doll stuck with pins, a piece of stone, and some lead. A book that had been taken away from a child because it was supposed diabolic turned out to be a common book of devotion. The Marqués gives no credit to accusations that Ana María de la Colina was depraved: "for having dealt with her and heard her speak, I do not find in her the slightest indication to presume so much malice." He did acknowledge, however, that she had been induced to hallucinate by Aramburu's fictions.[25]

10. On October 19, the order for Aramburu's imprisonment in the secret prisons of the Inquisition is issued, but she
cannot be found for several weeks. During this period her old
enemy Father Francisco Ynfantas is diligent in hunting her
down. Eventually she is discovered living with her husband in
the neighborhood of the Lagunilla market. When he takes her
into custody on January 27, 1803, the Marqués de Castañiza
is impressed by her serenity and the fact that "she went on
warming her hands in front of the brazier during the procedures." On the road to the prison she speaks "with poise and
moderation, but also with frankness and openness, without
showing fear nor even asking the reason for her imprisonment
nor any of the things the people usually ask under these circumstances" (p. 176). Before assigning her to cell number thirteen, the Inquisition makes a detailed description of her physical appearance and her clothes, which consist of a ragged
blouse, a *rebozo* (a shawl), some skirts, and a rosary which
she wears around her neck, "without having any other possessions in any place whatsoever."

11. After entering prison she is examined by a doctor who
finds an inflamation in the uterus and "fetid pus," which he
attributes to venereal disease. Since the infirmity could only
be treated by someone of her own sex, she is sent to the hospital of San Andrés, where she vomits blood, for which reason
a confessor is sent for. The confessor, Juan Díaz de Montoya,
reports that she "had not erred in anything touching the faith,
that she knows Christian doctrine, and has sufficient intelligence of the principle mysteries of our holy religion," and that
for this reason he has heard her confession and notes that she
has responded "with order and in detail" (pp. 181–182). Ana
de Aramburu's "delusion" is "cured."

12. On September 3, 1808, she writes to the Inquisition re-
questing to be admitted to the hospital of San Juan de Dios,
a request that is curtly refused on the grounds that she is due
to be released. So much for Ana de Aramburu.

Summarized in this way, the trial presents the story of a woman
who is an unsuccessful trickster and of an institution—the Inquisition—which is cautious in its verdict but nevertheless con-
siders her dangerous enough to have her imprisoned. Yet beneath

the often contradictory or incoherent evidence and the differing interpretations of Ana de Aramburu's behavior, another story can be mapped, the story of a woman who was not at all at home in the master discourse and who, indeed, tried to establish her own space. There is also the intriguing racial question. Ana gave one of her names as Moctezuma, which suggests that she was partly descended from an indigenous family. When she first appeared before the Inquisition she was described as "Spanish," i.e., as criolla, yet her skin was dark (*parda*). At the same time she claimed to have been humiliated by the fact that she was placed at one stage in the home of an Indian family where she was made to grind corn. All of this suggests not only the problems of a marginalized woman who was without family support but also the uncertain status of the mestiza who did her best to gain status in the only way possible. Her marriage to the tailor, Juan de Ortiz, probably took place just before 1800—that is, late in life, since she was already about thirty-eight when arrested, and it seems to have coincided with her move to Mexico City, where she entered into contact with the men and women of the artisan class who would become her disciples. At the time of her marriage she was already suffering from a strange "infirmity" upon which she based her claims to have unusual powers—a flux of blood that poured from her mouth. There is no reason to suppose that she could not have stayed with her husband, since he took her in when she was a refugee from the Inquisition. Hence it appears likely that she had deliberately chosen to fend for herself, perhaps because she really believed in her own powers, perhaps because she was averse to matrimony or even men.

But in the society of New Spain there was no place for women who had no estate unless they could rely on the charity of the clergy. At first Ana was sheltered by Father Esquivel; then she followed Father José María y San Joseph, who had been made prior of a Carmelite convent, to Toluca, where she was supported by members of his flock. At one point, she was placed in the home of one of his spiritual daughters, María de la Luz Rainaudo, whom she persuaded to hire a coach to take them both back to Mexico City where (she said) she intended to claim the Moctezuma inheritance. There is little doubt, however, that Ana had great expectations, and that some priests may even have encouraged her. Her friend Ana María de la Colina complained, "first they tell wonders of her and then turn against her, which drives me mad." Some of the young girls who were impressed by her activities even wrote down Aramburu's explanations of the mysteries of the Trinity and the Incarnation.[26]

It is de la Colina's evidence that suggests why Aramburu might have caused such a stir in the neighborhoods. Though she has difficulty in remembering the miracles, her evidence clearly suggests that her friend was upstaging the clergy, especially by claiming power over life and death.

De la Colina recalled the time

when the Aramburu died last year in the house of doña María de la Merced Alvarez, sister of a painter, who lives near the Carmen, close to the barracks in a tenement [vecindad] the latter had said to the witness that this time the Aramburu had seen dreadful things during her death but she did not remember what they were. And the same Aramburu had said that Our Lord had mercifully imprinted his five wounds on her and that blood flowed abundantly from them, which she had seen on several occasions. That she related that in Puebla she revived a child who had choked on a bun and a woman called Mariquita who had died without leaving a will, and that in Licenciado Esquivel's house she had forecast the day and hour of the death of señor Serruto,[27] as has been verified, and that after about seven days she got him out of purgatory and he came to ask Aramburu's forgiveness for having insulted her in life, and that in these days terrible noises were heard in the house belonging to Licenciado Esquivel in which Aramburu was living. (pp. 58–59)

Aramburu was also said to have postponed a woman's death when the confessor could not be there to perform the last rites. She condemned her enemies to long periods in purgatory and saved a woman who was about to be beaten by her lover by making her invisible. The despondent lover then became a novice in the Franciscan Order. She also forecast earthquakes.

Ana de Aramburu also played on her neighbor's belief in sympathetic magic, in animal spirits (or nahualismo).[28] She claimed that the image of a Holy Child had bent its head so that it would fit into a niche in her house and that it shared her suffering so that when her leg was swollen, the image swelled in sympathy.

All of these miracles respond to everyday problems of life, death, and sickness and are directed toward solving the practical problems of survival, of making a will before dying, of infidelity and sickness. At the same time they satisfy a desire for the miraculous and the sensational and perhaps feed a certain anticlerical resentment. For instance, Aramburu seems to have encouraged people to ignore the troublesome surveillance of the confessional, for she told one witness that

> at one time, without the guidance of any confessor and with only the help of books, she had greatly grown in virtue and that of course she would again take this path, abandoning the confessor, because the one who was her confessor, Father Francisco Jesús María y Joseph took no notice of her and she who answers [the witness] saw that in effect, he took no notice of her.[29]

Yet if we explain her away as a con woman or a *pícara*, we are likely to overlook the symbolic significance of Aramburu's performance and the way in which mysticism had been transcoded into popular lore. Indeed, two of her disciples, Juan Domingo Gutiérrez and de la Colina, mentioned mystical texts, and the latter even seems to have been familiar with the *Moradas* of Saint Theresa. Ana de Aramburu's own command of the language of mysticism was sufficient to impress at least one clerical witness, Licenciado Ignacio Pico (though he also claimed that the devil might have inspired her). He had heard her explanation of the mysterious significance of San Pedro's dream, saying that it was a figure or symbol of "slumbering, lazy souls, neglectful of their salvation," though he also found her amorous discourse with Our Lord too lukewarm (p. 99). Father Esquivel likewise noted that in her trances, despite "being a rough and ordinary woman in her everyday dealings, when she is in ecstasy she speaks with culture and of things which exceed her natural capacity," though she never committed an "error against our faith nor opposed to the discipline of the Church, nor anything ridiculous and dissonant and unworthy of the Majesty of God" (pp. 32–33). He suggested, however, that the "beautiful allegories of the garden and the countryside that she used when paraphrasing the Lord's prayer and the Ave Maria" could easily have been culled from the books she had read when young (p. 33). But such explanations only show clerical embarrassment at Ana's appropriation of "their" language. It is true that Ana's visions and holy dialogues copied down by Ana María de la Colina and included in the Inquisition evidence draw on common religious topoi—for instance, Christ as the divine gardener (the garden being the favorite space of contemplative theology)— but she transforms these commonplace sources in interesting ways.

For example, she describes Christ in detail, giving him all the physical attributes of the ideal lover and particularly emphasizing his fair skin:

> Your color is beautiful, but like a gentleman's, pink and proud. Your eyes are beautiful, peaceful, humble red. Your eyes rob hearts, Lord, your face, Oh Lord, is very honest, Lord, your beautiful red hair hangs down to your waist, You have a coral mouth so small and beautiful, very pink, Lord, your cheeks. It is true that your height is a meter and half, isn't that so, my Love? You have a fine body, thin, with small feet. How terrible to see your foot touch the ground, your hands are long, your nails well shaped, your brow wide. Is there anyone who doesn't love you? Just looking on you engenders love, your humility, your honesty, your patience, you are very peaceful. . . . I will give you my heart so that you will impress your passion onto it. (pp. 69–70)

Christ is not only "a gentleman" of European complexion but represents an androgynous ideal quite different from the swaggering machos and *léperos* of Mexico City. Ana uses rhetorical devices—the vocative, interrogation, response—to suggest that she was actually speaking to him, and does so in such a way that a listening public can imaginatively fill the gaps in the schemata. Instead of transcending the "I," like the mystics, in order to "melt" into the undifferentiated miasma of divine love, Aramburu draws attention to the performance itself[30] and to herself as the author of an amorous discourse.

But even more serious, in the eyes of the confessors, than this amorous language is her venture into dogma, for Aramburu is reported to have said to the Virgin that she was "daughter of the Father, wife of the Holy Spirit, and daughter of the Son, and that she was conceived without original sin before birth, during the birth, and after the birth." The Inquisition would characterize this statement as "the daughter of stupidity and the sister of verbosity" (i.e., the *female* relations of these undesirable qualities), for "what has original sin, which only occurs in the animation of the fetus, to do with the time before birth, during birth, and after birth, when no one can have any idea of whether the Virgin was conceived without the said sin?" (p. 128). Although Ana was offering a garbled version of the Virgin Birth and Immaculate Conception (which was not yet dogma), the issues involved are by no means trivial. The Inquisitors limit original sin to the sexual act, the "animation of the fetus," and deny any relationship between Virgin Birth and Immaculate Conception (i.e., the belief that the Virgin alone of mankind escaped original sin.) The Inquisition's excessively technical explanation is intended to put Aramburu in her place, but their rational correction cannot efface the symbolic charge of Ana's statement nor its significance as popular lore. From a contemporary point of view Ana de Aramburu's statements about Christ and the Virgin seem no more fictional than Sor María de Agreda's fanciful yet officially approved biography of Our Lady, which explained imaginatively how Immaculate Conception occurred.[31] But for the men who tried Aramburu, her statement unsupported by any "authority" could not but be incorrect.[32]

Ana de Aramburu attempted to overcome the "inferiority" of the human (and especially the female) lot and the outlawing of sexuality by using all the marks of her inferiority to advance her claims to have extraordinary powers. She could only become a valued person by transcoding the signs of social inferiority into a different discourse. Though there is no means of deducing her actual moral behavior from the Inquisition documents (the venereal disease she suffered from in the secret prisons could have been transmitted by her husband), it is certainly plausible to deduce that her body was her major resource. Though claiming to be a virgin, she had been seen suckling a child (which would mean that she had miscarried or aborted), and, when challenged with the contradiction, had claimed that she did this out of humility so that people would not know that she was a virgin. Many people saw her throw up copious blood or blood mixed with water, and even the clergy found this hard to explain. The vomiting is a carnivalesque inversion of mouth and vagina with blood taking the place of words. Menstrual blood, often associated with uncleanliness and therefore with women's devaluation, is here turned to different account, being used as a sign of special power. It makes Ana de Aramburu a unique individual, beyond the rules that bind others.[33] What is also significant is that even the charges of perverse sexuality that were brought against Aramburu (whether they were true or false) did not involve men. She was charged with kissing her adopted orphan (whose age was variously given as between six and ten) and taking him into her bed, with masturbating in public, with making women touch her sexual organs. Of course all this comes from evidence that wishes to stigmatize her as "unnatural."

To be persuasive Ana de Aramburu had to produce believable evidence of her supernatural powers, and from Ana María de la Colina's explanation quoted above it is clear that she relied on her gifts as a convincing storyteller. In this, she is the true predecessor of García Márquez' magician, Blacamán the Bad, who claimed to have risen from the dead.[34] Indeed, she claimed to have been resucitated on the day dedicated to the Sacred Heart, or the day of the Holy Trinity—after which she adopted the name Mariana de Jesús (p. 57). She could also be compared to Manuel Puig's spider woman, and, indeed, the Inquisitor described her activities as a "weave of entanglements, lies, and fictions" that "merited the greatest contempt" (p. 74). The very skills that produce her downfall are those that a century and a half later would be drawn on by writers to distinguish literature from more mundane pursuits.

The spider woman not only wove her stories but performed them, though not always convincingly. Even the credulous could not help observing that she smoked a cigarette when supposedly in a trance and that she frequently partook of mistela, a rather potent alcoholic drink. She even tried to stage elaborate performances, including one in which she tried to bring five people together so that they could exchange hearts with Christ. Father Ignacio Joseph Pico observed one such performance in which he found her

> lying down with her head on some pillows, her hands clasped on her breast . . . her eyes wide open and fixed on high, without blinking. I observed carefully for a long time and saw that she did not move her eyes, so I had them move a light from one side to the other, and, although this movement was made very close to the eyelids, she did not close or move them; after a quarter of an hour, she began to speak as if conversing with another person, giving us to understand that she was seeing Our Lord, Jesus Christ, since among other amorous things she said, "You are my beloved, you are my redeemer, you are my spouse, oh how gentle is your love." (p. 94)

Ana's performance bears some resemblance to other popular practices and lore—for instance, modern spiritualism, which also depends on a "medium" (often a woman). Such performances combine exhibitionism with a disavowal of authorship—a situation that at once puts the medium in the forefront of attention without her having to assume responsibility for her words.

What was at issue for the clergy, however, was controlling

meaning and establishing boundaries, one of the most important
boundaries being that between truth and fiction. The traditional
view was that fiction belonged to the devil, because

> the demon can fake ecstasy, raptures, spiritual conversations,
> words of the scripture, conversations between God and the
> soul, false prophecies of natural things, external shining, ex-
> terior effusions, and the appearance of blood, false obedience
> in which he wants the dominated person to obey in order the
> more surely to deceive, fake illnesses in which the person ap-
> pears to be dying, make them come to life. (p. 28)

Yet in order to determine the authenticity of such happenings,
the clergy had evolved—long before the modern state or the modern institution of medicine—a technology of the body. Of course
this could not be fully scientific since the clergy could not examine
the woman's body, but they learned to take into account plausi-
bility, the consistency of the visions with the subject's life style,
and anything else that seemed unusual. Father Esquivel thus notes
the periodicity of Aramburu's attacks, observing that they occurred "about once every month or two months," and that, "according to what they say," she expelled blood from her back and
sides. And he prudently adds,

> I say "according to what they say," because since chastity does
> not allow a priest to inspect these parts in a woman, I only
> perceived that they took out cloths stained copiously with a
> liquor as bright as vermillion and *as odiferous as balsam,* al-
> though with regard to her side, I did examine her many times
> in such a way that carefully covering all the surrounding parts,
> the nurses who were assisting her showed me it and I saw two
> or three marks as if from a scratch or some stripe as from
> inner blood or an external bruise. . . . And it is to be noted
> that according to my view she suffers these adversities when
> she wants to and convalesces from them at will, and during
> them she enjoys herself at the cost of the devout and some-
> times even drinks wine if she feels like it and even against the
> express order of the director. (p. 32)

He also deduces that she could not have been in a real trance since
she heard remarks that were made to her.

What is evidently at stake here is the delicate question of "fiction" and the troublesome problem of differentiating good from
bad "supernatural" events. It was precisely the authority to dis-

criminate that constituted clerical power.[35] Yet clearly that power was always felt to be fragile, and it was further threatened at the beginning of the nineteenth century by justifiable fears of an uprising of the subaltern classes—justifiable because such an uprising occurred in 1810 when the dissident priest Miguel Hidalgo led the first anti-Spanish revolt.

Some of this context is suggested by the lampoon that was pinned to Aramburu's door when she was living with the Orcolaga family. The lampoon is, in reality, a strip cartoon of drawings, showing a series of incidents in which Aramburu had tried to act as counselor to the Orcolaga girls, first attempting to make a match for one of them, and then advising them to enter a convent. There are even bubbles of speech that issue from the mouths of the characters, anticipating the comic strip. Because there is no way of reconstructing the incident to which the cartoon refers, it is impossible to decode it with any accuracy. Though the lampoonist finds Aramburu's pretensions ridiculous, the drawings clearly belong to the tradition of the "world turned upside down." One panel shows her seated on a dais, as if usurping the place of power, and saying, "I am mad and without sense." Underneath is the motto, "pride, vanity, majesty, and poverty," which sums up what happens when, in the lampoonist's view, women usurp the place of men.[36] As if to emphasize this threat, one of the figures in the cartoon refers to his *citoyen* (possibly the Phrygian cap, but certainly a reference to the French Revolution which had indeed turned the world upside down). Ana de Aramburu's pretensions are seen as potentially revolutionary.

Though it would be easy to represent the trial as an individual event in which an isolated woman was pitted against the Church, it is, in fact, an instance of a much more general problem: that is, the constitution of a subaltern culture as a bricolage of elements from mysticism, and the constitution of a space for bodily pleasure that was outside the sinful. Ana converted her own body into values that transformed the status of women, that turned the "low" into the "high." Only this can explain the reams of paper, the hours of time, and the bureaucratic apparatus spent on this lowly woman during a period of crisis. Unfortunately, in this particular struggle for interpretation, Ana's fragile instruments were no match for institutional power.

Yet Ana de Aramburu's case clearly marks the moment when the Inquisition is losing ground and when religion is no longer the source of power/ideology. That is what made her "fictions" so dangerous, for they responded to real needs. Decades later, when the Church came under attack, the clergy would shift their ground as they came to rely more and more on feminine "irrationalism" in their struggle against the secular state. This, in turn, inaugurated a new phase of the confessional relationship in which women would become the political instruments of the Church in its opposition to secularization. The emergent ideology of liberalism responded by inventing a new demonology in which the Church became the evil other. In his novel on the education of women, *La Quijotita y su prima* (Little Miss Quixote), written barely two decades after Ana's imprisonment, José Joaquín Fernández de Lizardi parodied female religiosity, pouring scorn on his protagonist, La Quijotita, when she mistakes a black cat for the devil (see chapter 4). Her religious and other caprices lead her to humiliation and finally into prostitution. One cannot help wondering if Lizardi, who had himself been imprisoned by the Inquisition, had come across Ana de Aramburu, whose strategies for survival would certainly not have endeared her to the secular intelligentsia any more than they did to the officers of the Inquisition.

The conclusions of the Inquisition make it clear that Ana de Aramburu was trapped, in part, because she had no status and made an illegitimate bid for power. Unlike the mystical nuns whose constant professions of obedience and humility generally warded off danger, Ana belonged to a class of people who had no place in the social text, no story and no power. It is all the more astonishing that she was able to put together her performance and even to invent a "romantic subject" constituted (as in a Buñuel film) by the very machinery (the amorous attachment to an ideal love object) that was supposed to control desire. The spider woman spins her web out of her own body, which is the only resource left to her when the official institutions have closed off or monopolized all other discursive space.

PART II

THE NATION

4

SENSE AND SENSUALITY: NOTES ON THE NATIONAL PERIOD, 1812–1910

Disintegration of paradise: nothing makes fatality more arbitrary. Absurdity of salvation: nothing makes another style of continuity more necessary. What then was required was a secular transformation of fatality into continuity, contingency into meaning. As we shall see, few things were (are) better suited to this end than the idea of nation.[1]

Nations, as Benedict Anderson has shown, are not only territories, peoples, and government, but are also "imagined"—that is, they articulate meanings, create exemplary narratives and symbolic systems which secure the loyalty and sacrifice of diverse individuals. In Mexico, as in other Latin American nations, the idea of the nation was grafted onto the bureaucratic network of the Spanish Empire. What made a substantial difference in the post-Independence period was the emergence of a new domain of discourse around the press and coffee houses and the emergence of a secular intelligentsia who aspired to replace the priesthood.[2] The nation may have been a fictional addressee, but by dint of being addressed it took on reality. Poets lovingly dedicated their odes to the "fatherland" or to the "mother fatherland" (*la madre patria*) as a creature new born out of the murky obscurantism of the colony.

In the year of Independence, 1821, the liberal intelligentsia had their eyes fixed on a homogenized modern society which they hoped could be mapped onto the diverse population of Mexico, a society dressed in European clothes and generally scrubbed and tidied up. A white society it would never be, but perhaps the "lepers" (*léperos,* the slang term for the lumpenproletariat) of the city streets and the wild Indians of the north and the descendants of the black slaves would eventually be symbolically whitened through education, through the influence of the press and civilizing literature.

The attack on the Church which helped to bring about the civil wars of mid-century was the logical outcome not only of the liberal idea of progress but of a struggle for intellectual hegemony, a struggle that gave the liberals victory in 1857 but left the Church still powerful in the provinces, among women and marginalized peoples. After the brief interregnum of Maximilian's French-imposed empire (1864–1867), churches and monasteries were closed, their lands seized, and the way was opened for the transformation of Mexico City into a modern metropolis. This was achieved during the long rule of Porfirio Díaz, which began in 1876 and ended with the Revolution of 1910. During his government, the heterogeneous provinces and peoples of Mexico began to acquire more than a phantasmagoric unity. Railways connected the provinces, there were determined attempts to subdue the rebellious indigenous populations, and Mexico City was turned into a showcase of modernization; left in limbo, however, was a vast proportion of the population—the peasantry, the underclasses, the clergy, and a great many women—some of whom must have wondered, like the inhabitants of Juan Rulfo's legendary Luvina, what kind of strange beast this entity could be when nobody knew its mother.[3]

Even in Mexico City the classical body of the Porfirian nation (displayed in the Palace of Fine Arts, the banks, and the statuary) was surrounded by pullulating markets and low music halls and theaters where the irrepressible diversity of this population was all too apparent. Yet the dark faces and the native dress, the non-European customs and languages of recent immigrants to the city, were mute witnesses to the real stratification within the nation. The economic development of Porfirian Mexico depended on the "backwardness" of sectors of the population, while its very idiosyncrasy as a nation made those same indigenous and mestizo masses symbolically central. One of the famous monuments of the Porfiriato was, as it happens, a statue of the defeated Aztec prince Cuauhtémoc.

This bizarre juxtaposition was not as arbitrary as it may seem. Indigenous communities in which symbolic production (artisan work, dance, fiestas), economic production, and reproduction of the labor force were all lodged in a single institution—the family—coexisted with plantation and mining enclaves in which the family was often broken up altogether.[4] Mulatto culture flourished alongside indigenous cultures. All the educational blueprints in the world could not alter the fact that the "backwardness" and heterogeneity of the rural population was the very basis on which the economy and cultural nationalism rested.[5] The statue of Cuauhtémoc placed at the very heart of the modern metropolis sublimated this cruel reality. But women's anachronism—their loyalty to Catholicism, their homebound existence—was, in the absence of a viable capitalist ethics, also necessary for the maintenance of the bourgeois household. The intelligentsia confronted such problems of heterogeneity by representing themselves as teachers and guides who would eventually (though not in the present) lead the indigenous, the blacks, and women out of the wilderness by means of education. And since the intelligentsia were the teachers, it followed that their readers were generally constituted as the pupils (and children) in the classroom of the nation.

THE DEPLORABLE EXAMPLE OF A FEMALE QUIXOTE

From the first, the need to recode the position of women in society was recognized by the intelligentsia. Women were especially crucial to the imagined community as mothers of the new men and as guardians of private life, which from Independence onward was increasingly seen as a shelter from political turmoil. Two aspects of the recodification of gender deserve special attention; the carving out of a territory of domestic stability and decency from which all low elements were expelled, and the displacement of the religious onto the national, which once again made "purity" the responsibility of women.

The need to modernize family life had been foreseen by the secular intelligentsia even before Independence. Yet they certainly did not want to undermine the hierarchy that made the ruler the father of the nation and the husband the ruler of the family. It was not woman's subordination within the family that the intelligentsia challenged but rather her devotion to the Church, which might lead her to pass obscurantist ideas on to the next generation. The intelligentsia set out to educate mothers so that they would instill in the new generation patriotism, the work ethic, and a belief in progress. Progressive politicians believed that the nation could be built only on the basis of productive labor for which the "colonial" family had left them little prepared. "Lazy habits" were the legacy of the colonial system and had been encouraged by the Church.[6] In colonial Mexico, upper- and middle-class children had traditionally been farmed out to wet nurses or left in the care of inexperienced servants. Women were now to be persuaded to "mother" their children by breast-feeding and educating them in early childhood in order to guarantee the future well-being of the nation.[7]

Because of this focus on the family, the progressive intelligentsia were eager to further some limited education for women, and to this end they used the didactic opportunities offered by the periodical press. The development of the press at the end of the eighteenth century had encouraged genres that did not depend on specialized knowledge or traditional erudition—in particular, the expository essay. And since anyone with access to imported books could acquire modern ideas, there was in theory nothing to stop both men and women from disseminating their opinions. The press potentially undermined the colonial hierarchy of knowledge. Correspondents addressed editors as their equals and felt free to make proposals for the good of the community.[8] Women, however, gained little from this new public space; in the first place they lacked the "cultural capital" of men, for they had not received the same schooling and were excluded from university training. And second, even when, by dint of self-education, they were able to argue on the level of the predominantly male audience, they were forced, as Sor Juana had been forced in the seventeenth century, to accept the fact that their intelligence could be put to only limited use, since their primary function was motherhood.

Given the paucity of women writers, men often wrote using feminine pseudonyms, thus asserting their control over the private as well as the public sphere.[9] Women came to participate in this discourse primarily as passive *readers*—recipients of didactic literature in which they were addressed as pupils to be taught or minds to be reformed; in this sense, they were classed with the rogues, thieves, prostitutes, léperos, and other heterogeneous elements who potentially constituted the new reading public in the eyes of such thinkers as Fernández de Lizardi.[10] This division between those who considered themselves the self-proclaimed *pensadores* of the new Mexico and those who merely occupied the benches in the imaginary classroom was determined by accessibility to cultural capital. It also gave those who had access to cultural capital a heady sense of power, a conviction of their ability to instruct in every aspect of life including conduct in the home—the domain that had traditionally been regarded as women's sphere.

Nowhere is this better illustrated than in *La Quijotita y su prima* (Little Miss Quixote and Her Cousin), a novel written by the journalist and indefatigable defender of the free press José Joaquín Fernández de Lizardi, and first published in 1818.[11] Though a "bad" (i.e., unsophisticated) novel by contemporary standards, it was paradigmatic not only because it presented the Utopian ideal of the new post-Independence family but also because the novel created two female paradigms—the good and obedient Pudenciana and the evil "little Miss Quixote."

Lizardi would insist on the "truth" of *La Quijotita*, describing it as a "true story that I witnessed and whose characters you know" (p. 12). Indeed, it is a veritable tract or blueprint for the new values of the secular family in which children were to be socialized by discipline and work, in which women were to find their own true career in marriage, and in which individual happiness could be achieved only when male and female spheres were firmly separated. In writing the novel, Lizardi drew freely on the vast literature on this subject, particularly French literature, though his source was not so much Rousseau as such earlier tracts as the Abbé Fénélon's *Traité de l'éducation des filles*.[12] He also quotes such writers as Jean Baptiste Blanchard and Antoine Leonard Thomas,[13] who belonged to a tradition of conservative thought that grounded women's subordination in their physical weakness and the need to protect them for childbirth. The more radical current of Enlightenment thought represented by Diderot and Helvetius does not appear to have reached early nineteenth-century Mexico.

Lizardi purportedly wrote *La Quijotita* in response to a request from a woman reader of an earlier novel, *El Periquillo Sarniento* (The Itching Parrot), who signed herself "La Curiosa" (the Curious Woman). She had asked him for a novel that would avoid the heavy sermonizing and obscure language of erudite tracts, "since girls who will someday be mothers are not usually attracted to this kind of serious reading that does not appear to be addressed to them" (p. 8). Whether the Curiosa herself was a real person or was invented by Lizardi is immaterial: in either case, he shows his sensitivity, at least in theory (as he had done in *El Periquillo Sarniento*), to a new class of reader whose culture was not the classical culture of the colonial period but was rather acquired through miscellaneous readings in periodical publications. In practice, he was unable to produce a pleasurable text because he assumed that his readers must be weaned from pleasure and turned to more productive forms of living through homily and rational dialogue.

The novel was, perhaps, not the appropriate genre for what turned out to be a series of secular sermons that attacked not only the habits of the old aristocratic family but also the modern "madness" of "little Miss Quixote." Fernández de Lizardi's concession to the novel form consists primarily in a first person narrator who, like a fly on the wall, is able to overhear women's gossip and report it to the paternalistic father of the text, don Rodrigo. This new paternalism was perhaps in part intended to foreshadow the as yet nonexistent secular state (the novel was published just before Independence). The burden of nationhood was thus placed on the family, which was responsible not only for internalizing Christian morality but also for developing the virtues necessary for the smooth functioning of a society that could no longer be policed by the Spanish imperial bureaucracy, the Inquisition, and the Church.

The French philosophes had distinguished between the absolute power of the old order and a new paternal power that was considered a duty as much as a right, a duty that followed inevitably from the natural superiority of the father within the family. What was new in their definition was the emphasis on love and benevolence rather than coercion.[14] And whereas in the aristocratic family women had exercised power through inheritance, in the bourgeois family they were obliged to conjugate love and marriage in a way that produced a new kind of dependency, one that was frequently embraced freely (in the name of love and in conscious rejection of the older type of forced marriages). In *La Quijotita* Lizardi presents the loving and orderly family of don Rodrigo, which he then contrasts with a disorderly "Dionysian" family—that of the appropriately named don Dionisio, which is dominated by women and the pleasure principle. The names of the members of these families indicate the function of each member. Rather than "characters" in the usual sense, they are like theses and antitheses in an argument. The good family is headed by a retired colonel with the good *castizo* (i.e., pure Spanish) name of don Rodrigo. His wife has the plain and unpretentious name Matilde, with its connotations of quiet respectability. The name Pudenciana epitomizes the modesty and reserve proper to the daughter's role. Matilde's sister and her family are quite the reverse. The father, don Dionisio, is lackadaisical, unable to manage his affairs or to resist pleasure.

His wife is Eufrosina, whose name symbolizes pagan frivolity. His daughter, Pomposa (the Quijotita of the title), is both pompous and a "bubble" (*pompa* in Spanish).

What is striking is that in this liberal tract, the ideal of domestic life has become, if anything, more circumscribed than that described by Fray Luis de León in his classic essay on married life, *La perfecta casada* (The Perfect Wife), written in the sixteenth century and the basis for the Catholic ideal of the family.[15] For Fray Luis the family was an economic unit as well as an alliance formed for reproduction. The perfect wife governs an army of servants and dependents who provide the household economy with food, clothing, and bed linen, and she has little time for idleness or repose. In contrast, in *La Quijotita*, Matilde no longer has any role in productive labor. She is first and foremost a mother who, once her child enters school, has little to do but attend to her religious devotions, to the moral instruction of her child and her maids, and to making her husband's life more comfortable. She describes her afternoons thus:

> After dinner, we rest for a while, until a little after three. He usually goes out and I go to my room [*estrada*] where surrounded by my family I work at my embroidery frame and cushion until they go for my daughter at four thirty; when she returns, we recite the rosary and I read them some of the catechism for my daughter, Tulitas, and the maids, since as you know it is the mistress's duty to teach the doctrine to their servants. Then it is time for prayers; the maids go about their tasks, the children play, and I busy myself with our affairs. At this time, Linarte returns, we drink chocolate and sometimes we converse; on other occasions, I play the clavichord or I go to your house and sometimes to the theater. (p. 102)

In one of his lengthy homilies, don Rodrigo Linarte (who, it is worth stressing, is a retired colonel, although he spends much of his day outdoors on unspecified business) justifies the restriction of women to these domestic tasks on the grounds of their physical weakness. For this reason, women cannot participate in active pursuits like men. A woman with a child in her arms could scarcely be expected to carry a gun, nor could she wield a chisel or pen or push a plough.

> Women's inferiority with respect to the man consists in nothing more than the weakness of her physical constitution, that

is to say, her body; with respect to the spirit she is in no way
weaker than a man; since the soul is neither masculine nor
feminine, it follows that with regard to the spirit, you are our
equals. (pp. 72–73)

Even so, this supposed spiritual equality is neutralized since woman's body affects her spirit. In adolescence women are susceptible
to *furor uterino,* that is, a "delirium or frenzy which makes them
commit by deed or word a thousand excesses shameful and repugnant to all honest and modest people" (p. 75).

When don Rodrigo's patient wife points out to him that despite
their capacities women have indeed been badly treated—a point
Lizardi could hardly fail to acknowledge—don Rodrigo answers
lamely that only barbarians beat their wives. He argues that civ-
ilized men had excluded women from the public sphere not out of
contempt for them but rather out of regard for their weak constitution and in order to reserve them for those objects for whose
care they are destined by nature (pp. 78–79).

Mothering is a gift of nature and the main justification for wom-
en's confinement to the home; it explains why they cannot be admitted to serious study of abstract questions, to university or Church
careers, and why their intellectual development must remain strictly
limited. The colonel allows his own daughter to go to school but
insists that from an early age she be segregated from boys. As she
grows older he himself and not the mother counsels her on courtship and the evils of adultery. Though Pudenciana is allowed to
dance (one of the few legitimate forms of courtship), she must not
waltz. She is encouraged to ride astride a horse instead of side-
saddle, since exercise is important to future mothers, and she is
also taught to repair watches in order to provide her with an occupation in case she is ever left a widow. Otherwise her education
differs little from that advocated by the Abbé Fénélon in the seventeenth century, and her life at home allows her less social life
than she would have enjoyed in most convents.

Since the novel is primarily a polemic that juxtaposes two contrasting life styles, Lizardi structures his novel around two girls
with very different characters. Pomposa and Pudenciana. Curiously, both girls are the only children of their respective families, a
fact that facilitates the polemical structure of the novel but strains
credibility, especially given the fact that motherhood is so highly
valued. In the case of Pomposa's mother, the frivolous Eufrosina,
the small family is explicable. She had put two children out to wet

nurses and they had died. But the virtuous Matilde, whom the reader might expect to have a large family, has a mysterious illness that leaves her sterile. There is no male successor to don Rodrigo, hence the great importance of Pudenciana's marriage. The colonel's small family, isolated from other relatives and looking inward upon itself, also anticipates the bourgeois ideal of a small self-sufficient group. As Philippe Ariès points out, "in the eighteenth century, the family began to hold society at a distance, to push it back beyond a steadily extending zone of private life."[16] The single-child family is a novelistic convenience which incidentally represents in Utopian fashion the extension of privatized space in which husband and wife are bound not simply by interest and inheritance but also by intimacy and affection. Thus, despite the limitations he places on women, Lizardi does advocate a family that is more humanitarian, in which parent/child relationships are governed by love and respect rather than by self-interest. This new form of rational upbringing, however, cannot coexist with older methods which had traditionally been handed down by women. Lizardi uses don Rodrigo to castigate old wives' tales, ghost stories and witchcraft, and other women's lore (p. 57).

It is therefore the husband who is given the final responsibility for education and welfare, which are elevated into disciplines and are thus no longer merely practices handed down by traditional means. The woman's sphere is confined to the home, where she looks after the corporal needs of children during the period when the child is still a slave to nature.

In Lizardi's novel, Pudenciana triumphantly justifies the colonel's method of child rearing. She marries don Modesto, a man without a family of his own, "absolutely alone" and therefore a self-made man who has no need of family connections to succeed. Lizardi gives him some vague occupation in trade and, "although he had little capital, it was enough to support a decent girl." The couple set themselves up on their own, thus forming a small self-sufficient family with the new female subject ideologically positioned as an instrument of nature. Her education is intended both to discipline her natural passions and to supplement the natural inclination for motherhood. The discipline has been made all the more necessary because of the seductiveness of consumer culture represented by Matilde's sister Eufrosina and her daughter, Little Miss Quixote, or Pomposa.

Because this is a didactic novel, Eufrosina and Pomposa cannot be given a fair hearing, for this might seduce the reader. Nor can

Lizardi let Eufrosina and her daughter get out of hand as comic
characters, since this might inspire sympathy. There is thus a vast
gulf between Lizardi's work and the Cervantine paradigm to which
it makes reference, for it is not only that Lizardi is a less skillful
narrator but that the pleasure text, the "delighting" that Cervantes
linked to the moral aspects of literature, has now become posi-
tively dangerous. The colonel who, as Eufrosina notes, acts as if
he were a missionary or priest, intercedes whenever the "Dionysian" discourse seems in danger of getting out of hand.

Since Eufrosina and Pomposa have to enact all the roles that
make women a threat to the social order, this also works against
their becoming "characters" in the full sense of the realist novel.
Eufrosina is more like a debating opponent who upholds not only
the superiority of women but their right to pursue pleasure liberated from male control. Only by reading the novel against the
grain of Lizardi's editorializing can we appreciate the libidinal energy that posed such a threat.

Eufrosina describes her life as a constant round of socializing
and entertainment, underlining Lizardi's fear that women's liberation could only encourage female license and thus threaten social
reproduction. Since she and Quijotita are the only actors who are
generated by the actant "disorder," they each have to enact very
different and often contradictory forms of disorder. For instance,
Eufrosina is both a snob and yet too intimate with members of
the lower classes. Pomposa, for her part, has to incarnate the contradictory roles of extreme religiosity and extreme licentiousness,
of love of luxury and unhealthy austerity, of snobbery, which makes
her look to the aristocracy for a husband, and a lack of discrimination, which blinds her to the signs of people's social status. Lizardi
attempts to lend verisimilitude to these violent contradictions by
attributing them to her "quixotic" character, which makes her act
out every caprice.

The nickname "La Quijotita" (Little Miss Quixote) is bestowed
on Pomposa by a certain Sansón Carrasco (named after a character in *Don Quixote*), who defines her form of madness as woman's madness of excess. Thus what might in some circumstances
be considered a virtue (her quickness, her imagination) is represented as a dangerous vice. She learns the catechism too rapidly
and therefore does not really understand it; she parrots pedantic
speech, thus aspiring imperfectly to male discourse without being
able to master it; her imagination turns a cat into a vision of the
devil. Her lack of judgment makes her hold a funeral ceremony

for her pet dog and run away from home in order to become a hermit. We note, however, that Miss Quixote's vices are all attempts to encroach on male territory, to acquire knowledge/power or status, and that Lizardi, in turn, converts this into a female form of madness.

When Miss Quixote's father loses his fortune and leaves home, she makes a bad marriage, and afterward, having no money, she is forced into prostitution by her mother, who thus turns out to be the real villain of the novel, the person most responsible for her daughter's disgrace and death. Such severe fictional punishment was certainly intended to serve as a warning against female mobility and individuality, while the contrasting success of Pudenciana underscores the superiority of an upbringing in which the father plays a major role. In Pomposa's case, mobility becomes a positive danger. When she runs away from home to become a hermit, she is exposed to unnamed horrors and has to degrade herself by taking shelter in the hut of an *indio carbonero* (an Indian charcoal-burner). Home, by implication, is the only safe place for the woman. Furthermore, in Lizardi's view, the virtues demanded by the Utopian society he envisaged—thrift, hard work, obedience, self-discipline—though supposedly rational and hence inherent in human nature, need the supplement of education, for untutored and undisciplined nature is always susceptible to the seductions of pleasure. Aside from general precepts on the education of women conveyed through the contrasting lives of the two daughters, Lizardi also prescribes what should be read and what recreation women should enjoy. Those activities which had formerly provided a space for women's creativity—gossip, fashion, story-telling, visions of saints or the devil, dancing and music—now come under the censorious eye of the father who insists that only practical and "rational" knowledge has validity.

Fernández de Lizardi's "new woman" as well as his harsh representation of the liberated woman was to be paradigmatic. In the nineteenth century there was a steady stream of moralizing literature, condemning the woman who was too much of a flirt to marry (in Nicolás Pizarro Súarez' *La coqueta*); as well as the moral dangers that came from indiscriminate social intercourse—for instance, at balls like the one described in José Tomás Cuellar's sketches, *La linterna mágica* (The Magic Lantern)[17] At the same time such texts bitterly ridiculed women who like La Quijotita had the temerity to read books and express opinions. As recently as 1946, the highly regarded novelist Mariano Azuela published *La mujer domada* (The Tamed Woman), a novel that parodies the attempt of a provincial girl, Pinita, to study and improve herself. When it was republished in 1958 by the Secretaría de Educación Pública, the introductory note insisted that its characters were drawn from reality.[18]

Throughout the nineteenth century the intelligentsia continued to "teach" women how to be domestic. One of the most significant vehicles for this reeducation was the "calendar" which adapted the religious calendar to secular purposes. Yearly calendars were published and edited for both sexes, but, for reasons that are not altogether clear, the 1840s saw a flurry of publications—both calendars and journals—destined for women. The publisher Mariano Galván, for instance, seems to have been a kind of one-man band producing calendars that included poems, short stories, advice, fashion notes, and scientific articles as well as a list of religious feast days. The calendar was thus a hybrid, both traditional and modern, preserving the religious calendar and emblems alongside romantic poems and stories and up-to-date advice.

Journals founded for the education of women tended to follow a similar pattern. *El Semanario de las Señoritas Mejicanas* (1841–1842) and *Panorama de las Señoritas* (1842) were both published by Vicente García Torres, though much of the material was written by Isidro Gondra.[19] It is hard to imagine women responding,with much enthusiasm to being coached in social decorum. One article began, "After having shown our amiable subscribers how they might perfect their talents through verbal instruction given by teachers [*maestros,* i.e., male teachers in Spanish] and professors today, we will touch on the advantages that may be acquired from conversation."[20] Women were told that they were being instructed so that they could resist worldly seduction and fulfill the destiny "that Providence has designed for them." They should

> understand the importance of their duties, both religious and moral, and should, from childhood and youth onward, acquire that knowledge which might console them for the passing of that time of life which is so full of illusions. The literary, moral, and physical world can enrich our Mexican women who today seem destined to vegetate, with all their treasures.[21]

The first issue of the *Panorama de las Señoritas* specifically separated the male interest in public affairs from the women's sphere. Women were to be recruited into a program of modernization not as partners but as beauties, as mothers, as lovers and spouses, as friends and consolers.

Frances Calderón de la Barca, a Scottish woman married to the Spanish Ambassador who arrived in Mexico in 1839, gave a more depressing view of this domestication, finding that women were cordial and warm but overdressed and intellectually limited. Schools and governesses were poor and mothers failed to offer any stimulus or encouragement to their daughters.

> They have no public diversion, and no private amusement. . . . When very young they occasionally attend the miserable schools where boys and girls learn to read in common, or any other accomplishment that the old woman can teach them; but at ten in this precocious country they are already considered too old to render it safe for them to attend these promiscuous assemblages, and a master or two is got in for drawing or music until at fourteen their education is complete.

As for the intelligentsia, they are content if their daughters "confess regularly, attend church constantly, and can embroider and sing a little. Nothing more seems to be required of them."[22]

The tone of condescension and the distance of the speaker from her material is characteristic of metropolitan travel literature of the period, which converted the entire peripheral world into the amusing or disgraceful object of a superior gaze. Yet the Mexican intelligentsia similarly adopted a distanced view when describing the backward behavior of their countrymen.[23] Though classing women with children, the intelligentsia also created an image of the home as an inviolate private sphere, one in which the woman ruled. Scenes of domestic life published in newspapers and written by prominant male intellectuals and journalists such as Guillermo Prieto and Manuel Payno celebrated the ups and downs of married life, often insisting on the myth of male subjection to women's wiles.[24] Yet there is ample evidence to show that domesticity did not always imply the apolitical and passive. At a time of civil war, women took on the political cause of their husbands, which often involved them in great personal risk. For instance when Concepción Lombardo de Miramón, the wife of General Miramón, supporter of the emperor Maximilian, learned that her husband had been condemned to be executed alongside the emperor, she pleaded and plotted for his release. This domesticated and deeply religious

woman undertook dangerous journeys through the battle lines; after her husband's execution and when she was living abroad as
the wife of a "traitor," she wrote two volumes of memoirs which
successfully combine the personal with the political, skillfully in-
terlacing the story of her sheltered upbringing, with her own and
others' accounts of the civil wars and political battles of mid-century.[25] What this demonstrates, however, is a dormant capacity
only awakened in extreme situations. The life of this conservative
widow is in its way exemplary. The widow seems to take on some
of the male power of her dead husband. No doubt there were many
similar examples on the liberal and revolutionary sides.

LITERATURE AND STATE FORMATION

One of the crucial changes that marked the period of peaceful stability during the Porfirio Díaz regime was the emergence of the
literary institution. As Peter Bürger describes this process in Europe,
that institution is only recognized as such once it has established
the autonomy of literature from everyday life. At that moment a
shift can be observed between an art that serves bourgeois society
(realism) to aestheticism, in which art not only sheds "all that is
alien to it" but becomes "problematic for itself. As institution and
content coincide, social ineffectuality stands revealed as the es-
sence of art in bourgeois society."[26] In Mexico this would occur
with the movement known as Modernismo, which corresponds to
fin-de-siécle aestheticism in Europe.[27]

Yet Bürger's remarks do not exactly match Latin American experience, since on that continent the pressing of literature into the
service of national formation coexisted with the aestheticism of the
Modernist movement whose exemplary figure was the ubiquitous
Nicaraguan Rubén Darío. Modernismo burst the narrow bonds of
nationalism, eschewed didacticism, and proclaimed an unabashed
aestheticism. Yet Mexico's version of Modernism was idiosyncratic, ranging from Manuel Gutiérrez Nájera's sketches of the
"modernity" of Mexico City life to the experimental poetry of Juan
José Tablada.[28].

Women writers all over the continent struggled to find spaces
for themselves within the debate on national formation or within
Modernismo. The Cuban Gertrudis Gómez de Avellaneda and the
Peruvian Clorinda Matto de Turner, to mention only two examples, allied themselves with the racially oppressed, rather as Harriet

Beecher Stowe did in the United States. In Uruguay, Delmira
Agustini made space within Modernismo for the woman bohemian. But there are no parallels to these women in Mexico. Traditionally strong in times of war and civil strife, Mexican women
were slow to challenge the domestication of women and often fearful
of taking a step into areas where their decency would be put into
question.[29]

The domestication and commodification of women were not only
discourses but were practices which belonged to the sites of everyday life activity—the home and the places of public spectacle such
as the Alameda, the central park, in which the fashionable paraded
their finery. But there were also other domains of discourse—notably the periodical press and the literary academy which offered
a different kind of public space—one in which the intelligentsia
could represent themselves as allegories of the new nation.

The educational system had, indeed, brought new men onto the
political and cultural scene of the nineteenth century, men like Benito
Juárez and Ignacio Altamirano, both of whom were from indigenous families and both of whom succeeded in representing progressive modernity.[30] Education and the press were the primary
tools that enabled such men to join the intellectual elite. But it was
in literary circles that the blueprints for national literature were
developed. There were dozens of these literary circles formed between the 1830s and the end of the century. Even though some
women participated in the circles and were respected as poets, these
were predominantly male institutions, and the tone of lectures was
highflown and patriotic.[31]

A characteristic example is the 1851 lecture at the Liceo Hidalgo
delivered by Francisco Zarco in which he described the object of
literature as the redemption of humanity: "To teach luminous truths,
correct the harmful vices of humanity, give a little faith and hope
to those who suffer on Earth, that is the grandiose mission of literature in our time."[32] Toward the end of the century, the tone of
these literary academies had become even more exaltedly nation-
alistic; thus the novelist Ignacio Altamirano described the literary
evening as the "sanctuary" of the future prophets of civilization,
as well as places where the memory of the patriarchs of the past
would be preserved, and he promised they "will sleep peacefully
in their graves because they leave worthy disciples in the nation,
disciples who will remember them with tears and will repay them
with the most gratifying of tributes—the imitation of their works
and virtues." The novel was the Bible of this apostolate and the

means of initiating lower orders into the "mysteries of modern civilization."[33] Interestingly, Altamirano's advice to women writers was to write with passion and feeling but not to imitate Sor Juana's obscure jargon.[34]

However, it was not only a question of whether women had access to literary life. Rather, the problem was the separation of the public from the private sphere and the incorporation of national literature into the former, leaving women primarily with a duty to the hearth and to the expression of private feeling. There is no doubt that Latin America's lowly place in the world system led to a compensatory "virilization" of literature and a high valorization of those genres that responded to what were perceived as important national questions (i.e., social, philosophical, and historical novels and essays on social questions).[35] Women in their domesticity were no doubt struck by the triviality of their own preoccupations in comparison with such pressing national needs and were, understandably, reluctant to venture into areas that were foreign to their experience. Those men who had an interest in encouraging women to write were indeed hard put to find them a place within nationalist literature. This is clear from a lecture given by José María Vigil, director of the National Library and a man sympathetic to women writers. He clearly believed that inner feeling and domesticity were women's privileged territory, though he did not deny that one or two women had risen to the heights of heroism. Ideally woman's feelings, her creativity and domesticity should be in harmony:

> [Woman] feels the flame of love with great intensity but in her rapture, in the delicious ecstasy that envelops her soul, no unchaste image sullies the purity of her flight; and when disappointment wounds her adolescent illusions, when the brutal hand of someone who misunderstands her withers the spring flowers of her life, she resignedly bows and turns her tearful eyes toward that otherworldly region of eternal justice where those who weep are the fortunate. The warmth of the hearth holds an ineffable enchantment for her; for there the purest and most profound feelings are born and develop—filial affection, conjugal and maternal love, which fortify the soul, infusing it with heroic abnegation to support the reverses of fortune and the miseries of life. . . . The Mexican woman writer is above all a woman and woman in Mexico is, liter-

ally, the angel of the house, of that sanctuary which has not
been penetrated by those theories harmful to family which is
the most solid key stone of the social edifice.[36]

Vigil's anxiety to promote women writers seems to have been
inspired by a desire to balance the public role of literature with its
feminine counterpart, a literature both patriotic and domestic. When
he delivered a lecture to the Mexican Academy in 1882, he spoke
on a woman poet, Doña Isabel Prieto de Landázuri—a surprising
choice for this period. However, he represented her as an exemplary woman, author of a play, El Angel del hogar (The Angel in
the Home) and of poems on motherhood. He compared her fa-
vorably to Sor Juana, who did not reveal "the slightest motherly
feeling." Doña Isabel, however, died of breast cancer at an early
age, a fortuitous but ironic ending for this heroine of motherhood.[37]

THE NAKED CORPSE AND THE FASHIONABLE SKELETON

The intelligentsia of the Porfiriato moved between the high and
the low, from respectable society to the brothel, though the latter
was fraught with risk. A rather disapproving hygenist of the period, Dr. Luis Lara y Pardo, may possibly have exaggerated when
he estimated that one hundred and twenty of every thousand women
were registered prostitutes and declared venereal disease to have
reached "epidemic proportions," yet his warning that men should
take the maximum precautions during intercourse could scarcely
be considered radical at a time when sexuality and death were so
closely associated in literature.[38]

The separation of public from private, in fact, produced something of the same effect on women's sexuality that religious discourse had done, making it either heretical or impossible. For men,
on the other hand, the bohemian life allowed them to cross over
into the low and forbidden world of sexual promiscuity. "Bohemian" becomes the euphemism for this contamination in which
physical risk commingled with religious guilt. The literary text is
often a teasing peep show in which sexuality is either introduced
only to be repressed by the moral code (typically in the novel) or
disguised by euphemisms (typically in poetry). As Stallybrass and
White have pointed out with regard to England,

whilst the "low" of the bourgeois body becomes unmentionable, we hear an ever-increasing garrulity about the *city's*
"low"—the slum, the rag-picker, the prostitute, the sewer—
the "dirt" which is "down there." In other words, the axis of
the body is transcoded through the axis of the city, and whilst
the bodily low is "forgotten," the city's low becomes a site of
obsessive preoccupation, a preoccupation which is itself intimately conceptualized in terms of discourses of the body.[39]

In Mexico, this transposition can also be effected by more traditional means by applying the code of religious morality. A brief
but telling illustration will perhaps suffice. It takes the form of an
entry in the diary of Federico Gamboa, man about town, skeptic
reconverted to Catholicism, diplomat, author of a famous novel,
Santa (Saint)[40], which is strongly reminiscent of Zola's *Nana* and,
in his personal life, an upholder of the prevailing double standard.
  Gamboa's diary indeed merits comment, since, on the surface at
least, it would seem to belong to the "private" writing that was
left to women. Gamboa, however, "masculinized" the genre, writing his diary for publication and revealing his inner life in order
to construct a public persona that can transcend the death and
corruption around him. Nothing illustrates this better than a passage in the diary in which he describes a visit to the morgue where
the body of the murdered prostitute, Esperanza Gutiérrez, better
known as La Malagueña, is laid out naked on a slab. She had been
killed by a rival soon after a masked ball that Gamboa had at-
tended and where he had actually conversed with her. He is thus
able to suggest that he has sinned in order to prepare the ground
for his purification. Accompanied by a friend who has decided to
sketch the naked body, Gamboa finds himself contemplating the
"absolutely naked" and "untempting" body on the slab, "the
bloodless feet looking something like old ivory: her face with a
horrible hole under the left eye, a wound that took away her cares;
her lips half open with the grimace of those who have gone forever."[41]
  In Gamboa's novel *Santa,* the female prostitute symbolizes the
inevitable corruption of the provinces under the corrosive effect
of city life. Here, in his diary, the naked body becomes the grotesque low with its gaping careless apertures, drained of all attraction. But Gamboa's attention is now attracted to the "hundreds
of persistent flies half drunk on the setting sun, with their suspi-
cious odors and ancient dried up blood" which passed over and

flew around "the naked defenseless body." He meditates on the decomposition of the body, a fate that awaits us all. Most of all he is "fatally attracted" to "the scar of her wounded eye, the diminutive scar over which fell her proud, disordered blonde hair, now disheveled and dirty." What fascinates him? Is it the fact that she cannot return the look because there is no eye? The dead Malagueña makes Gamboa uneasily aware of the scopic power of the male look because here the object offers no barrier, no distance. There are no clothes, no lowered or defiant gaze. For once, the powerful male eye hesitates. But only for a moment. The diary becomes the place of public penance where sexual guilt can be exorcised as a meditation before the *mementi mori*. In other words, the transcoding of the low sexual into the social allows Gamboa to reaffirm traditional values.

In contrast, the Modernist elevates sexuality and turns it into aesthetic contemplation. Here, the exemplary writer is Manuel Gutiérrez Nájera, Modernist journalist, poet, and writer of urban sketches. In his stories, as in Gamboa's novels, the city offers an opportunity for promiscuity, for the mixing of different social types. A short sketch about a tram ride is a celebration of heterogeneity.[42] Yet "contamination" still lurks close to the surface—tuberculosis being the transposition into readable terms of an unmentionable problem. But Gutiérrez Nájera also found ways of transposing sensuality into the readable, displacing it from the naked body to the luxuriously clothed body-as-commodity.

For the liberal intelligentsia, commerce was a social cement, the sign of a modern mentality. While the moralists traditionally criticized women's fashions as indulgence and the index of social decay, many of the progressive intelligentsia saw fashion as the positive symbol of modernity. Here was a domain where women could take the initiative. While male dress had become more sober and uniform, women were allowed such irrational extravagances as the crinoline and the bustle. But the significance of fashion went beyond dress. It was the aesthetic counterpart of the market, the first system of signifiers that appeared to have no reference to anything other than differentiation. If each new fashion nudged out the last, then where could one find a stable grounding of values? The consequences of the commodification of culture, which reduced everything to subjective choice and personal taste, seemed to point toward chaos. Kant had anticipated the problem by separating the universal category of the beautiful from subjective evaluations that apply to the pleasurable. Modernismo incorporated taste into the beautiful but reserved the scopic and evaluative glance for the male. The feminine allegorized both the purity of poetry, its release from the crude world of commerce, and at the same time the retention of a sensuality that could now be indulged because detached from any human reference.

It was through beauty, fashion, and taste that literature liberated itself from the retrograde didacticism of the naked cadaver, turning the clothed female body into a fetishistic object of desire. Though this transformed women into something other than a function of family life or an outcast low body, it also emphasized the link between women and commodification, as is clear from one of Gutiérrez Nájera's delightful sketches. In this fantasy, the poet imagines himself shrinking to the size of an elf and plunging into a trunkful of his mistress' clothes:

> I am in the middle of silky underwear, white linen, light Indian cotton all warm, amorous, and perfumed. Inside the great trunk I smell a delicious scent of violets. . . . Here is the lovely morning robe with its rose colored ribbons, here her lacy cap which gives such a coquettish and picturesque aspect to her blonde hair; here the light colored stocking with beautifully embroidered flowers and leaves. . .[43]

In this orgy of sensuality, woman becomes an aesthetic object and can be conjured up metonymically by each one of her garments. The writer luxuriates in this, thanks to his magical transformation into an elf. No longer a teacher, he becomes a playful voyeur, and in this capacity constitutes feminine sexuality as a site of pleasure. In "objectifying" sensuality in this way, literature ensured a constitution of Woman that avoided troublesome dialogue with women and invented a Modernist aesthetic that was transnational in scope.

WOMAN'S PLACE

The Argentine critic Sylvia Molloy speaks of the *aniñamiento*— the reduction of women to the status of children at this period.[44] This was encouraged by the mentor position adopted by intellectuals such as Vigil. One of the most prolific woman writers to emerge at the turn of the century, María Enriqueta, would thus adopt the mask of ingenuousness and childishness and a subordinate position. "I am resigned," she wrote in one poem.

to the obscure name
of the one who carelessly intones her lament.
In the harmonious nave,
my song does not aspire to leave any trace.

[Yo me conformo con el nombre obscuro
del que entona, sin miras, su querrella.
Bajo naves acordes con la acustica,
no pretende mi canto dejar huella.][45]

And a talented woman writer of the period, Laura Méndez de
Cuenca, gave her short stories the title *Simplezas* (Simple Pieces),
thus deliberately guarding herself against heavy-duty criticism.[46]
The contribution of Mexican women to their pavilion at the Chicago
World's Fair illustrates the bizarre channeling of talents and a ten-
dency to miniaturization. Cristina Ramírez contributed a model of
a silver mine complete with miniature workers,[47] which was displayed among samples of carefully embroidered butterflies and
sumptuously crafted ecclessiastical garments. In the separation of
"art" from "craft," the latter was left to women and the popular
classes.

But some of the poems included in Vigil's anthology reflect,
though timidly, nonconformity with domestication. A poem by Ester
Tapia describes a soul ascending to heaven while another is about
to be incarnated in human form. The ascending soul advises the
other that if it wishes to enjoy love, it should not become the soul
of a woman, since women spend their lives weeping, enslaved to
male whims.

If for a moment her beauty he adores
Cruel indifference she swiftly meets
Remembered only in his sorrow
forgotten in his happiness.[48]

This timid murmur of rebellion is an indication that women did
not feel at home either in the national narrative or in Modernist
liberation. The stories of Laura Méndez de Cuenca, author of one
of the few novels written by a Mexican woman in the nineteenth
century, reflect this discomfort. Though imbued with the literary
ideologies of the time—a third person narrator, a moralizing intention, and an unadorned workmanlike style—they depict human relationships which are not, as in most of her male contemporaries, allegorical signposts for the state of the nation. Moreover,

she does not confine herself to scenes of marital life. Rather, many of her stories seem to revolve around the problem of upward mobility—the painful attempts of peasants and lower-middle-class people to keep themselves afloat or to rise in the world. Several of her stories indirectly deal with women's emancipation. One of them concerns woman's situation outside the usual trials of marriage, love, and infidelity, and one, "Heroína de Miedo" (Heroine of Fear), is a brief convincing account of woman's imprisonment within the home. In this story, the newly married María Antonia tries her best to live the enclosed life that is expected of her while her husband spends most of his life outdoors. But she is well protected by the servant Casimira, and is resigned to a life "of obedience and irresponsibility" whose monotony is relieved only by her hope of having a son whom she intends to educate to be "free and responsible." One evening, when left alone, she sees a robber with a knife waiting under the bed and, instead of screaming, she outwits the thief. In "La tanda" (The Stage), the daughter of a woman who works in a cigarette factory attempts to better herself by becoming an actress and giving recitals which are so good that they make the poetry of inferior male poets sound better. Her career, however, comes to an abrupt end when she dies of consumption. Both stories reflect, though timidly, on wasted talent.

It would be a mistake to see this frustration as the only way nineteenth-century women were able to confront the master discourses of domesticity. Women were often at the forefront of rebellions against capitalist modernization. It was a Chamula woman, Augusta Gómez Checheb, who became the "Mother of God" during the so-called caste war of Chiapas in 1868 (see chapter 6). In 1889 Teresa Urrea, the illegitimate child of an *hacendado* in Cabora, began to have visions and to cure people, and two years later the rebel community of Tomóchic declared her its patron saint. Rebellious mayos and yaquis battled Federal troops shouting "Long Live the Queen of the Mayos and Yaquis, the Saint of Cabora." Despite the fact that she did not participate directly in these events, Teresa was exiled to the United States where she lived until her death and became a nationally known healer.[49] A few decades later another woman, the Madre Concha, would be charged with instigating the assassination of Obregón.[50] All these women, however, were connected with ethnic movements or with Catholic resistance to modernization. We also have to take into account, therefore, a tradition that is only now coming to light of women's struggles in Independence and Reform movements and in the anarchist and workers' movements of the late nineteenth and early twentieth centuries. It would be a long time, however, before the national literature could accommodate women who were something other than symbols of purity or corruption, perhaps because, as Octavio Paz was to point out in his well-known 1950 essay, *The Labyrinth of Solitude,* the very construction of national identity was posited on male domination.[51]

This question of identity was to be sharply redefined with the Mexican Revolution of 1910–1917. Women's active participation in the Revolution and feminist congresses held during the revolutionary period for the first time brought the debate on women's emancipation into the public sphere.[52] In the following chapters, I shall be examining a different kind of struggle for interpretive power, one that attempts to displace the mythical Woman of post-revolutionary discourse.

5
BODY AND SOUL: WOMEN AND POSTREVOLUTIONARY MESSIANISM

The Revolution of 1910–1917 was publicly presented as (and indeed had been) a major social transformation. A million people had died in the Revolution, many more had seen their lives transformed. Women had followed armies, fought, fled from their homes, lost their men, survived, had nursed and fed troops.[1] Further, during the Revolution an incipient feminist movement had taken shape.[2] Yet the Revolution with its promise of social transformation encouraged a Messianic spirit that transformed mere human beings into supermen and constituted a discourse that associated virility with social transformation in a way that marginalized women at the very moment when they were, supposedly, liberated.

Nothing illustrates this more clearly than the contradictory figures of José Vasconcelos and Diego Rivera. Vasconcelos, as Minister of Education during the presidency of General Obregón (1920–1924), introduced an ambitious plan for educating the illiterate rural masses. Literacy "missions" were sent to the remote areas, and he commissioned murals for public buildings in order to instruct people in national ideals.[3] Vasconcelos' Messianic vision drew support and admiration from all over Latin America. The celebrated Chilean poet Gabriela Mistral was one of those who came to participate in the "evangelical crusade," and when Vasconcelos resigned as Minister in 1925 she described him as the "best of your men . . . the most constructive man that the race of Adam has produced in this poor America."[4] Vasconcelos drew women recruits into the literacy campaigns and sent them on educational missions to the rural areas, realizing that as teachers women would not only create a new social space for themselves but would alter education itself by giving it a more maternal image. Women who were often unable to complete long careers in medicine or other disciplines flocked into teaching. Vasconcelos sought to dignify the career by transforming it into a social mission and the teacher (*maestro* or *maestra*) into national heroes and heroines. "In the whole history of Mexico," writes José Joaquín Blanco, "there does not exist any official project for the redemption of women comparable to or as practical as that conceived by Vasconcelos. . . . For the first time, it gave ordinary women an important function in the social and political life of the country not as the chorus but as actors."[5]

This is an optimistic conclusion, however. The missions, in fact, placed women in a position that was rather similar to that of the nuns in the colonial period serving their redeemer. They were expected to be unmarried and chaste, they had little expectations of rising in their profession, and motherhood was still regarded as woman's supreme fulfillment. Gabriela Mistral contributed to this myth. The anthology *Lecturas para mujeres* (Women's Readings) that she compiled for the Mexican Ministry of Education consisted predominantly of works by male writers, many of them the great culture heroes of modernity. The section in her anthology titled "The Higher Life" included only one woman, Sor Juana Inés de la Cruz. The few contributions by women did nothing to dispute the view that it was men who were destined to become the apostles of the new world order. In the introduction she argued that, whatever her social status, woman's only reason for existing was motherhood, which united the material and the spiritual. Women who could not become mothers could only devote themselves to the spiritual.[6] She also embraced the conventional view that men acted and women felt, declaring that women's patriotism was more sentimental than intellectual, inspired more by landscape than by the story of heroic deeds.[7]

Vasconcelos had more advanced ideas about women's liberation (he chafed under the restrictions of family life). Yet he also considered himself a culture hero, identifying himself at different times with Prometheus, Ulysses, and Quetzalcóatl. His autobiography, even though it was written after his failed election campaign, is the work of a man whose every public gesture was a message to posterity, and the title of the first volume, *Ulíses criollo* (Creole

Ulysses),[8] emphasized his own role as an epic hero who would someday return to reclaim his Ithaca. He also compared himself to Quetzalcóatl, the culture hero who had left his tribe with the promise that he would one day return and restore plenty.[9] And, as if this were not enough, he also depicted himself as the archetypal hero and redeemer, Moses.

Unlike the biblical Moses, Vasconcelos was not found in the bulrushes, yet he found a way of describing his own childhood in terms of this paradigmatic hero myth. The son of a customs official, he spent his childhood in a remote outpost of northern Mexico where stories of Apache raids and kidnapped children periodically terrorized the population. His mother tried to dispel the terror by inventing a comforting fairy tale. She would show her son a Bible engraving that

> represented little Moses abandoned in his basket among the Nile bulrushes. A slave who had heard his cries could be seen preparing to take him to Pharoah's daughter. My mother placed great emphasis on the story of the lost child because we lived in Sasabé, which was less a village than a frontier post in the desert of Sonora, near Arizona.

His mother taught him that should he be captured, he should use the opportunity to "bring Christ's message to the heathen, the savages: that is the supreme mission." And,

> If the Apaches come and take you away, fear nothing, live with them and serve them, learn their language and speak to them of Our Lord Jesus Christ who loved for us and them and for all men. The important thing is not to forget; there is an Omnipotent God and his only son is Jesus Christ. . . . When you grow up a little more and learn the roads, travel South toward Mexico and ask there for your grandfather who is called Stephen. . . . However, if you cannot escape or, after the passage of time, you prefer to stay with the Indians, you can do so; only do not forget that there is only one God and his only son, Jesus Christ; this is what you must tell the Indians.[10]

The story is perfectly credible, but it is not hard to imagine that Vasconcelos might have modified it to fit into Rank's account of the hero's adoption by an alien tribe.

The postrevolutionary period had a wealth of such redeemers. When Vasconcelos recalled Diego Rivera from an eleven-year exile in Paris and recruited him to paint murals on the walls of public buildings, his Messianism proved infectious. Diego too thought of himself as larger than life, a giant who painted vast walls thanks to his superhuman energy. In Paris he described feeling his studio closing in on him, and he would press against the walls and corners "till he would throw open the window and feel himself spreading out all over Paris."[11] On his return to Mexico he depicted himself as a force of nature, an incarnation of the cosmic race.

Yet it was precisely at this time of superhuman redeemers that the problem of women's identity surfaced in an acute form—and not only in Mexico. All over Latin America women seemed torn between contradictory demands. We think of the suicide of Alfonsina Storni in Argentina, the murder of Delmira Agustini in Uruguay, the paranoia of Gabriela Mistral in Chile. Literary criticism asks us to separate the work from the life, but violence or the representation of violence to the self is not simply a problem of textuality.

The two women I discuss in this chapter, Frida Kahlo and Antonieta Rivas Mercado, belonged to a small group of "advanced" women. The most advanced of the group was the photographer Tina Modotti, who had come to Mexico in the twenties with Edward Weston; she became the lover of the Cuban politician Julio Antonio Mella and was vilified after his death as a free-loving Communist. The claim can be made that Kahlo and Rivas Mercado, who lived under the shadow respectively of Diego Rivera and José Vasconcelos, symbolically performed in their lives a response to Messianism that is occulted or transposed in their art. Despite the fact that both Vasconcelos and Rivera wanted "liberated women,"[12] Frida Kahlo and Antonieta Rivas Mercado both came up against the fact that there could be no liberation within the symbolic order in which woman always represented the fictional Other. In Rivas Mercado's writing, the noncoincidence of women and Woman is not only made visible, but the phallic organization of meaning and of sexuality produces a schizophrenic response, a dramatic splitting in her self-representation.[13] Kahlo's liberation was more extreme than Rivas Mercado's: she had an affair with Trotsky and several lesbian adventures. Yet both of them accepted at some point in their lives the myth of the birth of the hero, while at the same time forging an identity in some space that was outside history and the nation.

THE OTHER FRIDA

In 1935 Diego Rivera painted his mural *Modern Mexico* on the walls of the National Palace. In the panel showing the campaign against illiteracy, he depicted his wife, Frida Kahlo, wearing a red star and holding a book for a dark-skinned working-class boy to read. Her sister Cristina, who was then Diego's mistress, is in the foreground; she is also holding a book and has her two children by her side. Frida's face is nunlike in its intensity. Cristina has the voluptuous look and upturned eyes of a woman in orgasm or of a mystic. In another panel Frida as comrade is shown handing out arms to workers.

Rivera's iconography is interesting both for what it does and what it does not depict. On the one hand, it suggests that postrevolutionary women have a new social space. They are teachers, comrades, and revolutionaries (*maestras* and *compañeras*), although in these positions they are still represented as "helpers" in the epic narrative; on the other hand, women are not only mothers but sexually liberated mothers.

That these multiple images of women should appear on the walls of the most important government building in Mexico City seems at first sight an unequivocal message for the postrevolutionary state. Yet Rivera's mural is not only a social message but also a male polygamous fantasy, which objectified his different and conflicting representations of women. The fact that Diego was a revolutionary and was presumably representing an advanced political position makes the fantasy all the more interesting.[14]

Kahlo's own painting at this time showed something rather different. In *A Few Small Nips* a female corpse laced with stab wounds lies on a bed over which stands a fully clothed murderer, indifferent as a butcher over a dead animal; in *Suicide of Dorothy Hale* Kahlo shows a woman jumping from a building and then lying dead on the ground. In some of her "recurring" self-portraits,[15] she shows her body bared for an operation, mutilated, decorated, or bound in some way to nature. As critics have often observed, her painting is a dramatic example of the gulf between the male depiction of *jouissance* as a mystical trance and her own sense of the socialized female body penetrated by technology. Despite their revolutionary themes and depictions of death and violence, many of Rivera's murals are distanced, serene, and even Arcadian. Frida's paintings on the other hand shock because they reveal the painter's "inner" life not as spirit but as bodily organs. She often turns the body inside out, placing the heart and the organs on the outside. Woman's inner life is on display because her inner life is her inner body.

Kahlo's paintings also reveal a deep split in her personality, explicitly acknowledged in *The Two Fridas,* in which her dual selves, dressed as if they belong to different generations, are joined by an artery that leads from the open breast of one into that of the other. This split made it impossible for Frida to recognize herself as a unitary subject. Is there a private self so different from the displayed self? Is there a "private" self at all? Are men never split in this way? In some of her self-portraits, she is adorned in beautiful and exotic clothes, "dressed up" as a Tehuana and therefore visibly different from any bourgeois Western beauty. But in other paintings there is a naked, mutilated, and helpless Frida whose inert body appears to be controlled by science. The unclothed body is not a "self" but a socialized body, a body that is opened by instruments, technologized, wounded, its organs displayed to the outside world. The "inner" Frida is controlled by modern society far more than the clothed Frida, who often marks her deviation from a norm by defiantly returning the gaze of the viewer. The naked Frida does not give the viewers what they want— the titillation of female nakedness—but a revelation of what the examining eye does to the female body.[16]

Given the power of this self-representation, it may seem perverse to discuss a painting in which Kahlo does not appear and which, unlike her other paintings, tackles a vast historical and social theme. Yet the painting *Moses* (or *The Birth of the Hero*) represents an allegory of the unsolved problems of sexual division which puts women on the side of anonymous nature and men on the side of culture and "immortality."[17] Despite the vast theme, which encompasses the history of humanity, the canvas is small, thus giving the effect of a miniature version of the massive public murals painted by Diego Rivera, Clemente Orozco, and David Siqueiros.[18] The topic of the painting—the birth of the hero Moses—was suggested by the patron, but before painting it Kahlo read Freud's *Moses and Monotheism* with some enthusiasm. This curious text owes much to Otto Rank's account of the birth of the hero, according to which culture heroes are generally "found" and adopted rather than being parented in the usual way. The hero is "motherless." Not only that, Freud's Moses initiates one of the great historical transformations, the shift to monotheism (and patriar-

chy), a task that is described as a culture journey away from home—
family, race, and tribe—into a strange land. Freud's version of
the Moses legend makes the male child's separation from the mother
the paradigm for historical change.[19] Kahlo's attempt to be faithful
to this version could only be contradictory.

Kahlo admitted that she took the events and images that left the
greatest impression on her after reading the book. "What I wanted
to express clearly and intensely was that the reason why people
need to invent or imagine heroes and gods is pure fear. Fear of life
and fear of death." She then launches into an unusually prolix
description of each of the images:

> I began by painting the figure of Moses as a Child (Moses in
> Hebrew means he who was taken from the water and Moses
> in Egyptian means child). I painted him as described in many
> legends, abandoned in a basket and floating upon the waters
> of the river. Plastically I tried to arrange that the basket cov-
> ered with animal skin should be as close as possible to a womb,

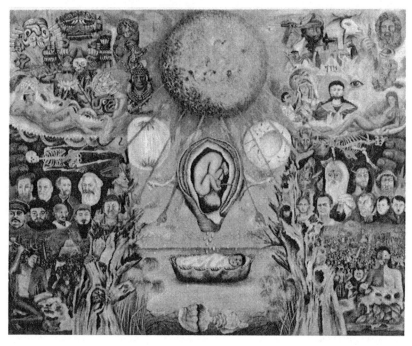

Frida Kahlo, *Moses.*

but according to Freud the basket is the exposed womb and
the water signifies the maternal source as it gives birth to the
child. To emphasize this fact I painted a human fetus in its
last stage in the placenta. The tubes, which are like hands,
extend toward the world. By the side of the already created
child, I placed the elements of its creation, the fertilized egg
and the cellular division.

Two aspects of Moses interested her particularly—first, that his
birth represented the origin of all heroes, "that is to say heroes
who are more persecuted than others—for this reason I placed a
monitoring eye over them. Sargon, Ciro, Romulus, and Paris belong to this group." Second, she is interested in the fact that he
gave the chosen people a religion that was not Jewish but Egyptian.
"Amenhotep IV revived the cult of the Sun, adopting the ancient
religion of Heliopolis. For that reason, I painted the sun as the
center of all religions, as the first god and creator and reproducer
of life. That is the relation between the three principle figures in
the center of the painting."
She next goes on to describe the hierarchical distribution of the
human heads in the painting:

> Like Moses there have been and there will be great men who
> transform religions and human societies. One can say that they
> are like messengers between the people they rule and the gods
> they invent to rule them. I make reference to these gods; nat-
> urally I could not fit them all in and I arranged them on one
> side or the other of the sun. On the right, those of the West,
> and on the left, those of the East. A winged Assyrian bull,
> Amon, Zeus, Osiris, Horus, Jehovah, Apollo, the Moon,
> Venus . . . and the devil. On the left, lightning, thunder, and
> the track of lightning, that is to say, Hurakan, Kukulkan, and
> Gukamatz; Tláloc, the magnificient, Coatlicue, mother of all
> the gods, Quetzalcóatl, Tezcatlipoca, Centéotl, the Chinese
> dragon god, and Brahama, the Hindu. I needed an African
> God, but I couldn't find one. I could have made a little space
> for him.

Having painted the gods which did not fit in their respective
heavens, I wanted to divide the celestial world of imagination and
poetry from the terrestrial world of fear and death, so I painted
the human and animal skeletons you see. The Earth hollows her
hands to protect them. Between the dead and the group of heroes,

there is absolutely no division since they also die and the earth takes them generously back without distinction. On the same earth, with their heads painted on a bigger scale to distinguish them from the multitude, there are the portraits of the heroes (few of them, but well chosen), the transformers of religions, the inventors and creators of religions, the conquerors, the rebels, that is to say, the real big teeth. On the right (I ought to give this figure more prominence than any others) is Amenhotep, later called Ikhnaton, a young Pharaoh of the eighteenth Egyptian dynasty (1370 B.C.) who imposed on his subjects a strictly monotheistic religion that was contrary to tradition and against polytheism which stemmed from the cult of On, the religion of Aton, in other words the Sun. They not only adored the sun as a material entity but as a creator and conserver of all living creatures, inside and outside Egypt, whose energy was visible in his rays, thus anticipating modern knowledge of solar energy.

As there was no way that Kahlo could convey "monotheism" in plastic terms, she depicted something like a Catholic hierarchy of cherubims, seraphims, and saints, with a hierarchy of heroes— Christ, Zoroaster, Alexander the Great, Caesar, Mahomet, Tamberlain, Napoleon and the "lost child" Hitler. "On the left," she wrote, there is

the marvelous Nefertiti, wife of Iknaton. I imagine that as well as being extraordinarily beautiful she must have been quite a case [hacha perdida] and a most intelligent collaborator of her husband. Buddha, Marx, Freud, Paracelsus, Epicurus, Genghis Khan, Gandhi, Lenin, and Stalin. The order is weird, but I painted it according to my knowledge of history which is also weird. Between them and the multitudes I painted a sea of blood with which I signify war. And, finally, the powerful and not well-considered human mass, composed of every kind of animal; warriors, peaceful people, learned and ignorant, those who build monuments, the rebels, the flagbearers, the happy and the sad, the healthy and the sick, the poets and the stupid ones, and anyone else you want to put in this big mess. You only see those in front clearly . . . as for the rest, what with the noise, you cannot tell.

On the left, in the foreground, is Man the constructor in four colors (the four races). On the right, the Mother, the creator, with a child in her arms. Behind her the Monkey. The two trees which form an arch of triumph are the new life which is always burgeoning and the trunk of old age. In the center, underneath, the most important for Freud and for many others, Love, which is represented by a shell and a snail, the two sexes, covered with roots which are always new and alive. That is all I can tell you of my picture.[20]

Now this is an extraordinary description, for Kahlo seems to endorse heroes and hero worship and Freud's version of the transition of society to monotheism and the patriarchal order. Yet the painting itself (and parts of the description) cannot gloss over the rift in her thinking between nature and culture, even though she attempts to take birthing away from women. The space of creation, which includes the sun, ovary, sperm, fetus, and the newly born child, the snail and the shell, combines references to Christian myth, to Host and Nativity, with a nonpersonal sexuality. Except for the tubes (like pointing hands) that issue from the sun, this process of generation and birth is independent of the gods and humans, and even of the primal pair who occupy the bottom left- and right-hand corners of the painting. The child thus appears to be a gift of nature, born of the sun, curled in leaves, rocked in animal skins. The whole of the center panel separates this "natural state of affairs" from the figures on the right and left of the painting, each of which are divided into strata, the sphere of the gods and culture heroes. It is not only that heroes are separated from their bodies, but that, unlike the masses, they are individualized. In this Frida was faithful to her source. And the absence of women (except for Nefertiti) among the heroes shows that she encountered some difficulty when it came to putting women on the side of history and social change.[21]

But although Frida separates the world of nature from that of culture and divides culture into gods, heroes, and masses, she also distances herself in significant ways from the hero myth. To begin with, compared with Diego Rivera's monumental murals, this canvas is minuscule (24″ × 30″). The effect is to miniaturize the heroes, whose isolated heads seem pathetically removed from the impersonal source of life—the sun. The organization of culture, on the other hand, is hierarchical, as in the religious paintings that inspired her, and she makes no attempt to separate the "good" from the "bad." The living immortals, Stalin and Hitler and Gandhi, are placed impartially alongside Christ, Napoleon, and Marx, for what matters is not their ideologies but the difference between the hero and the masses, between those who have names and those without names (which includes nearly all women).

What are we to make of this? There is clearly a separation between the anonymity of creation and the personal immortality of the hero. Kahlo accepts, even if only indirectly, a complementarity in which women are closer to nature but men are heroes of culture. At the same time, anonymous creation is the center of the painting and here, hollowed out, between the heroes and the masses, are the sun (as the origin of life) and the primary couple. This couple is, however, prior to subjectivity. It is in other paintings that the problem of women's subjectivity comes to the fore. In *The Love Embrace of the Universe and Earth: Diego and I,* Frida paints the two vast arms of the Universe (whose sex is undetermined) and of nature (as Goddess) and in front of them herself holding a naked baby Diego in her lap. It is Diego's head, however, that bears the mark of the prophet, the eye. For women sex is destiny. In *Diego and Frida* (1944), the half-face of Diego does not match with Frida's half-face and the phallic snail has grown much larger than the shell. The dream of equality is here seen to be shattered.[22]

It was logical perhaps that Frida Kahlo should be a nonparticipant in the hero-race; that instead, she should use her own body as a work of art that she dressed up and adorned and painted. In this self-creation, there was no pretense that human beings could transcend mortality.

SUPERMAN

A different but equally compelling collapse of the dream of the hero occurred in the life and writings of Antonieta Rivas Mercado, who committed suicide in 1931. She is the author of a handful of short stories and a series of political articles that recorded José Vasconcelos' unsuccessful 1929 presidential campaign, first published in his journal, *La antorcha,* and of some passionate love letters to the painter Manuel Rodríguez Lozano.[23] A gulf separates the "public" Antonieta who becomes the ventriloquist of a nationalist discourse of which Vasconcelos is the hero and redeemer, and the "private" Antonieta of the autobiographical stories and the love letters. Like Frida Kahlo, she tried to enunciate the

Messianistic nationalism of postrevolutionary Mexico, but, at the same time, subverted it at the deepest level.

Antonieta Rivas Mercado's life and writing are riven by this duplicity. She was the wealthy daughter of an architect of Porfirian Mexico who was separated from her mother. Antonieta adored him and became his companion on extended travels to Europe. On their return to Mexico she gravitated toward intellectual and literary circles before marrying Albert Blair, an engineer from the United States who had settled in Mexico. He was a Christian Scientist who refused to let their child, Antonio, be treated by doctors.[24] But Antonieta had other reasons to be unhappy as can be gathered from an autobiographical story, "Páginas arrancadas" (Torn Pages), which offers an unusually frank and brutal picture of married life. The story is written in the form of a diary. Its treatment of sexuality is unusually frank for the time since it describes the unwanted physical demands made by the husband (who is likened to a "repulsive beggar"). Their sexual encounters leave her "cold and hard; insensible and detached." When he is inside her, she has an urge to strangle him. So extreme is her disgust that it brings on a nervous breakdown, but after her recovery she has no alternative but to return to him, her only consolations now being religion and the child inside her.[25]

The real life Antonieta was able to leave Albert Blair, though the separation caused her terrible problems to the end of her life and certainly contributed to her suicide. After the separation she accompanied her father to Europe and, after their return to Mexico, moved in with him until his death in 1927. Their home was on the appropriately named Street of Heroes. In effect her independent life lasted for only four years.

Thanks to her wealth, she was able to act as patron to members of the *Contemporáneos* group, especially Salvador Novo and Xavier Villaurrutia, and in 1928 she helped fund the first avant-garde theater (presciently named Ulysses).[26] She funded the publication of three books: Gilberto Owen's *Novela en forma de nube* (Novel Like a Cloud), Andrés Henestrosa's *Los hombres que dispersó la danza* (The Men Scattered by the Dance), and Xavier Villaurrutia's *Dama de corazones* (Queen of Hearts). Rivas Mercado thus found a space for herself among the small group of writers who represented (though modestly) a bohemian avant-garde. Several members of the group were homosexuals, including (probably) the painter Manuel Rodríguez Lozano, with whom she was in love.

In an article on Mexican women that she contributed to a Madrid newspaper, she made a clear-eyed analysis of how women stood with regard to the social and intellectual world. Commenting on the passivity of Mexican women and their reputation for "goodness," she draws the conclusion that it is these various qualities that make Mexican men what they are. Since there is as yet no feminine logic, because women have not invented one, women can only rise above their passivity by using masculine logic which, however, they will have to modify if they are to make their presence felt and to influence others.[27] Rivas Mercado took this to its logical conclusion when she joined Vasconcelos' election campaign.

She was introduced to Vasconcelos in Toluca on March 10, 1929, when he was about to make a triumphant entry as a popular presidential candidate into Mexico City. His return from the United States was intended to imitate that of Francisco Madero, whose entry into Mexico had sparked the 1910 Revolution, and he made a protracted journey toward the capital. Antonieta, already an enthusiastic supporter, had driven to Toluca in a fine motor car, accompanied by several friends, including Manuel Rodríguez Lozano. It was in her car that Vasconcelos made his entrance to the outshirts of Mexico City.

In his autobiography Vasconcelos refers to Antonieta by a pseudonym, Valeria. He had always liked "emancipated" women and was attracted by Antonieta's glamor and modernity. He believed her, no doubt sincerely, to be "one of the greatest women of our time."

> When she came to see us, she was in Toluca at the end of an illustrious social career that had been sustained by her talent, her beauty, and by a considerable fortune which she had wasted, partly on bad business deals, partly because she had given it away—to support the symphony orchestra, to pay for the publication of select literary reviews, or for the upkeep of an avant-garde theater, Ulíses. Dark-skinned, with a fine supple figure, an example of the fine native race, her strength was, nevertheless, in her spirit.[28]

He described her as the "muse" of the avant-garde, a woman who was dedicated to work and study and went everywhere with her ten-year-old son. For her part, Rivas Mercado described Vasconcelos' entry into Mexico City as like that of Christ on Palm Sunday:

> Like the Levite, this civil servant, this simple man arrived in
> the Mexican Jerusalem after stirring, as Christ had done be-
> fore him, the depths of the soul of the humble of the valley
> with his preaching, in which he adapted for his own people
> the inspired and terrible word of the Nazarene. (*La campaña*,
> p. 64)

Vasconcelos must have been delighted at finding someone who could
portray him as the Messiah with such wholehearted enthusiasm.
Her articles on his campaign, the early part of which she recon-
structed from his recollections and that of others, not only appeared in the journal *La antorcha* but were also used in the third
volume of his autobiography, where again and again he refers to
her "masterly style." He would again draw on it to write parts of
his political "novel," *La flama*.[29]
The style was indeed "masterly," and perhaps consciously so.
Rivas Mercado mimics a long-standing masculine tradition of heroic writing, for there was no "feminine" tradition on which she
could draw. She writes a third person account of the campaign
from which she herself is conspicuously absent, except as the witness to this Messiah.[30]
Her articles on the election campaign begin with a description
of the year 1928 and the campaign journeys through Mexico, and
end with the debacle of election day, November 17, 1929. Though
written in a language that is too exalted for modern taste, they
comprise a conscientious piece of partisan reporting in which
Rivas Mercado even improves on Vasconcelos' mythic version
of himself. In defeat, he is "Prometheus Enchained," and, as if
this were not enough, the articles are headed by quotations from
Aeschylus' tragedy *Prometheus*. The story she tells is, of course,
that of the redemption of a people from captivity. The Mexicans
are described over and over again as living in "confusion" as they
wait for salvation to come to them. They need to be awakened
and reminded of their destiny by a hero with a "virile conscience
and a strong will." At times she depicts Vasconcelos not only as
a Moses or Prometheus but as a Christ clearing the merchants from
the temple. And she faithfully observes that Vasconcelos also rein-
carnates the indigenous culture hero Quetzalcóatl. She even takes
a leaf out of Vasconcelos' own mythic book by identifying his enemy, the caudillo General Calles with Quetzalcóatl's foe,
Huitzilipochtli.[31]
But Rivas Mercado goes further than this, for she makes

Vasconcelos into the Father of the nation, the supreme phallic power, converting the nation itself into the body/woman through which the hero passes. "Oh power of desire," she exclaims, at once identifying herself with that power and with the "feminized" masses. Those masses were represented for her by an "ancient Indian woman" who approached Vasconcelos after his speech, threw herself at his feet, and, "embracing his knees, unconsciously repeated the gesture with which Thetis greeted the father of the Gods, and a single word filled her mouth and moistened her eyes, 'Father.' Father, who is strong, who knows everything, who guides and who defends his child through life's turbulence, Father."

Because Vasconcelos occupies the phallic position in her discourse, the place of the Father and of Law, Rivas Mercado is effaced and de-faced. The discourse speaks for itself, only occasionally through an "emphasis'" or interruption indicating the mode of its production. One such interruption (significantly, in an essay that Vasconcelos did not include in his autobiography) occurs in the course of an analysis of the United States' intervention in Mexican affairs, where Antonieta's bitter experience of her marriage to a North American suddenly becomes a metaphor for the relationship between the two countries. She depicts the United States as courting Mexico by making false promises and then attempting to undermine its Catholic traditions by infiltrating Protestant sects such as the Christian Scientists (Blair, it will be remembered, was a Christian Scientist). She calls for a resistance to capitalism based on Catholic and Hispanic tradition. "We have to learn from so-called obscurantist Spain the secrets of the great builders of this continent, whose works we have not even been able to rival since our Independence" (*La campaña*, p. 70).

Both Vasconcelos's and Rivas Mercado's belief in the hero myth seemed to withstand the final debacle, when Vasconcelos' campaign collapsed before the onslaught of bribery and intimidation that culminated in the assassination of the student leader Germán del Campo. Vasconcelos found himself increasingly isolated. He left Mexico City a week before the election, and on election day, November 17, he was traveling by train, unable even to get off for fear that he would be killed. Calles' protegé Ortiz Rubio was elected and Vasconcelos went into exile in the United States, trailing, according to Antonieta, mythic clouds of glory behind him. He was, inevitably, "Prometheus chained to the hard ungrateful rock from which without repose he would watch the hands that his faith had raised up sink into the pit. Prometheus Bound" (*La campaña*, *p. 140*).

THE OTHER ANTONIETA

Antonieta Rivas Mercado was not an eyewitness to Vasconcelos' defeat. She had already left for the United States, ostensibly to further Vasconcelos' campaign by organizing support in New York, but also apparently because the press had begun to lampoon her.[32] Vasconcelos had opposed the journey, saying "I did not wish to see her uprooted from Mexico and publicly compromised."[33] She had been forced to take the dangerous step of forging her husband's signature on her passport, since, without it, she would not have been allowed to leave.

All this would be anecdotal were it not for the fact that throughout the whole period, when she was reporting on Vasconcelos' campaign and during her exile in the United States, she was writing a very different kind of prose—passionate love letters to the painter Manuel Rodríguez Lozano, letters in which the discourse is not one of mastery but of abjection. The public and the private Antonieta seem to be two different people.

The letters to Rodríguez Lozano begin in 1927 and continue throughout the Vasconcelos campaign, the last being written just before her suicide. In her essays on the Vasconcelos campaign Rivas Mercado had transcoded the language of redemption into that of national change. Her letters to Rodríguez Lozano resemble those of a mystic confronting a confessor who is guiding her along the "road to perfection" (her words), but he also takes the place of God. "I was worth nothing. I was the clay waiting for the impulse that would give it shape," she writes. Or again, "And God said, 'let there be light' and there was light" (*Cartas*, p. 38). One curious aspect of this abject writing is the position of the addressee. For Rodríguez Lozano occupies the same unattainable position in her private discourse as had Vasconcelos in her public discourse. Unable to accede to her sexual demands, Rodríguez Lozano must have found that he could divert her physical claims on him by urging her to sublimate her desire for him into the spiritual. Indeed, it is evident that he himself suppressed his own sexual preferences by dedicating himself to his work, acquiring an aura of Doric austerity in Antonieta's eyes. Her letters refer to his suspiciousness, his inability to give himself to others, his reticence, all of which could be attributed either to a homosexuality he wished to keep secret or a chastity he imposed on himself because his desires were socially unacceptable.

But the painter's stance of celibacy gave him power over Antonieta, like the power of a priest; Rodríguez Lozano came to represent the Law in its purest form, and she, for her part, fell into the role of spiritual daughter. "I begin to feel life as a road to perfection and you are [that road] for me. . . . With you, life becomes the narrow road that goes to heaven, but who would choose not to take it? And by your side, one must be transformed into the fountain that floweth over in silence" (*Cartas*, p. 49). She has become a visionary:

> I have seen your truth resplendent, luminous as an angel, and my own just as clear. I felt God speaking through my mouth, true and pure. I have had the rapture of seeing God in your eyes, of hearing him in your lips, and I ask myself if, like *Moses,* the light that shines from me will not blind the ones who have not been chosen. You sanctify life, and my supernatural, happiness comes from my consciousness. (*Cartas*, p. 50; my emphasis)

Thanks to Manuel, Antonieta is reborn. The seed that has fallen on his disciple Abraham (i.e., his friend Abraham Angel) she demands for herself. She too wishes to be the fertile ground on which seed will fall. But there was to be little in the way of fulfillment except in her imagination. Her life became one of constant waiting and rejection, a situation in which Manuel had the upper hand, able to torment her by refusing to write or see her, or by referring to her sexual history, her reputation as a "modern woman." At times it was as if he were making her do penance for this. He put her through purity and loyalty tests, forcing her to declare at one point that she would kill herself rather than let him down (*Cartas,* p. 56). For her part, Antonieta was intelligent enough to realize that perpetual self-abasement was counterproductive: "Here I am in love with a man for whom, sensually, I do not signify any emotion. Besides working what am I to do? 'Divide myself'? 'Find my integrity in division'? Suffer?" (*Cartas*, p. 59). Women are supposed to "feel," but they cannot demand reciprocity.

On Manuel's recommendation she went away and imposed a strict work schedule on herself. She was now "on the narrow road that leads to the paradise of the righteous" (*Cartas*, p. 59). On September 25, however, she took a decisive step, one that she could only describe in agitated telegraphese—she had joined Vasconcelos in his election campaign. A public Rivas Mercado was born. "Destiny awaits me. I was born yesterday—or today, perhaps? Of the birth, the memory of mortal anxiety, of myself, I know nothing" (*Cartas*, p. 63). Life became a constant round of meetings as she and Vasconcelos traveled across Northern Mexico to Monterey and Saltillo and then into Tampico. Despite her own enthusiasm and that of the crowds, it was clear to her that armed struggle was probable and perhaps even inevitable. In a letter to Manuel she described the campaign as "magnificent and terrible" (*Cartas*, p. 67). Nevertheless the excitement was alluring. "A sea of people were waiting, a palpitating generous sea which, with passion and desire, went out to receive a pure man" (*Cartas*, p. 67). Yet the new Rivas Mercado could not erase the notion that her authentic self was elsewhere: "I want to go deep, seek something within myself far from all fictitious exaltation. . . . I want to find you" (*Cartas*, p. 66).

It was perhaps this painful division as much as the growing escalation of violence that led her to leave Mexico for the United States on September 28, 1929, in order to "discover herself" (*Cartas*, p. 70). Once in New York her interest in Vasconcelos' campaign seemed to weaken:

> I have left behind that anguished country that is ours where I was caught in the trap of political passions, and I do not feel the slightest inclination to go on with it. Vasconcelos' adventure appears hopeless. I hope it ends well. I feel that I have settled accounts with my country, that it is no longer mine, that I am outside countries and beginning to live a universal truth. (*Cartas*, p. 72)

She had a hundred projects—to write a novel and articles, to translate, to promote Rodríguez Lozano's painting and Vasconcelos' cause, to visit museums and Harlem. She met the Spanish poet García Lorca, whom she liked and who would describe her hyperbolically in his letters as a "millionaire,"[34] and she met the entire Hispanic community, including José Clemente Orozco—though she quickly fell out with Anita Brenner, the chronicler of the Mexican muralist movement.[35] Her letters from New York give a vivid picture of the feverish twenties.

Antonieta was scarcely an unprejudiced observer, however, since the modish muralists overshadowed Manuel, while her support of Vasconcelos made her an oddity in circles that believed in the socialism of General Calles. As if this were not enough, Vasconcelos accused her of deserting the cause, and she herself felt that she had betrayed "the prostitute mother," Mexico. She had "suicidal" longings to go there and die, and the equally strong conviction that she and Manuel should save themselves from what she saw as an increasingly dark political future. She vacillated between hopes of seeing her love for Manuel reciprocated sexually and abjection. All this brought about at least two breakdowns in November (*Cartas*, p. 79).

The breakdowns were marked by a religious crisis that Vasconcelos chose to believe represented a healthy return to her Hispanic roots. According to his account, she went to pray at the Chapel of Guadalupe on 140th Street: "A great mystical effusion penetrated her soul. On the following day after mass, she asked a priest to confess her. Later she took communion with a fervor that transported her beyond the temporal," and, apparently, into a renewed commitment to Vasconcelos' cause. "To save Mexico, it is necessary to restore the basis of its traditional faith."[36] Vasconcelos put his own interpretation on this "conversion." In his autobiography he wrote:

> In Valeria's soul . . . something happened that shows the quality of a noble and brave heritage; though before, she had been less than diligent in the struggle, now she took on herself the entire weight of the hopeless task. Taking an extreme position to strengthen the force of her attack, and also out of sincere conviction, she became a Catholic, broke with her former friends, and dedicated her entire strength to revealing the immediate truth of the Mexican situation and to her writing projects.[37]

That part of her was indeed engaged in this renewed political activity is demonstrated by a letter she wrote from Los Angeles to Gabriela Mistral, which was published in the *Diario de Panama;* in it she accused the American government of sabotaging the election of Vasconcelos and supporting Calles.[38]

Meanwhile the story she was telling Rodríguez Lozano was altogether different. In a letter to him she described a far more hopeless crisis.

I went mad with pain; I lost my head during attacks which I never believed were those of a mad woman; my structure for living here was healthy, balanced, and a tropical storm undid everything—I went mad—and I have returned, renewed—the crisis passed—into this new world, in which only you who are eternal and permanent persist out of the values of yesterday and my will to work which will justify the care, attention, and tenderness that you have showed me. I will be all that you expected of me. (*Cartas*, p. 79)

It was during her second breakdown that Rivas Mercado had a brief affair with Vasconcelos—whether for the first time it is impossible to tell.

He came for me with the docility and greed of a child who had lost his only support and consolation. This is not the time to stop and consider whether I did right or wrong in giving him, without your knowing, and as someone gives bread out of charity, something that you yourself rejected for so long. (*Cartas*, pp. 90–91)

It is a revenge. Having always insisted that their love was spiritual, Manuel could hardly object to her carnal affair with Vasconcelos. She has done what she thought she would never do—divide body from soul.

Her numerous literary projects of this period obsessively center on treachery (she wants to write on La Malinche and Antigone) and on women's sexual emancipation. But to judge from her unfinished novel, "The One Who Ran Away," she identified more readily with the male Mexican character than with the emancipated American woman. The novel was dedicated "for ever" to Manuel Rodríguez Lozano. In yet another project she outlined the story of a dominating mother who was apparently based on an acquaintance, though the story could also have reflected her own ambiguous relationship with her adored son (*Cartas*, p. 100). It was indeed the son who precipitated her last desperate journeys—first to Mexico and then, with him, to France. She had smuggled him out of Mexico without her husband's consent and, after installing him in Bordeaux under the care of Vasconcelos' literary agent, Deambrosis, she set out on her final journey to Paris.

THE BULLET HOLE IN THE TEXT

Rivas Mercado was to make her own intervention through self-destruction. Her suicide was carefully planned, the scenario deliberately chosen. Notre Dame de Paris had to be cleansed after the sacrilegious event. In her final diary entry, which Vasconcelos later published in *La flama,* she speaks of her decision to kill herself "so that my son can return to his father."[39] This seems odd when she had just gone to such trouble to take the son away from the father, but may be explicable in the light of one of the articles that was about to appear in Vasconcelos' journal, *La antorcha,* and that in all likelihood she had read. It was an article on Freud's oedipal theory, and it happened to stress the crucial moment in the boy's development when he must free himself from the "effeminate" and become more "manly."[40] Many of her friends believed that the financial difficulties to which she was certainly not accustomed precipitated her decision, and certainly, on the final morning, she was preparing a return journey to Mexico at Vasconcelos' suggestion, to reclaim her jewels and money.[41] But her final actions and her suicide note indicate that she was unable to live a freedom she found impoverished without love. Suicide was a calculated sacrifice that took her beyond the austerity of Rodríguez Lozano and the empty bravado of Vasconcelos.

Ostensibly planning to return to Mexico to put her financial affairs in order, Rivas Mercado went to the consulate to pick up her passport, and there took the opportunity to reproach the consul, Arturo Pani, for serving the Calles government. She then returned to the room in the hotel where Vasconcelos was staying to look for his pistol. Throughout his electoral campaign Vasconcelos had made much of the gun and his need to carry it against possible assassins. But he had never used it. No action was better calculated to put a hole through Vasconcelos' own myth than Antonieta's use of his gun to kill herself. The entry in her diary underlines her deliberate betrayal:

> I feel sorry to leave him; he will feel wounded, I would almost say, betrayed, but it will soon pass and he will forgive me and perhaps underneath he will feel relief. . . . He does not need me. He told me that himself when we talked on the long night of our reunion here in this same room. At the height of the discussion, I asked him, "Tell me the truth, the real truth—do you need me?" I don't know whether he foresaw my des-

peration or whether it was out of sincerity that he said, "No soul needs any other, no man or woman needs anyone other than God. Each person's destiny is linked to the Creator alone."

At the very moment when Antonieta could have become "herself," she finds the self depends on a man who does not need her, a son who will be better off without her, and a love object who refuses to respond to her. Did Antonieta, a reader of Hölderlin, aspire to be one of those "tender, noble souls" who would take their place next to the heroes and the gods? Her last act was guaranteed to ensure that Vasconcelos "will never be able to forget me. I will be in his heart until the hour of his death." And she was right.

In the final paragraph of her diary, she coolly outlines the plan that she carried out to the last detail:

> I will end my life looking at Jesus; in front of his crucified image. I have already reserved my seat on a bench that faces the altar of the Crufixion in Notre Dame. I will sit down in order to have the strength to shoot. But first I shall have to hide my intention. I am going to bathe [now] because it is already getting light. After breakfast, we will all go to the photographer's to pick up passport photographs. Afterwards I shall pretend to go to the consulate, which he refuses to enter. I will have him wait for me in a café on the Avenue. Deambrosis will be with him. I don't want him to be alone when the news arrives. (*Cartas*, pp. 111–112)

Shooting oneself is not a form of suicide favored by women. But Rivas Mercado knew what she was doing. She was proceeding with male logic. If there was no place in which she could speak, she would make one. This was how she finally escaped from all of them—from Manuel, from Vasconcelos, from her husband and her son. But it was Vasconcelos who would turn her suicide to productive use.

HE LOOKS FOR A NAKED BODY AND FINDS HIMSELF CUCKOLDED

"C'est un triste souvenir." (The French police, alluding to the gun with which Rivas Mercado killed herself.)

Suicide is a particularly disturbing form of death. For Vasconcelos, Rivas Mercado's act was traumatic, which was why he tried to bury it in a torrent of words, writing three different versions of it. The first appears in the third part of his autobiography; there is a second, more schematic version in *La flama,* and a third in the form of an allegorical play also included in *La flama,* in which Vasconcelos depicts Antonieta (or Valeria as he calls her) in purgatory.[42]

In these different versions, he first of all exorcised his own guilt, then gradually shifted the blame to the evil intellectual influences on Antonieta's life. Nowhere does he recognize her conflicting selves. He had cast her as his Diotima and was determined that she should fulfill that role, and indeed, when they were reunited in Paris, she placed in his hands the manuscript of her essays on the electoral campaign that he believed "would put her in the first rank of women writers of Spanish America."[43] Vasconcelos was clearly looking forward to a renewal of their liaison. He was sensible to the agreeable touch of their bodies as they walked along together, deluding himself that this was "a harmony of souls united in the illusion of eternity."[44]

Instead, she wrote her suicide note, addressed it to the consul, Pani, and set out for Notre Dame. One of the last people to see her was a bookseller, who saw her stop and glance at the books in his window before proceeding to her death. The rest of the day proceeded exactly as she had planned.

When Pani learned of her death he telephoned Vasconcelos, who accompanied him to the police station, not without some anxiety in case anyone should connect him too closely with the dead woman. The French police, however, knew what was expected. In *El proconsulado,* Vasconcelos quotes the commissaire as saying, "If you agree, we will give the apparent cause of death as suicide while the balance of her mind was momentarily disturbed owing to matrimonial difficulties." This was a neat solution for a lifetime of contradiction.

The problems of the funeral, of informing the family, were disposed of in like fashion. "We have a refrigerator in the morgue," the French official reassuringly informed Pani and Vasconcelos. "It completely preserves the body." There remained one other problem—the gun, which had belonged to Vasconcelos and which he was understandably reluctant to reclaim. Sighing, the magistrate observed, "Ah you are right, *c'est un triste souvenir.*"

Vasconcelos himself was devastated and even had suicidal thoughts. Yet, the anxiety he felt at the thought of reading Antonieta's papers inspired sexual metaphors. He actually referred

to this reading as a *rape*—"the rape [*estupro*] of a defenseless soul."
What did he expect to find? Why did he have to rape the dead to
get at the plunder? "Wasn't I perhaps throwing myself downhill
into crime?" he asks, a question that hardly seems appropriate to
the event unless we conjecture that he wanted to engineer a cover-
up. The only possible crime was the obliteration of any mention
of his own connection with "the deceased."

The cover-up, paradoxically, begins with an "undressing."

> Rapidly I undid wrappings, opened notebooks: put everything
> in chronological order. There was correspondence, recent notes,
> and a diary of scarcely ten or twelve pages begun in Bordeaux.
> The letters were, for the most part, from a masculine confi-
> dant. From what he said it was easy to guess that she had
> written in order to invoke certain responses of healthy advice,
> erudite, ingenious, and loyal elucidation. They were the letters
> of a cultivated man to a superior woman, though not without
> certain cautious allusions provoked by feminine coque-
> try. . . . There was nothing or almost nothing that referred
> to the inner motives, the profound disillusionment that doubt-
> less broke the spirit of that great person who had disappeared.

The undressing had failed to reveal the clue he was looking for,
even though he was holding Manuel's letters in his hand. For the
clue he sought was some reference to himself. Even Antonieta's
diary "was reserved, but in the sense that it did not reveal a naked
soul. It was written in the intervals of intense literary activity and
contained observations on books and readings, little or nothing
intimate." Between the lines of the autobiography, written years
later, we can sense the entire process—the feverish anxiety, the
puzzled discovery that there is nothing intimate, the settling down
into a more detached reading of Antonieta's diary which even allows him to appreciate her prose style, which has something of
Gide, but something of the languid quality associated with the
paintings of Botticelli (how far away "the deceased" must now
have seemed). He permits himself a comparison between Botticelli's
Simonetta and Antonieta which favors the latter.

> Simonetta was a stupid fool who died of consumption, while
> Valeria was a talent who approached genius. Her portrait was
> on my table—one of those faces marked by misfortune and
> greatness. Perhaps greatness that is brought about by misfor-
> tune; ideas flowed from her brain like the print in a news-
> paper, firm and clear without a shadow of complaint or lament.

Marked by misfortune. Uncompromising. Thus step by step the reader follows Vasconcelos in his reading of Rivas Mercado, as now, somewhat reassured, he persists to the very end. Vasconcelos has become a mere reader, no different from the reader of any pulp novel who must find out what happens next. It has begun to dawn on him that he is not even the main character, that the main character is a certain "So-and-so," whose name appears in the diary:

> She spoke of the person with fervor but it seemed that they never became intimate; still, a jealous urgent curiosity made me devour the pages which were left to read. Was it possible that she said nothing about me? Ah, of course, there was my name on the page before me. Let's see, "Today I finished my account of Vasconcelos' campaign. I have reread it and found it good, only that it amuses me to think that my readers will believe me to be very much in love with Vasconcelos. . . . "

The secret is finally out. Far from her being raped, she has cuckolded him. The treachery of women! He allows himself a little ironic reflection, "So her devotion to the cause that had united us was amusing, her loving abandonment of the past was trivial and superficial and so was the subsequent deep affection." And still he goes on reading. The mystery is not complete. Such duplicity must have some explanation, and he finds it—in Nietzsche. "I went on reading, pages of a commentary on Nietzsche. There was the poison she had taken in."[45] She had written, "if as Nietzsche says, the genius is the one who feels himself identified with everything, whether with his own or his adopted offspring, then Vasconcelos is a genius." That was what he wanted to hear, but perhaps it was not so very satisfactory after all. She had upstaged him with a bullet.

The night he dreamed of walking with her in the rain under the same umbrella. In the morning he has already forgiven her. Forgiven her for what? For being the hero? But Vasconcelos triumphed in the end. It is he who now becomes the chief mourner at the funeral, who places flowers on the grave and receives the condolences of the handful people who attend. The death has become, in his mind, a noble sacrifice. He even permits himself a little erotic *frisson*. Visiting a friend of his, a rather racy widow and actress, he pictures her dead husband and Antonieta silently witnessing the flirtation. What a sense of self-satisfaction there is in resisting the flesh "because of his instinctive posthumous fidelity."[46]

The significance of Rivas Mercado's suicide increased for

Vasconcelos, if anything, as he grew more conservative. Once more it would be recycled into his memoirs—this time to prove the deadly effects of women's and gay emancipation. By this time he had come to regard her as a "virile" character whose feminine nature had forever been distorted by her parents' separation. And on top of that she grew up in a period of women's liberation.

> The glorification of action and the pursuit of beauty; the Faustian ideal which attracted so many to the superficiality of the merely human, all these currents contributed to transform Valeria into the legendary woman emancipated from prejudice and capable of erotic adventures as well as for enterprises of talent and greatness.

But, he now claims, she had also been influenced by the worst French decadence (in which Vasconcelos included Picasso, Gide, Anatole France, and Debussy): "The City of Light had replaced the City of God." After the divorce and the squandering of her fortune, she was abandoned by all her friends except for gay men.

> In Valeria's literary circles, the Gide of The Narrow Gate was cast aside in favor of the immoral teacher of Corydon and The School for Women. There was talk of a new humanism. . . . They had decided to fight for freedom but once they had it, they did not know what to do with it and they finally corrupted it.

And this is from the same man who had wanted a sexually liberated mistress. In this account Valeria is redeemed from bohemia by the Vasconcelista campaign. And then the suicide, which is now squarely blamed on "decadence": "All the collected works of Nietzsche and Hölderlin were on her desk in the last weeks of her solitude. Dangerous, tempting, they offer the cup of definite annihilation." Her situation, and the triumph of the unworthy, brought on incurable disgust. "If life was like this, better give it up." This nihilistic example is, however, not without its exemplary aspect:

> When she shot the pistol into her heart, sitting on a bench of the Church, her final look invoked the Crucifixion. Thus the sexton found her, bleeding, her eyes open, fixed on the face of the Savior. She must not have been damned. The sin she committed when she fired the pistol was redeemed by the look of adoration, the cry for mercy which never fails the repentant sinner.[47]

Even now Vasconcelos cannot leave her alone. There has to be yet another version of the suicide, perhaps the most significant of all if the patriarchal front is to be maintained intact. This time he writes an imaginary dialogue which takes place in purgatory, where Antonieta meditates on the difference between her death and that of the Hero. In this dialogue, Antonieta/Valeria admits the futility of her suicide: "The hero dies so that something can live. To die for oneself is egoism and cowardice. Especially in my case." In purgatory she must learn not to rebel against her destiny but to become part of the harmony of the universe.

Vasconcelos' versions of Rivas Mercado's death represent a long obsession which only the power of her suicide can explain. She had transgressed the rules by trying to become the superman, wresting control, once and for all, from those Fathers who had dominated her life. Yet this personal liberation left interpretive power in Vasconcelos' hands. From Diotima Antonieta descended rapidly into a figure exemplifying the evils of emancipation.

Both Frida Kahlo and Antonieta Rivas Mercado tried to live through powerful men. Of the two, Kahlo became a true artist, but only when she was thrust out of her matrimonial dream. Her obsession with the self-portrait is a long and never-completed struggle to understand female identity. For Rivas Mercado the only identity was in destruction. There was no possible way to combine motherhood, public service, and sexual satisfaction. Vasconcelos' confession that he did not need her, just before her suicide, increases in importance as we realize that she could not envisage any woman's space that was outside the shadow of a man. Like Frida, whose liaison with Trotsky seems also to have been inspired by the need to conquer the hero, Antonieta found sexual emancipation to be a new form of enslavement. Like Frida, she was to find a devastating way of interrupting the immortal hero's journey to fulfillment by displaying her own mortality.

6

ON THE IMPOSSIBILITY
OF ANTIGONE AND
THE INEVITABILITY OF
LA MALINCHE: REWRITING THE
NATIONAL ALLEGORY

The political scientist and feminist Nancy Hartsock observes of the hero that he emerges quintessentially in the *Iliad* in the person of Achilles, "the best of the Achaeans," a man whose purpose is "the achievement of undying fame whether through glorious victory or glorious death."[1] She goes on to argue that the link between death, sacrifice, and heroism continues to underlie the concept of the polis today; this claim has some validity when we think of Latin American politics and narrative, especially in the sixties, when there was a resurgence of the hero myth around guerrilla leaders like Che Guevara. In literature, too, there was an exploration of heroism, sacrifice, and failure, whose obituary was written by Vargas Llosa in *Historia de Mayta,* translated as *The Real Life of Alejandro Mayta.*[2] A whole book could be devoted to these themes of loyalty and treachery, death, memory and oblivion as they relate either to the real society caught in the stagnation of colonial time and only salvageable by a violent seizure of power, or as they relate to the ideal polis of literature, the community that narrative plot holds out as its lure and its unattainable goal.

Death and the commemoration of the dead is central to the hero myth, for the uncommemorated are by definition unhonored and therefore written out of the historical record. Those novelists who wish to mark their distance from official history do so by remembering the unsung dead. For instance, one of Carlos Fuentes' novels, *La región más transparente* (1959; translated as *Where the Air*

Is Clear), includes a litany of all the unhonored dead of Mexican history.[3]

The imperative to commemorate the dead is all the more pressing when, as Nietzsche pointed out, the narratives of the victors inevitably prevail, an unpalatable truth that García Márquez turned into comic fantasy in a story called "Blacamán the Good, Salesman of Miracles," in which two rival magicians vie for power. The victor not only attains fame and fortune but is able to bury his rival alive in a tomb that he visits merely to have the pleasure of hearing the cries of the vanquished. Here the narration of history is owned by the dominant power. García Márquez' first novel, *La hojarasca* (1955; Leaf Storm), it should be remembered, was prefaced by an epigraph taken from Sophocles' drama *Antigone*— Creon's decree condemning the body of Polinices to lie unburied outside the city walls.[4] The same passage from *Antigone* is also evoked in the opening lines of Augusto Roa Bastos' *Yo el Supremo* (1978; I the Supreme);[5] and the themes of death, heroism, and anonymity are announced in the titles of many contemporary novels: *Sobre héroes y tumbas* (1961; Of Heroes and Tombs), by Ernesto Sábato; *La muerte de Artemio Cruz* (1962; The Death of Artemio Cruz), by Carlos Fuentes; *Para una tumba sin nombre* (1959; For a Tomb Without a Name), by Juan Carlos Onetti; *El luto humano* (1943; Human Mourning), by José Revueltas. Mourning the fate of Polinices, these novelists become surrogates for Antigone herself.

The Antigone myth complements the Oedipus myth in important ways, as was recognized by Hölderlin, Hegel, and more recently by Derrida, Lacan, and George Steiner. Steiner has even argued that "since the fifth century B.C., Western sensibility has experienced decisive moments of its identity and history in reference to the Antigone legend and to the life in art and argument of this legend," and he cites an extraordinary example from recent history in which a girl in Germany in 1941 sprinkled earth on the body of her executed brother, saying, "He was my brother. For me that is sufficient."[6] Unlike the Oedipus myth, which Freud tried to read in terms of male and female development ("the dream of symmetry"), *Antigone* seems to divide the sexes along the axis of separation between state and family.

The usual reading of the tragedy emphasizes Antigone's stern refusal to temporize with ancient ritual. Her duty to the dead comes before reason of state, a duty that Hegel, in particular, identified as woman's.[7] For this, Creon condemns her to a terrible death, but he also brings ruin onto his own house, for Haiman his son (and Antigone's lover) hangs himself. But the interpretation of *Antigone* undergoes a sea change in Latin America, where Polinices is identified with the marginalized, and the role of the one who commemorates the dead and does not permit them to be consigned to oblivion is taken by the writer who "masculinizes" the Antigone position.

Mexico did, nevertheless, produce an anti-Antigone legend: that of "La Malinche" or Doña Marina, the indigenous woman who was given to Cortés by a Tabascan tribe and who became his mistress, mother of one of his children, and an interpreter or translator ("translation" being closely related in its Latin root to "treachery"). Without her, one critic suggests, the conquest would have been difficult and perhaps even impossible, and another describes her as "the most hated woman of the Americas."[8] She was from the first regarded as an icon, both by the indigenous people who ascribed extraordinary power to her and by the Spaniards for whom she was the exemplary convert. Yet it was not until Mexico became an independent nation and the problem of national identity surfaced that Doña Marina, transformed into La Malinche, came to symbolize the humiliation—the rape—of the indigenous people and the act of treachery that would lead to their oppression. It was Octavio Paz, in his well-known essay on the Mexican national character, *The Labyrinth of Solitude* (1950), who argued that the Mexican male subject had been constituted as a violent rejection of this shameful mother. "Doña Marina," he wrote, "has become a figure that represents those Indian women who were fascinated, raped, or seduced by the Spaniards, and, just as the child cannot forgive the mother who leaves him to go in search of his father, the Mexican people cannot forgive the treason of La Malinche. She incarnates the open, the raped [*lo chingado*], in opposition to our stoic, impassive, and closed Indians."[9]

The problem of national identity was thus presented primarily as a problem of *male* identity, and it was male authors who debated its defects and psychoanalyzed the nation. In national allegories, women became the territory over which the quest for (male) national identity passed, or, at best, as in Juan Rulfo's *Pedro Páramo* (1955), the space of loss and of all that lies outside the male games of rivalry and revenge.

Under these circumstances, national identity could not but be a problematic terrain for women novelists, although it was not something they could avoid. How could they plot themselves into a narrative without becoming masculine or attempting to speak from the devalued position, the space of the marginalized and the ethnic, which was not the space of writing at all? This is the dilemma of the novelists I discuss in this chapter, both of whom, in different ways, attempt to write women into the national narrative, yet, in doing so, repeat La Malinche's "betrayal."

Before proceeding with my argument, I would first like to make clear that "treachery" is not only a political term, for in Latin American literature betrayal of one's roots or origins, especially if they are in indigenous communities and orally transmitted cultures, is often considered tantamount to a rite of entry into the literary institution. Orally transmitted narratives, such as folk tale and romance, have their roots in a community where treachery means threatening the very existence of the community to which storyteller and listener belong.[10] As soon as stories are written and published, however, a different contract between storyteller and reader is established. In much modern fiction, too, there is another type of betrayal—that of the community between writer and reader, as the avant-garde writer tends to destroy the reader's preconceptions and any loyalties that preexist the text. Here "treachery" can be enabling and emancipatory. Indeed, Borges made it a mandatory move in the affirmation of literature's autonomy from social and familial references.[11] In such writers as Carlos Fuentes and Mario Vargas Llosa, lying (a form of treachery) becomes equivalent to fictionalizing, and is accompanied by a privileging of the fictional (and imaginative) over the preconstructed "real."[12]

In the novels I discuss in this chapter, on the other hand, treachery takes place not so much between writer and reader as on the level of the enunciated—that is, in the space where plot, character, and novelistic time are interwoven. These novels therefore register the first type of treachery, that which takes place in the shift from the community bound by orally transmitted culture to the nation. The two novels I have chosen to illustrate this point are *Los recuerdos del porvenir* (translated as *Recollections of Things to Come*) by Elena Garro, and *Oficio de tinieblas* (Tenebrae) by Rosario Castellanos. Both novels combine some version of realism with romance, fairy tale, and legend, and both were written in the 1960s and thus coincide with the "heroic" phase of the Latin American novel. I shall concentrate primarily on their plotting and particularly their endings, since it is precisely the closure of the novel that is the place of ideological ambiguity. What is at stake is whether a "heroine" is possible at all within the terms of the epic or master narratives of the nation. As Teresa de Lauretis has written, women, as readers, are always torn by these narratives, since they are invited to identify with the hero but must also identify with woman as boundary or obstacle or territory through which the hero passes on his road to self-transformation. Both novels make it clear that rewriting master narratives around a heroine is fraught with difficulty.[13]

Elena Garro, the author of *Los recuerdos del porvenir*,[14] was, at the time of writing the novel, the wife of Octavio Paz, whose *The Labyrinth of Solitude* was already a classic discussion of Mexican character. He had vividly portrayed the Mexican's defensive *machismo* and his need to repress the "feminine" in himself and others. It was an analysis that owed more to Jung than to Freud. In his essay, Paz had listed the female stereotypes—prostitute, goddess, great lady—invented by men. Women, he claimed, "transmit and conserve but do not create the values and energies which nature and society pass on. In a world made in the image of man, the woman is only a reflection of male will and desire."[15] Paz is, of course, critical of this. But because he makes no distinction between representation and the real relations of women, his argument locks male Mexico into permanent negation of part of its self, and, since that part is idealized Woman and not women, there seems to be no arena of struggle.

Garro's novel aligns women with the marginalized and gives them central importance as plotters against the state. The setting is a regional town occupied by a victorious revolutionary army which is the instrument of the new postrevolutionary nation. This alien force destroys the traditional structures, yet unites all marginalized groups in silent opposition. The period is the 1920s, when the militant secular state attempted to undermine the power of the Church and instead brought on the armed conflict known as the Cristero War.

Interestingly, Garro did not try to tell the story as a realist novel. Instead, she chose the fairy-tale plot. This is an interesting choice, since contemporary narrative theory has drawn heavily on Vladimir Propp's *Morphology of the Folk Tale* (1958) in order to build a narratology. Yet if we attend to surface rather than to deep structures, we find that fairy-tale plots, unlike epic narrative or the classical realist novel, often have feminine protagonists and that the fairy-tale romance has deeply influenced women's popular fiction down to the present.[16]

The narrator of Garro's novel is not a person but a collectivity— the town of Ixtepec, or rather its orally transmitted collective

memory. But that memory is activated by a monument—a stone—
which is the only remaining vestige of one of the two heroines of
the story, Isabel Moncada. The choice of this collective protagonist has the advantage of giving voice to all the marginalized elements of Mexico—the old aristocracy, the peasantry (and former
supporters of the assassinated revolutionary leader Zapata), the
indigenous, and women; in sum, all those left behind by modernization and the new nation. Excluded from this collective memory
is the official history propagated by the "new men" who have forged
postrevolutionary nationalism and who, in the period covered by
the novel, are engaged in the war against the Catholic Church whose
militant arm is the Cristero guerrilla army.

Jean Meyer, one of the foremost authorities on the Cristero War
of the 1920s to which Garro's novel refers, has criticized *Los recuerdos del porvenir* for its ideological bias. He writes: "The author offers an interesting vision of the problem. For her, it is all
about the death of the agrarian movement brought about by Catholic reactionaries (Porfiristas) and atheist revolutionaries," and he
quotes a sentence from the novel: "The Church and the government fabricate a cause to ruin discontented peasantry. While the
peasants and the priests prepare themselves for terrible death, the
Archbishop was dealing his cards to the wives of atheistic rul-
ers."[17] Though Meyer is correct in showing that the author's politics are foregrounded in passages such as these, to select such
metadiegetic statements is to miss the point. Despite the historical
references, *Los recuerdos del porvenir* is not altogether a historical
novel but rather, like *Antigone,* it challenges the state's appropriation of meaning by evoking more ancient loyalties—to family,
religion, and "imagined" communities which do not coincide with
the nation. In this respect, it is more deeply subversive of official
history than the better-known *La muerte de Artemio Cruz* by Carlos
Fuentes. This subversion is partly conveyed through the different
temporalities at work in the novel—the disjunctive time of revolutionary change, the nostalgic time of memory, frozen time, fes-
tive and ritual time. The title itself is disturbingly ambiguous, for
it suggests both the future's memories and anticipated recollections. The novel often shifts into a different time warp, and this
is evocative of Latin American temporality where different temporal modes (cyclical, linear) and different historical modes often
coexist.

The novel is structured like a double-sided mirror. We look into
one side and see a projection of the fairy prince and the happy

ending. We look into the other and see the dark fairy tale, the one with the bitter ending. At the novel's start Ixtepec is occupied by the victorious army headed by General Rosas, who had fought with Obregón. The officers have installed themselves in the town's hotel along with the women who have followed them or whom they have kidnapped or seduced.[18] All the desire and resentment of the occupied town are focused on the General's mistress, Julia, and on a mysterious stranger, Felipe Hurtado, who, like all fairy-tale heroes, appears mysteriously out of nowhere and who has some inexplicable link to Julia (possibly simply the fact that they came from the same place and had shared the same community). This first part of the novel is narrated as the magical romance of Julia's rescue. General Rosas had attempted to subdue Julia by using his power; his rejection of romance corresponds to the actant *machismo*, which is also actualized by several other of the military characters who vainly try to dominate their woman, all of whom are "elsewhere," living in a world of romance.[19] But machismo also implies a code of death and honor. The General must assert mastery over the rival, Felipe Hurtado, by killing him, and he sets out to do it in the most public way possible, by going directly to the house where he is staying and challenging him. But Hurtado magically escapes with Julia on the legendary white horse, taking advantage of a cloud of darkness that surrounds Ixtepec even during the daylight hours.

Because fairy tale and romance have been the most persistent mode of representing female desire, many women writers consciously reject them because they appear to amount to a seduction of the reader. In their book *The Madwoman in the Attic,* Gilbert and Gubar describe how both Charlotte Brontë and Emily Dickinson felt themselves to be slaves of the romantic plot and the patriarchal structures that plot reflected.[20] European and North American popular literature for women used these romantic plots, turning them into the formulas of a marketable product. In Mexico, however, it was the popular song, cinema, and orally transmitted culture that kept romance alive, although by 1962, when *Los recuerdos del porvenir* was published, popular print romances and *fotonovelas,* photo novels—popular narratives in a comic-strip format, but using photographic stills—had become the favorite reading of the newly literate.[21] Garro's appropriation of romance in the first part of her novel satisfies the desire for a happy ending which the second part of the novel disappoints. Romance is one way in which Utopian feelings repressed by tyranny and machismo can be expressed, and it allows the liberation of the courtesan, Julia, the "public woman," whose disappearance with Hurtado makes her into a legendary heroine.

In the second part of the novel, Garro turns the whole issue around. Now the army, still headed by General Rosas, who has become more repressive since his loss of Julia, enforces the government decree that bans the Church of Rome. This episode is based on historical events that led up to the Cristero War and began when President Calles announced his intention of replacing the Church of Rome by a national church, the Orthodox Mexican Church (La Iglesia Ortodoxa Mexicana). The persecution of "their" church unites the entire population of the town—the aristocratic Moncada family headed by don Martín and Ana and their children, Juan, Nicolás, and Isabel; Juan Cariño, the president of the defunct municipal council; the sacristan, don Roque, and the displaced priest; the Indians; a doctor; old *beatas* like Dorotea; and prostitutes.

The antiheroine of this part of the story is Isabel Moncada, who passionately loves her brother Nicolás, resents the fact that she is a woman, since this condemns her to inaction, and invests her desire for power in the abandoned and solitary General Rosas. In short, she becomes a traitor. As Catholic resistance grows in the town, Father Beltrán disappears and the sacristan don Roque is stoned at night by anonymous attackers and left to die. His wounded body mysteriously disappears, carried off, we learn later, by the priest who is hiding in the hut of a *beata,* doña Dorotea. There is no point in exploring every detail of a complex and somewhat melodramatic plot. It is enough to know that the entire town participates in a plan to help the priest escape; that Juan, one of Isabel's brothers, is killed during the escape, which takes place during a ball organized in the hope of hoodwinking the military; but the military outwit the populace and keep them dancing all night while the army rounds up the conspirators. Isabel's brother, Nicolás Moncada, is caught with the priest and condemned to be shot along with several other conspirators. Those who betray the Cristero cause are all women—a servant, a prostitute, and Isabel Moncada, who puts her own dream of power and seduction above the interests of the community and allows herself to be carried off by the General on the very night that his troops kill her brother Juan.

Isabel is thus the reverse of Antigone, having chosen reason of state over family and community. Her one chance of redeeming herself is by using her sexual power and appealing to the General to save her brother Nicolás. In the mirror opposites of the novel, the prostitute, Julia, had refused to practice seduction on the General and had escaped from him. In the second part, the aristocrat, Isabel, tries to win power through seduction but fails. The General, out of self-disgust rather than affection for Isabel, invents a plan to substitute another prisoner for Nicolás, thus allowing him to save face while "repaying" Isabel. But the "hero," Nicolás, refuses to participate in the deception and is shot with the other prisoners. Isabel has failed to save him and now fails to save herself. She is taken by her old nurse, Gregoria, to a sanctuary dedicated to the Virgin, but defiantly asks only to see Francisco Rosas again. However, the last moments of Isabel and her metamorphosis are known only because the servant Gregoria lives to relate them. In her version, a cloud of dust blows up, recalling both the darkness that had allowed Julia and her lover to escape and the cloud of dust that had surrounded Antigone as she reached the body of Polinices. But in Isabel's case, the dust conceals her shameful metamorphosis from a living person into a stone on which the servant Gregoria writes the epitaph and the last words of the novel:

> I am Isabel Moncada, born of Martín Moncada and Ana Cuétara de Moncada, in the town of Ixtepec, the first of December 1907. Into stone I was transformed on the 5th of October, 1927, before the horrified eyes of Gregoria Juárez. I caused pain to my parents and the death of my brothers Juan and Nicolás. When I came to beg the Virgin to cure me of my love for general Francisco Rosas who killed my brothers, I vacillated and preferred the love of the man who ruined me and my family. Here I shall stay alone with my love as a memory of the future forever and ever.

Gregoria's story turns Isabel into the monument of betrayal, a betrayal of the family. Her sin is that of *malinchismo*. Yet the constant shifts of the narrative, the undecidability of the point of view allow us to read Isabel's tragedy in another way. For Isabel's problems start from the moment when, after an idyllic childhood, she is separated from her brother Nicolás and designated a female. She had never really reconciled herself to the social consequences of gender differences nor to the fact that only men work, travel, and become heroes. The family cannot fulfill her desires because of the incest taboo. She desires her brother, and, therefore, cannot be completely loyal to the family or to the state. The family constitutes her as a woman and thus separates her from her brother, but her attempt to cross over from the traditional community into the new postrevolutionary world is also a failure because her assertive gesture is not acceptable to traditional and communal values.

Garro's novel thus represents an impasse. Women do not enter history—only romance. Either they are legends like Julia, the elusive phantom of male desire, or like Isabel they are the undesired surrogates who are not objects of desire but who allow themselves to be seduced by power. Such women do not wrest interpretive power from the masters and are not commemorated by posterity, except as traitors to the community that has been forever bonded by memory and speech. The fact that Isabel's treachery becomes inscribed in stone while Julia's legend remains a legend only underlines the fact that both are outside history.

Much of Garro's writing down to the present is preoccupied with exile and the homelessness of marginalized peoples and those who have been vanquished. And this often involves her in attempts to interrupt the measured time of history.[22] But in *Los recuerdos del porvenir,* she takes on the confrontation between oppressive patriarchy and all of the informal knowledge, belief, and experience that it would try to repress. One of the women in the novel, for instance, finds no difficulty in being silent under investigation because her father had taught her that women should not open their mouths. Yet as Garro also shows, women's plotting is undermined because power seduces them. This finally is for her the lesson of La Malinche.

Oficio de tinieblas (Tenebrae) by Rosario Castellanos was published in 1963, a year after *Los recuerdos del porvenir.* The author, who came from a white, land-owning family in the predominantly indigenous state of Chiapas, was a pioneer feminist, author of many essays and poems protesting women's subordination. Indeed, in one of her poems, "Meditación en el umbral" (Meditation on the Threshold), she rejects a whole series of female stereotypes from the mystical Saint Theresa to Sor Juana in her cell, from Emily Dickinson to Jane Austen, concluding,

> There has to be some other way that isn't called
>   Sappho, or Messalina, or Mary of Egypt, or
>   Magdalene, or Clementia Isaura
> Another way to be human and free.
> Another way to be.[23]

It was particularly in her poetry and in her essays that she revealed a deep sense of her own devaluation as a woman, describing herself on one occasion as

> a woman of good intentions
> who has paved
> a straight and easy path to hell.[24]

Castellanos' novel is an ambitious attempt to show the complexity of race, class, and gender relations. Yet, as in Garro's novel, the resolution of these complexities turns into a story of female treachery. *Oficio de tinieblas* is written in the historical realist style that was at that time favored by many Latin American writers, with characters representing social clasess or racial stratification. It is written in the third person, using traditional narrative devices to depict subjectivity—interior monologue or free indirect style—and it can be considered one of the most ambitious attempts by a Mexican writer to create a historical novel in the Lukacsian sense.[25] Lukacsian typicality, however, often lapses into the stereotypical—the macho landowners, submissive wives, exploited Indian villagers, and rich merchants who are the stock characters of the *indigenista* novel.[26]

What interests me here is that, like Garro, Castellanos first identifies women with other groups marginalized both in older patriarchal structures of the landowning class and in modernized Mexico. In *Oficio de tinieblas,* she tries to work through the divisions between women of different classes and races who, in some sense, as women, share the same problems. Yet the realist novel elided her own subjectivity beneath the voice of the omniscient narrator. It would be in her poetry, and particularly in her later poems, that the problem of women's sexuality would surface most explicitly.

Before writing the novel, Castellanos had worked in her native Chiapas for the national institute that dealt with Indian affairs (the National Indigenist Institute) and was therefore implicated in its policies, which at this period involved intense acculturation and modernization. Her experience working with an educational puppet theater in San Cristóbal brought her into direct contact with people she described as "scandalously poor and radically ignorant."[27] In common with other members of the Institute, she believed that the only road for the Tzotziles was acculturation, but she was frustrated by their resistance to the literacy program and the narrow-mindedness of the bureaucrats in charge of the programs. The conflict between an oppressed indigenous group who were nevertheless "light years away from modern civilization," and the "bureaucracy without ideals" was to be deployed in *Oficio de tinieblas*. Yet this conflict was also filtered through her growing preoccupation with the issue of gender, especially the issue of motherhood.

Her choice of a historical realist novel to depict this conflict is therefore understandable, since the third person narrative and the historical raw material allow her to transpose a personal into a national problem. Yet, though she could not have known it, she chose a dubious historical anecdote as her source, an anecdote that somehow impressed her and yet would undermine the verisimilitude she strove for. Though the novel is set during the period of agrarian reform under General Lázaro Cárdenas (between 1934 and 1940),[28] the indigenous uprising which is the central episode of the novel was based on events that took place between 1868 and 1871, the accounts of which were written by those sympathetic to the ruling landowning caste, who depicted the Indians as bloodthirsty and savage in order to justify repression. The highlight of this apocryphal story was the Indians' crucifixion of one of their own children.[29] Castellanos was not alone in accepting the veracity of the legend. The reputable anthropologist Ricardo Pozas, who did field work among the Chamulas in the 1950s, includes this legend in his book *Chamula* as if it were true history. He even mentions the crucifixion as an example of a tradition of human sacrifice going back to the ancient Mayas.[30]

What had alarmed the landowners in 1867 was not so much an indigenous uprising but the fear of an uprising in the wake of the caste wars of Yucatán,[31] and their alarm was exacerbated by the activities of the followers of a religious cult. Pedro Díaz Cuscat, helped by a woman, Agustina Gómez Checheb, reportedly made a clay figure in Tzajalhemel, adorned it with ribbons, and claimed that the idol had come down from heaven to satisfy the needs of the indigenous community. The idol was placed on a box and Cuscat, from inside the box, would make it speak. Here he followed a tradition of Maya resistance, in which speaking boxes and speaking crosses had figured prominently.[32] The priest of Chamula persuaded the Indians that the saint was false and took away its clothes. But soon afterward Pedro Cuscat and Agustina Checheb made and adorned new idols. This time Agustina was said to have given birth to these figures and was named the mother of God. Cuscat was arrested on suspicion of inciting rebellion but then freed.

According to the legend, Cuscat began to claim that the indigenous community needed a crucified Christ to make them equal to the Christians. They chose Domingo Gómez Checheb, who was supposedly crucified on Holy Friday, 1868. The priest was ambushed and killed, marking the beginning of the Indian rebellion, which was joined by Ignacio Fernández Galindo, a native of San Cristóbal. The Indian rebels set fire to ladino stores and houses, killing men, women, and children, and spreading alarm in the entire province. Galindo was taken prisoner, whereupon Cuscat attacked San Cristóbal. Galindo and Benito Trejo were eventually executed and the Indians retired, defeated, from their positions around San Cristóbal. Cuscat escaped but died in the mountains.

This account, which formed the basis of Castellanos' novel, is a mixture of truth and fiction. Similar legends always seem to spring up where there is racial oppression—at this same period, in La Habana, whites quaked at stories of blacks killing white babies. Even in the 1960s when Castellanos read the account of the 1868 "uprising," she accepted it as the true record of a "brief collective 'Dionysian'" orgy of blood "which quickly spent itself without being able to generate any lasting results."[33] What undoubtedly attracted her to the legend was the major role played by a woman, Agustina, the maker of idols.

Yet what mars the novel is, perhaps, not so much the shaky source of the story or the transposition from the nineteenth century to modern times but the fact that in making the child's crucifixion central to the novel, Castellanos tacitly acquieses in the view of the literal-mindedness of the indigenous population propagated by positivism. In her novel the Indians sacrifice a real child because they cannot understand the symbolism of the Eucharist, whereas, as anthropologists point out, the symbolic systems of those very indigenous peoples are of the utmost sophistication. Finally, her choice of the historical realist novel with a third person omniscient narrator contributes to the ideological closure of the novel and its pessimistic view of the outcome of both the struggle of the indigenous people and of women. *Oficio de tinieblas* is therefore in many respects an interesting failure, but a failure that allowed Castellanos herself to work out her own ambivalences about women, power, and seduction.[34]

Around the nucleus of an Indian uprising, Castellanos constructed an entire provincial society—with its landowners, teachers, students, bureaucrats, priests, and the landowners' wives, their servants, and their mistresses. The novel opens with a violent act— the rape of an indigenous woman by a member of the landowning class. This woman will bear the child who will eventually be crucified. This unwanted motherhood stands in sharp contrast to the sterility of most of the women in the novel. Indeed, motherhood is to sterility what virility is to impotence in the male. When motherhood is thwarted by sterility or by choice, then female energies go into compensatory creations. One of the central characters, Catalina, is a barren Tzotzil woman who adopts the child of rape and eventually organizes his crucifixion. The attractive and sexually liberated "La Alazana" (The Mare), the common-law wife of one of the bureaucrats of Cardenas' land reform program and the mistress of the wealthy Leonardo Cifuentes, is also childless and compensates for this with a fruitless attempt to break into Chiapas society. Cifuentes' stepdaughter, Idolina, is unmarriageable because she has lapsed into hypochondria because of her father's death and her mother's remarriage to Cifuentes; she lives a prolonged bedridden childhood in the company of her old Indian nurse. The Indian nurse, Teresa, had borne a child who died because, after becoming Idolina's wet nurse, she was unable to nourish it.

The emphasis on sterility among the female characters obviously indicates that Castellanos herself regarded maternity as a form of feminine fulfillment. It is because she was committed to the historical novel and the "typical" character, that the actant "sterility" surfaces in so many different characters from different social classes and races. Yet this does not mean that mothers are necessarily idealized. Idolina's mother is a sinister character who married the opportunistic Cifuentes after he had murdered her husband. Even more sinister is the "new woman" of postrevolutionary Mexico, La Alazana, who becomes Cifuentes' mistress and whose affair with the landowner has a destabilizing influence on the course of affairs. It is she who ultimately acts as a Malinche, betraying her common-law husband who is in Chiapas to bring about agrarian reform, and therefore betraying the ideals of the Revolution.

Even this brief summary suggests the immense ambition of the novel and the sheer amount of compression necessary to bring together problems of class and race on both the personal and the public level. Not only this, Castellanos attempts to transpose an event of the nineteenth century into the near present of the late 1930s, when Lázaro Cárdenas was attempting to introduce land reform in the teeth of opposition from the landowners. Thus, to the themes of the marginality of the indigenous community and women, she adds that of the failure of postrevolutionary society to achieve its goal of social justice.

Nevertheless, it is the sterile Catalina, the wife of one of the leaders of the indigenous community, whose bid for power dominates the novel. It is she who manipulates a marriage between her own idiot brother and the raped Tzotzil woman, a marriage that allows her to adopt the child Domingo. But this surrogate motherhood is denied her. As a male child, Domingo must learn to do a man's work and must be separated from Catalina and initiated into male society. Bitterly disappointed at this second thwarting of motherhood, Catalina retires to a cave, where she develops her visionary powers and becomes known as an *ilol* or female prophet. She has discovered idols in a cave and organizes a cult around them. Though Catalina leads a movement of resistance, she cannot become a true resistance leader but must remain an isolated figure. The one public role that is open to her is that of prophet, but she is deprived of this too when the priest destroys the idols and she is arrested. When she is released she returns to the cave, this time to create her own idols, a process equated with giving birth (p. 249). When the priest tries to intervene a second time, she resists, and, following her leadership, the community stones him to death. The fact that Castellanos has these fictional events occurring at the time when the Cárdenas government was seizing lands and redistributing them to the peasantry gives added reason for the tensions in the region and accounts for the militant organization of the landowners against the indigenous population.

The major confrontation occurs at Easter, when the tribe deserts the idols and returns to the Christian Church for the reenactment of the Passion, a myth that has more power over them than Catalina's invented religion. This leads her to conclude that she can only revitalize (recreate) the indigenous community by crucifying her godchild, that is, by destroying the genealogical succession on which the community is based in order to create a new and more powerful community in imitation of that of the dominant classes. The scene of the crucifixion is one of incredible cruelty. The nails are rusty. "When they penetrate his flesh, they pulverize the bones, break open the arteries, and tear his tendons." As they carry him on the cross, "Each vibration of the wood is painfully prolonged in Domingo's flesh, and they wring from him his last groans, cut his last ties to life" (p. 323).

Castellanos dwells on the pain and humiliation of the boy whose sacrifice causes a senseless and ultimately suicidal uprising which separates the tribe from its lands and reduces the survivors to homeless and fugitive nomads.

Castellanos secures the ideological closure of the novel not only through the diegetic conclusion but also by showing how the events passed into popular myth. In fact, she introduces two myths—one a myth of writing and the other a myth of telling. In the first of these, the dispersed Tzotziles meet in a cave (the Platonic reference is inescapable) and incorporate into their rituals a book they cannot decipher but which is a copy of the Military Ordinance; unwittingly, they worship the very system that has defeated them, thus ensuring their continuing exploitation. In this myth, writing is the instrument of domination. The second myth is told by the Indian nurse, Teresa, to the childlike Idolina, who is a member of the upper class and who has helped to bring about the social disturbances by writing anonymous letters. In Teresa's story, an Indian woman gives birth to a child of stone, acquires magic powers, and is severely tested. Her pride causes her to demand human sacrifice. (She thus recalls the Aztec's "terrible mother" goddess, Coatlicue.) The lords of Ciudad Real pursue her in vain, but finally defeat her by tying up the stone child, whereupon the *ilol* destroys herself. The novel ends thus: "The name of that *ilol*, which everyone had once pronounced with reverence and hope, has been proscribed. And anyone who feels tempted to utter it spits, and the saliva wipes out the image and its memory." Clearly Catalina, like Isabel Moncada, is punished by being turned into an example of female hubris, but her punishment is to lose her proper name, to become anonymous. This second myth illustrates the failure of orally transmitted legend to provide a collective memory around which further resistance could be mobilized. Writing belongs to the dominant classes, but orally transmitted culture is also penetrated by dominant values.

The ending of Castellanos' novel seems to reflect a belief that subaltern cultures (including that of women) cannot become counterhegemonic because they do not have access to writing, and because even their oral culture is penetrated by myths of submission. Teresa's mythic interpretation of Catalina's actions, transmitted not to her own people but to Idolina, who belongs to another social class and race, demonstrates the fact that all transculturation is destructive to the indigenous community and that woman's bid for power, when it is not linked to national consciousness, can have devastating results. The sterility of all the women in the novel is damaging. Yet the communities that it damages—whether Catalina's indigenous community or La Alazana's postrevolutionary nation—are themselves founded on the devaluation of women. Both Catalina and La Alazana suffer from the double standard.

Important questions are thus raised, though not resolved, in *Oficio de tinieblas*—one of the most basic of which is the question of women's marginality and its relation to identity. For though apparently a tragedy of the indigenous people, who at the end of the story are dispersed and have lost their community, the novel clearly depicts the inability of the nation to cope with either the marginal culture of the indigenous community or the marginality of women. What gives Castellanos' novel some validity, despite its anachronistic picture of women and ethnicity, is the fact that she at least poses the contradictory and antagonistic nature of gender relations as they intersect with race and class. But it is a validity undermined by a third person narrative that masks an ideological positioning. Her story is not official history, yet it is structured by the master narrative of the landowners in ways in which she was not even aware. Her omniscient voice puts her outside the orally transmitted cultures of the indigenous community and women and allows her to speak from a place—the national novel—in which there are no heroines, only heroes.[35]

Does Catalina do what Castellanos did not dare to do? Sacrifice family to attain tribal power? And is the destruction that Catalina brings upon the tribe hyperbolic because in this way Castellanos assures herself as well as her readers of the terrible consequences of this step? Certainly her later poems suggest that women have a fundamental difficulty in asserting power. Unable to identify with the father, they are trafficked by the mother. In a moving poem, "Malinche," she depicts La Malinche as a princess expelled

> from the kingdom
> from the palace and the warm womb
> of her who gave legitimate birth to me
> and who hated me because I was not her equal
> in looks or rank
> and saw in me her image and detested it
> throwing the mirror to the ground.

Self-hatred is woman's most powerful emotion.

In both of these novels of the early sixties, ambitious women are expelled (or expel themselves) from the polis and thus fail to "author" themselves or acquire a name for posterity. Isabel

Moncada's treacherous self-incorporation into the state turns her into an admonitory inscription, not an exemplary hero/author. Catalina brings destruction on the tribe and with them is condemned to homeless wandering. What strikes us in each case is that the woman acts in isolation, exploiting traditional women's spaces of romance and religion, yet without ever being able to institutionalize an alternative discursive practice outside oral tradition. Both Garro and Castellanos seem caught in a predicament. Garro escapes from verisimilitude through fairy tale but thereby cannot insert her heroines into history. Castellanos' attempt to be true to history means that she dooms her protagonist. In both cases, the problem is rooted in their attempt to appropriate the then hegemonic genre—the novel as national allegory. In such novels the personal lives of the protagonist generally represent the problems of the nation as a whole.[36] But as these novels show, it is simply not possible to retain verisimilitude and make women into national protagonists. Women's attempts to plot themselves as protagonists in the national novel become a recognition of the fact that they are not in the plot at all but definitely somewhere else.

7

OEDIPUS MODERNIZED

With modernization everything has to be recoded, for now people
are on the move away from home territories and genealogies. There
are new "modern" discursive practices—radio and cinema—able
to interpolate large numbers of people hitherto marginalized by
illiteracy and to create a national iconography that idealizes the
mestizo, the peasant, and the indigenous. Mexican cinema during
the presidencies of Avila Camacho (1940–1946) and of Miguel
Alemán (1946–1952) was as efficient as the classical Hollywood
cinema in creating spectator identification and relaying it by means
of a narrative plot that mapped the spectator into a process of
change.[1] If as de Lauretis suggests, identification is "not simply
one psychical mechanism among others, but the operation itself
whereby the human subject is constituted,"[2] then this explains why
cinema was able to constitute an ideal national identity that incorporated the masses by revising the oedipal narrative.

In this chapter I examine two films from the 1940s and a well-
known sociological family history of the period, Oscar Lewis' *The
Children of Sánchez* which offer different displacements of the
oedipal myth onto the national narrative. The film *Enamorada* (In
Love) belongs to the "Golden Age" of Mexican cinema.[3] It is unusual in that it explicitly comments on the power of representation
to put to rights a world turned upside down by Revolution. The
broken family, the cult of violence, and the independent "masculinized" woman have to be transformed into a new holy family

in which women accede voluntarily to their own subordination not to a biological father but to a paternal state. The limits of this benevolent and paternalistic state are dramatically revealed in a film that appeared at the same time as *Enamorada,* Luis Buñuel's *Los olvidados.*

Here the mythic family of the nation is revealed to be indeed mythic, for as Stallybrass and White point out, "the very drive to achieve a singularity of collective identity is simultaneously productive of unconscious heterogeneity, with its variety of hybrid figures, competing sovereignties, and exorbitant demands."[4] Such hybrid figures which resist modernization are "delinquents," a classification as essential to the modern state as "delusion" was to the Inquisition. The delinquent "leaves undone"—that is, he or she does not do what the state demands. The delinquent is therefore the place where the state fails and the one who introduces the disorder of death into its Utopian and essentially masculine project. Yet, even among the delinquents, the circulation of power is between males, while women are the objects of desire and the guardians of death.

Can women tell their story? Oskar Negt and Alexander Kluge argue that the modern culture industry prevents individuals from interpreting the self and the world.[5] In this chapter I offer a counter example, though an ambiguous one. In Oscar Lewis' life stories of a Mexican family, *The Children of Sánchez,* Consuelo creates her own family narrative, successfully separating herself from her biological father and transferring her allegiance to a surrogate father, the representative of modernization.

THE HOLY FAMILY OF THE POSTREVOLUTIONARY STATE

Enamorada (1947) was directed by the "Indio" Fernández, whose career as a director spanned the years between 1941 and 1978. It brought together a major triumvirate of the Mexican cinema— Fernández himself, the cameraman Gabriel Figueroa, and the screenwriter (and novelist) Mauricio Magdaleno, as well as two of Mexico's most popular stars, Pedro Armendáriz and María Félix.[6] The story is roughly based on *The Taming of the Shrew.*

The film can also be seen, however, as an intervention in a recent polemic. Feminine militancy had increased during the regime of Lázaro Cárdenas, but women had failed to get the vote partly because Cárdenas believed that they would support the conservatives.[7] *Enamorada* presents an exemplary resolution of this conflict, for it shows how militant conservative women can be won over by a postrevolutionary regime that has left the violent past behind.

The film takes place during the Revolution. It opens when a peasant army led by the revolutionary General Juan José Reyes (Pedro Armendáriz) is about to invade and occupy a town. The General's energetic character is immediately established by his bucking horse and the swift manner in which he has the town's rich citizens rounded up. Among the first to be interrogated is the priest, Father Manuel, who turns out to be a childhood friend of the General's, and the wealthy don Carlos Peñafiel, whose fiery daughter Beatriz is about to be married to an American. The American is conveniently absent for most of the film, having obtained a safe-conduct to travel to Mexico City for Beatriz' wedding dress. In his absence, Beatriz and the General meet in a head-on collision. In this conflict, religion, in the person of the androgynous and classless priest, becomes the only logical mediator between the old landowning class and the new revolutionary leadership, and between the sexes. Though the film's title, *Enamorada,* with its feminine ending, suggests that it is the woman who is in love, it is in fact the lower-class General who first falls for Beatriz. This puts him doubly at a disadvantage, both because of his lower social position and because his character is rendered more sensitive by love. Beatriz, on the other hand, is "masculinized" because of the power of her class position and her own independent and proud nature. The narrative therefore must restore the balance by affirming the General's masculinity and subduing the "virile" female.

In their initial encounters, it is always Beatriz who fearlessly humiliates the General. These violent confrontations are generally followed by a cut to the church. In the first of these the camera lingers over the sumptuous baroque roof and altar while Father Manuel sings a sugary *Ave Maria.* Yet the film does not simply dissolve the class conflict and the conflicting ethical codes through the mediation of religion. Rather, it foregrounds its own system of representation. In a long and crucial sequence, the priest takes the General to the sacristy and shows him an old painting which depicts the Magi bowing before the Christ child. The priest points out that this painting, which shows the powerful of the world humbling themselves before the Church, was the work of a certain

Juárez. The uneducated General jumps to the conclusion that the painter was Benito Juárez, the nineteenth-century politician who attacked the Church during the Reform Movement.[8] This misrecognition is crucial to the film since it is a pun on Juárez, a pun that substitutes a painter (and his representation of classlessness) for the sectarian anticlerical politician, and substitutes a work of representation for revolutionary social change. The General is moved by the painting and has the priest take the picture out of the darkness and place it where it can be seen.

Now this scene points to the importance of representation as a way of mediating conflicts. Indeed, portraits were commonly used in Hollywood films when emphasis was being placed on the work of representation.[9] In this case, the theme of the painting is the "feminine" quality of humility which is lacking in both the General and Beatriz. It is precisely the fact that this sequence seems to have no immediate bearing on the development of the action that thrusts it into the foreground of the viewer's attention. Diegetically, it is simply an incident in the gradual "softening" of the General, who persists in his pursuit of Beatriz despite her violent rejection. But at the metadiegetical level, it privileges representation (and the cinema) as an agent of social transformation.

Beatriz' transformation is more difficult. The death of her mother has left her in sole possession of her father's affection—and the American fiancé will clearly not be able to displace this oedipal relationship. However, the first step in her transformation occurs when her father reveals to her that he had stolen her mother from her family. The revelation awakens in Beatriz a recognition of the "rightness" of this male assertion of dominance, but she cannot identify the General as a potential lover because of his lower social class. She continually refers to him as a *pelado*, a lower-class ruffian, whose proper partner would be a female camp follower (a *soldadera*). The taunt provokes the General into praising the *soldadera* as the supreme example of womanhood, and when Beatriz responds by slapping him, he strikes her in turn and then hits the interfering (but forgiving) priest. The following sequence again foregrounds the painting. Father Manuel tells Beatriz of the General's reverence for the painting and his respect for her. This enables Beatriz to recognize that the lower classes might harbor "noble" feelings.

As is now widely recognized, the identification of the spectator in classical cinema is heavily dependent on the "look." *Enamorada* handles this in exemplary fashion. In a scene in which the lovesick General serenades Beatriz, who is lying half asleep in her bedroom, the camera alternates between her face and especially her eyes, which flutter open and shut as she is awakened by the music, and the General seen from overhead, looking upward toward her balcony. A group of serenaders who have accompanied the General sing "La Malagueña" ("How beautiful are your eyes"—"¡Qué bonitos ojos tienes!"). The entire sequence is a play of looks, with the camera cutting between the General, Beatriz, and the singers, whose falsetto seems to mime the softening of the male under the influence of love (the theme of the painting again). The General looks up toward Beatriz' window but cannot see her. When Beatriz goes to the window and looks out, the General is no longer looking. Her eyes fall on her fiancé's picture as she turns away from the window. The General looks up and she is not there. She goes to the window once more, only to see the General walking away. This play of eyes indicates a misrecognition which makes us, the audience, wish for an exchange of looks between the two, and, significantly, this exchange will first occur in the church, thus guaranteeing its purity and holiness.[10]

Beatriz, her head covered with a shawl and looking like the Virgin of Sorrows, is praying before a baroque altar when the General enters the church dressed in his fighting uniform with the bullet cases crossed over his chest. This time their eyes meet. A speechless Beatriz listens while the General pours out his feelings, telling her that he will always carry his love for her in his heart "like the image on this altar." Love and religion are analogous. Beatriz hurries out, but not before turning back to look at him again as he turns away from her toward an altar painting.

The General now becomes almost sublime in his abnegation. He returns money and jewels to the wife of the merchant he had shot at the beginning of the film and allows Beatriz' fiancé to return to her with the wedding clothes he has brought from Mexico City. Finally, when the Federal troops attack, he agrees to abandon the town to avoid bloodshed. The sound of the retreat interrupts the civilian marriage ceremony in which Beatriz, dressed in black, is about to be united to her American fiancé. The roar of enemy cannon wakens the subdued Beatriz, who throws down the pen just before signing the marriage contract and runs into the street. Against the gigantic shadows of the marching peasant army thrown onto the background of white walls (and reminiscent of the murals of Orozco), Beatriz searches for the General, then turns back to say goodby to her father. The General, still believing that she has rejected him, stoically leads the retreat. But Beatriz runs across the battlefield, among the humble *soldaderas*. In the final sequence, she has placed her hand on the rump of the General's horse. He turns and meets her gaze, then, sitting upright, he looks ahead while Beatriz, holding on to the horse's rump, marches behind him. The proper hierarchy of male/female has not only been restored, but the "exchange" of Beatriz signals the change from the old order to the new and the necessary separation of this new family from older rooted communities.

Ideologically the film realigns the family that had been torn apart by the Revolution. Most of the characters belong to broken families. Carlos Peñafiel is a widower, Beatriz is motherless, the General an orphan. The theme of orphanhood is further accentuated by the General's mascot, a war orphan whose name, Adelita, refers to a famous love ballad of the Revolution—and by an episode in which an aged lonely combatant tells of his regret at having abandoned the woman he should have married.

The ideological problem of the film is how to uphold the need for family life without sacrificing revolutionary nationalism. In other words, the film has to found a revolutionary ethics. The narrative resolves this by introducing the priest and the Church as the space in which a new ethics will be founded. Yet it is clear that the Church "blesses" and therefore gives authority to the new form of representation—the cinematic spectacle—as well as to the secular family which unites members of different social classes. At the same time the absence of mothers in the film suggests the lack which Beatriz promises to fill. The economy of the plot requires the elision of a traditional mother who might evoke associations of home and roots. It is the motherless and tamed Beatriz who is destined to become the mother of the new holy family by separating herself from her old family ties to follow the General. Together they can become the icons of the new migrant work force. The cinema thus provided a powerful technique for shoring up the family (at least in theory) at a time when large numbers of immigrants were drifting into the city and finding themselves without the social censorship and the religious and political control that prevailed in the provinces.

THE FORGOTTEN

Los olvidados (English title, *The Young and the Damned*),[11] is a now classic film by the well-known surrealist and avant-garde Spanish director Luis Buñuel, who lived and worked in Mexico during the late forties and early fifties.[12] Indeed, the directors of *Enamorada* and *Los olvidados* used the same cameraman Gabriel Figueroa, who injected a certain lyricism into Buñuel's film. Buñuel had been struck by the poverty of Mexico but wanted to make a film that would avoid sentimentality. In *Los olvidados*, all that *Enamorada* suppresses or resolves—that is, the violence of gender relations—is brought to the surface. The modern is grafted onto archaic and destructive death drives, and the adventure unfolds with all the inevitability of classic tragedy.

This juxtaposition of the modern with the archaic is established through the mise-en-scène—the adobe houses on the outskirts of the city in which new high-rise buildings are under construction, and the markets, fairgrounds, and a small farm with cows and chickens, are close to the modern buildings and contrast with the tidy "modern farm" that the government has set up to rehabilitate delinquents.[13]

Because the film subverts the official image of a Mexico making a smooth transition into modernity, it was provided with an introduction that showed stock shots of New York, Paris, and London, and a voice-over that explained that delinquency was a problem in all modern cities, not just in Mexico City: "Mexico, a great and modern city, is no exception to this universal truth, and this film, based on real life, is not optimistic but leaves the solution of this problem to the progressive forces of our time." What the film shows, however, is not only the hypocrisy of this benevolent and paternalistic authority but its inability to deal with the archaic demands of Eros and Thanatos.

Almost all critics of *Los olvidados* have commented on the film's classical antecedents and its literary allusions, which range from Oedipus to the picaresque novel *Lazarillo de Tormes*. Few critics, however, dwell on the fact that it is predominantly a male tragedy of fraternity and treachery, which obviously undermined the then socialist aims of the Mexican government. The delinquent Jaibo brings death and disorder and is therefore the scapegoat that must be killed if society is to be held together. But it is the mother, ambiguously presented as object of desire and as the castrating woman, who motivates this tragedy.

Buñuel heightens the tragedy by giving the characters a certain archetypal quality,[14] though he never allows us to forget that he is depicting a historically specific situation. For instance, all the characters, except for the victim Julián, are fatherless, which recalls the orphaned protagonists of the Spanish picaresque. Yet they are fatherless at a particular historical moment—when the Mexican state is consolidating its paternal authority over its citizens. This double dimension allows Buñuel to depict an antisocial hero, Jaibo, without idealizing the benevolent reformist solution of the state; for Jaibo's evil genius is far more powerful than the feeble solutions of reform school and education.

In this situation, the devalued woman becomes the mother-provider *and* the object of desire. One of the protagonists, Pedro, is indeed the living reminder of woman's prisonhouse, for he is the child of rape, fathered by a man his then adolescent mother had scarcely set eyes on. In Buñuel's film, women are not born into the role of the Great Mother, it is thrust upon them. Their sub-

From Luis Buñuel's *Los olvidados*: Jaibo confronts Pedro's mother.

ordination is secured by rape, but it is a rape that breeds a mute resentment expressed in gestures of rejection.

This conjunction of the archetypal with the historically specific also applies to the women characters, Pedro's mother and her younger counterpart Meche, who lives with her grandfather, her hypochondriac mother, and an older brother in a stable surrounded by the city. Both women are objects of desire, Pedro's mother being the motive of her son's rivalry with Jaibo; and both are caught between their conflicting roles as objects of desire and as providers of maternal love and affection (although barely adolescent, Meche protects an orphaned peasant boy, Ojitos, and is already coveted by both Jaibo and a blind beggar).

In the plotting of *Los olvidados*, women are both helpers and opponents in the male quest for identity. The plot can be briefly summarized as follows: Jaibo escapes from reform school, convinced that he had been denounced by Julián. Jaibo is not only a delinquent but a destructive force utterly at odds with liberal-humanistic values. In the course of the film, he has his gang try to

Meche searches for a pair of scissors to fend off the blind man (*Los olvidados*).

rob a blind beggar, and when the beggar strikes back, he attacks
him and wantonly destroys the musical instrument on which the
beggar depends for a living. Jaibo overturns the cart of a legless
cripple and sends it rolling down the hill, leaving the cripple strug-
gling on the ground like a helpless beetle. In neither of these episodes does Buñuel seek to inspire sympathy for the victim—the
beggar is as vicious as Jaibo.

Jaibo acts out his desires as if law and society did not exist. He
recruits the rape-child Pedro as his accomplice, making him the
unwilling witness to the murder of Julián. This uneasy alliance is
quickly demolished by Jaibo, who seduces Pedro's mother and then
incriminates the boy by stealing a knife (which of course can be
read as the phallus) from the place where Pedro is working, thus
causing him to be sent to a model farm—reform school. The headmaster of the school is the spokesman for the paternalistic and
reformist state. The school's answer to delinquency is work and
responsibility, so the headmaster tries to win Pedro's trust by giv-

The blind man is attacked by Pedro, Jaibo, and the gang on the edge of
the city (*Los olvidados*).

ing him money and sending him on an errand. Jaibo is waiting
outside and steals the money. The next time they meet there is a
bloody fight. Pedro takes refuge in a stable where he is killed by
Jaibo. His body is found by Meche, the young girl whose grandfather owns the stable. The grandfather is fearful of the police,
and with Meche's help puts Pedro's body in a sack and carries it
off on the back of a donkey to a ravine where it will be left, "outside the polis, a prey to birds." As they make their way out of
town with the body hidden in a sack, they pass Pedro's mother,
who is looking for her son. Meanwhile Jaibo has been denounced
by the blind beggar and is shot by police as he runs away. As he
dies, superimposed over him there appears the figure of a stray
and mangy dog.

What undermines any hope of social progress then, is women's
role as a sexual object, and this ambivalent role is also transposed
to various symbolic objects that are circulated in the film. One of
the most important of these is milk. In an scene early in the film,
Jaibo, Pedro, and Ojitos sleep at the stable owned by Meche's
grandfather. They are hungry. Jaibo tries and fails to milk a donkey. Ojitos, the little peasant, gets under a goat and drinks directly
from the udder. Thus the difference between urban and rural life
is underlined. This scene alludes to the infant's symbiotic relationship with the milk-providing mother, which is transposed,
however, into a sense of loss and desire. But milk is constantly
exchanged throughout the film—having lost its original status as
a gift between mother and child. Like sex, it has become a commodity. The blind man is given milk in exchange for curing Meche's
mother. Jaibo catches Meche washing her legs in milk—thus
transforming the innocent liquid into an aphrodisiac. In another
scene, Meche takes milk to the blind man, who makes her sit on
his knees, whereupon she seizes a pair of scissors and, with Ojitos
watching, makes a gesture as if to kill him. Thus milk is constantly
being exchanged for death and sex. Cocks and chickens similarly
serve as symbolic objects. Pedro hugs a hen and takes one of its
eggs when he gets home from beating up the blind man. When at
one point he tries to kiss his mother's hand, she lashes out at a
black cock who is mating with one of the hens. Just before sleeping
with Jaibo, she picks up a couple of chickens, unconsciously bar-
ing her legs as she does so. At the model farm Pedro looks after
chickens but acts in an "antisocial" fashion, sucking the eggs which
are communal property. When one of the boys protests, he breaks
the egg and then begins to hit the chickens. Afterward he draws

a picture of the chicken massacre on the wall. Milk and chickens suggest the pre-Oedipal, yet both are also exchanged as economic values and as signs within the symbolic order. Thus the film constantly shifts between nature and culture. When Jaibo seduces Marta, her children are watching a couple of dressed-up dogs dancing.

But nature implies not only life but death. In the much commented on dream sequence of the film, Pedro sees the murdered Julián's blood-covered face under the bed. As he rises in horror, his mother seductively floats across the room. When he asks her why she had refused to give him meat, she turns and offers a bleeding lump of flesh, at the same time closing her eyes. But the meat is snatched away by a laughing Jaibo, who has taken the place of the dead Julián. Here the mother provides not milk but a cadaver. The other face of the Mother is the face of mortality.

Buñuel reproduces here the patriarchal representation of Woman, but, unlike in *Enamorada,* this representation is not shown only in its idealized aspect, for the alignment of Woman with nature also means that she must represent death. Buñuel offers no explicit criticism but rather takes to the limit the consequence of patriarchal gender differences. Modernization exacerbates the problem by lodging the paternal function in the state, which is also the repository of immortality. In Buñuel's version of the transition to modernization, the old mythic stories are still acted out in these as yet unredeemed and unredeemable areas that the rational modern city has ejected from its body, as it will eject the corpses of Pedro and Jaibo. The all-male, hygienic model farm symbolizes the rationality that marginalizes the intractable elements that cannot be put to productive use. Yet it is woman who is the Trojan horse. The state cannot run without women, and women do not simply fulfill a reproductive function but also represent the "mothering" and the desire which the state cannot provide. Thus Buñuel shows exactly why analogies between families and states break down in their exclusion of desire.

In Buñuel's films, people are always looking for the lost mother's breast that will give them absolute fulfillment. His very film technique therefore depends on the shock tactics of showing the return of what has been repressed by modernity. It is women who are more in touch with the reality of these archaic drives than the men, but women's desire is never symmetrical with that of the men. In the final scenes of the movie, Marta is seeking the son who, unknown to her, is dead. She has finally become a mother to Pedro, but her gaze falls on the sack in which his corpse is hidden. Is this sacrifice what woman, in her incarnation as Coat-licue,[15] really wants? I would read the conclusion of the film rather as the avant-garde response to the bourgeois holy family—though it is an answer that once again aligns Woman with nature (as life and death), with mortality, with forces more archaic than either the authoritarian paternalism of the Porfiriato or the benevolent paternalism of the reformist state. In this inexorable system there is no way for women to tell their story.

HER STORY

Classic cinema often seems to position the woman spectator as accessory to her own subordination. Yet we have no means of knowing how women spectators saw *Enamorada*. Did they simply enjoy the spectacle of powerful María Félix without bothering about the ending? As Teresa de Lauretis points out, women bring to such spectacles a whole repertoire of previous "experiences."[16] Yet, how do we know what women's experience is, unless we are prepared to accept behaviorist or empiricist accounts? Experience of other women is given to us through discourses—life stories, case histories, or ethnographic studies which carry their own ideological freight. With these reservations in mind, I shall examine one of the female voices that make up Oscar Lewis' *The Children of Sánchez,* an ethnographic account of the lives of the poor in Mexico City tape-recorded during the 1950s, the same period of transition to which *Enamorada* and *Los olvidados* belong.[17]

With the passage of time, however, it has become possible to reread *The Children of Sánchez* not as a reflection of the "real Mexico" nor as an illustration of the "culture of poverty" thesis but rather as a demonstration of the unresolved problem of interpreting subaltern cultures. Lewis himself was not even aware that this might be a problem. Indeed, in order to give the narrative more spontaneity, he omits his own questions, and he does not reveal that some of his primary texts consisted of written material, not oral interviews.

In this chapter, I read against the grain of Lewis' text by isolating one of the children's voices—that of Consuelo—since it is through a rereading of her story that the textual conflicts between voice and writing, spontaneity and design can be appreciated. However, I also wish to stress that I believe *The Children of Sánchez* to be a unique document and, indeed, almost the only text of this

period in which women of the subaltern class "speak." It was the
very originality of Lewis' approach that made the work contro-
versial in Mexico, so much so that there was an unsuccessful attempt to suppress the translation on the grounds that the Sánchez
family bore little resemblance to the idealized poor represented in
literature and on the screen. In the United States *The Children of
Sánchez* was a best-seller, and numerous editions appeared. It was
turned into a motion picture with Anthony Quinn playing the part
of the father, Jesús Sánchez. Some editions display shots from the
movie on the cover and advertise it as the book of the film. Further, despite the initial censorship, it was eventually published and
circulated in Mexico. The Sánchez family became celebrities. But
by this time, they were no longer the same family. Consuelo did
not even attend the funeral when her father died in 1986.[18]

Lewis began to study the urban poor of Mexico City after com-
pleting research on the village of Tepotzlán. Observing the migration of families to Mexico City, he decided to embark on a follow-
up study of the new urban immigrants. In this way, he stumbled
upon a class of Mexican society that had until then been ignored
by anthropologists. Concentrating on the *casas de vecindad*—that
is, the multifamily dwellings grouped around courtyards and in the
area of Tepito not far from the center of Mexico City—Lewis
embarked on an intense description of every detail of the inhabitants' lives, much of the information being supplied by tape-recorded interviews. Over a period of years, he collected a body of
information far in excess of the published *Children of Sánchez* and
A Death in the Sánchez Family.[19] At the same time, he believed
that he had found an explanation for underdevelopment in the
family life of the poor and, in particular, in the transmission of
fatalistic attitudes that prevented individuals from progressing.

This "culture of poverty" thesis has been challenged by many
subsequent studies and was eclipsed in the 1960s by the dependency theory that related the underdevelopment of the Third World
to the overdevelopment of the industrial nations.[20] In the fifties,
however, Lewis was not alone among social scientists in believing
that changes in attitudes would bring about modernization and
progress.[21] Nevertheless, *The Children of Sánchez* transcends the
ethnographic thesis; first, because Lewis evidently got a great deal
of enjoyment out of the Sánchez family, while disapproving of their
relapses into fatalism; second, because the life stories often undermine the very culture of poverty thesis they are supposed to
illustrate. For example, the father, Jesús Sánchez, who was born

in a small village and raised in a tradition of authoritarianism, moved upward in the social scale, whereas some of his children, though exposed to the ideology of upward mobility, did not. The culture of poverty thesis was, in fact, theoretically lame from the start, and perhaps in the final analysis is important only as the enabling device in Lewis' telling of the life stories of the Sánchez family.

Lewis' interviews with the Sánchez family continued through the 1950s to 1959, and follow-up interviews were made after the publication of the books. Because of his long relationship with them, he came to be "part of the family," a surrogate parent. This hierarchical arrangement was reinforced by the environment in which the interviews took place—that is, in the office or in his home rather than in the "Casa Grande." No doubt this contributed to what Lewis describes in the introduction to *The Children of Sánchez* as the family's "positive image of the United States as a superior country." This positive image, he says, "placed me in the role of a benevolent authority figure rather than the punishing one they were so accustomed to in their own father" (p. xxi).

Oscar Lewis sees himself as the representative of a paternalistic and benevolent power and, indeed, this was one face that the United States presented to the world in the 1950s, when its prosperity could be linked to liberality and the export of commodities. The attitudes that were supposed to have made this prosperity possible were thought of as "development," and the social sciences were instruments of what many believed to be a progressive foreign policy. It is not within the scope of this essay to comment on a form of development that has now exploded into debt crisis, inflation, runaway shops, unplanned urbanization, and even more desperate poverty. What is fortunate is that Lewis produced a body of material that goes far beyond the ideological constraints inherent in his "development" philosophy.

Lewis' "life story" approach to anthropology was, of course, not without precedent. The Chicago school of sociologists had long been interested in the lives of working-class people, and their studies of "deviancy" had a profound effect on literature. Lewis' originality consisted in studying the family as a unit, an approach that was guided in part by his desire to "offset the subjectivity inherent in a single autobiography" by producing a collage of people who had shared the same experience. As a social scientist, he was interested in the accuracy and truth of the data he collected but also in conveying "the emotional satisfaction and understanding which

the anthropologist experiences in working directly with his subjects" (p. xii). Lewis' aspirations, therefore, went beyond those of
the social scientist, for he believed that the tape recorder had made
a "new kind of social realism" possible: "With the aid of the tape
recorder, unskilled, uneducated, and even illiterate persons can talk
about themselves and relate their observations and experiences in
an uninhibited, spontaneous, and natural manner" (p. xii).

Lewis writes that the "children of Sánchez"—Manuel, Roberto,
Consuelo, and Marta—"have a simplicity, sincerity, and direct-
ness which is characteristic of the spoken word, of oral literature
in contrast to written literature" (p. xii).[22] From the vantage point
of the 1980s, there is little need to comment on this phonocentrism
nor on a view of oral literature that makes it the voice of the marginalized. Indeed, Lewis believed that it was precisely because the
novelists had failed to be truthful to this raw material that the
anthropologist had to step in and become "the student and spokesman of what I call the culture of poverty" (p. xxiv). Lewis not
only described his interviews as "stories" but also believed that
they represented a truer form of social realism than contemporary
Mexican novels, and that there was something in them of both art
and life. The hierarchical nature of Mexican society had "inhibited
any profound communication across class lines" (p. xiii). "Today,
even most novelists are so busy probing the middle-class soul that
they have lost touch with the problems of poverty and the realities
of a changing world" (p. xxiv).

The *Children of Sánchez* was composed as a polyphonic text in
which the life stories of the four children of Jesús Sánchez (two
boys and two girls) are interwoven. Each child takes up the story
in turn to recount stages in life that roughly correspond to childhood, adolescence, and adulthood. These stories are framed within
the father's narrative. This not only breaks up the chronological
narrative but also constitutes a point of reference against which
the reader can evaluate the stories of each of the four children and
their relationship to the father. The four participants in the narrative, Roberto, Manuel, Consuelo, and Marta, are first and foremost the "children of Sánchez." The question of why Lewis selected this particular family is interesting, for there is no reason to
suppose that the Sánchez family was "typical." A great reader of
Mexican literature, Lewis was no doubt familiar with Octavio Paz's
influential *The Labyrinth of Solitude* with its graphic discussion
of the Mexican macho ideology. Whether for this or for some other
reason, he selected a family with a strong father and with no mother.

The story thus concentrates on the way the male children live the rivalry with the father and the way the female children vie for his attention.

The editing is skillful, for the life stories carry the reader along a linear path in which the anthropological digressions go almost unnoticed or become absorbed into the life story. At the same time, the adoption of only one "voice" in each section conceals the hierarchical structure of the original interview in which Lewis himself played an extremely active and dynamic part, relaying gossip, jogging memories, asking after friends and relatives, and thus contributing to the construction and maintainance of the collective memory.[23] Out of this heterogeneous interview material (and writings, including detailed descriptions written by his assistants of homes, clothes, utensils, and appliances)[24] Lewis constructed a family "autobiography," which included both the typical and the individual, the common experiences of Mexicans living in the barrio, and the idiosyncratic experiences of each of the children.

Of the four Sánchez children interviewed, Consuelo stands out as an anomaly, for, although Lewis presents his material as if it all came from interviews (no doubt identifying orality with poverty), in fact Consuelo wrote down her own life story in a 170-page autobiography that forms part of the edited material of the finished book. It is true that but for Lewis she would never have written her life story, yet the process of its production and the elision of that process in Lewis' introduction speaks for itself. The anthropologist does not regard Consuelo's autobiography as "writing" but as raw material. Consuelo also contributed several essays on themes suggested by Lewis, describing her dreams, the houses she had lived in, her sister and brothers. Indeed, she felt her meeting with the Lewises to have been a turning point that altered her whole conception of the self. She tells them:

> Before, I thought that I did not want to live. I always refused to live (it was the title I thought of for my book), thinking that I was living life like a robot, after having gone through so many events that had left an indelible mark on my past and in the story of my life; and for that reason, I suffered bitter moments of lethargy: caught in a spiral in which I whirled, I whirled, I danced the scenes, the words, the actions that I lived.[25]

Writing and the ability to distance herself from the family play an important part in this transition. In *A Death in the Sánchez*

Family, Consuelo describes the typewriter as "the thing that brings self-respect and order to my life."[26] The drama of Consuelo is that on becoming an "author," she distances herself from her past. For instance, in *A Death in the Sánchez Family,* which was written two years after the publication of *The Children of Sánchez,* when Consuelo was living an independent life in Nuevo Laredo, she describes her return to her old neighborhood as follows:

> The scene in front of my aunt's *vecindad* will always be engraved on my mind. It made me suddenly realize the truth about poverty, exposing its raw ugliness openly to the eyes of the world. The red brick wall of the *vecindad* framed a group of beggars huddled near the entrance. Some were standing, their lowered heads covered with long matted hair full of lice and filth growing down into stiff, spiny beards. Their round, reddened, motionless eyes and open mouths had the idiot expressions of alcoholics.[27]

Consuelo "frames" the picture from the point of view of an affluent world for whom poverty is the ultimate sin. One could say that she had been successfully converted.

Consuelo's mother had died suddenly at the age of twenty-eight when Consuelo was four, and her father, Jesús, was left to bring up the two boys, Roberto and Manuel, and Consuelo and her younger sister Marta. At the same time he kept another "wife" by whom he had several children and whose existence was kept a secret from the rest of the Sánchez family for some time. After the death of his wife, he also took in Elena, a young woman who later died of tuberculosis, and he had other relations, first with a woman who worked as a servant in the house and later with Manuel's sister-in-law, Dalila. Clearly, Sánchez' family life is very different from the model family presented in didactic films and popular narrative.

Jesús puts work before everything, his sense of worth being intimately related to his role as family provider. He is thus patriarchal in the true sense. It is not feeling or sentiment that unite him to his children but his responsibility as "head of the family." He takes in Manuel's wife and children, refuses to allow Roberto and Manuel to exercise what they see as their rightful authority as males, and is hostile when Consuelo tries to contribute to household expenses. The need to provide takes the place of affection toward the children, and when at the end of *The Children of Sánchez* he sums up his life, he declares that he can no longer treat his sons and Consuelo affectionately: "They have made me spend a lot of money uselessly." His one remaining ambition as he grows older is to build a house for his children. "Just a modest place that they can't be thrown out of. I'll put a fence around it and no one will bother them. It will be a protection for them when I fall down and don't get up again" (p. 499).

Sánchez represents what Jean-François Lyotard calls "customary knowledge." He passes this knowledge on in the form of proverbial wisdom—"as we say here, after twenty-four hours, a corpse and a house guest begin to stink." "Well, as some people say, 'Where everything else is wanting, God steps in.'" Sánchez' narrative corresponds to Lyotard's "narrative post," of the sender which

> is based upon the fact of having occupied the post of addressee, and of having been recounted oneself, by virtue of the name one bears, by a previous narrative—in other words, having been positioned as the diegetic reference of other narrative events. What is transmitted through these narratives is the set of pragmatic rules that constitutes the social bond.[28]

Although Lyotard's examples are drawn from traditional societies, his description could be applied to Sánchez in his character as "father" and in his understanding of what this implies. As the framework for Lewis' study, however, Jesús' narrative knowledge serves as a contrast, not a continuity. His children, Manuel, Robert, Consuelo (though not the youngest, Marta), will obstinately refuse (or be unable) to take up their appropriate roles.

The structuring of *The Children of Sánchez* is interesting for the way in which the stories are interwoven. Each son or daughter relates the first part of his or her life up to adolescence; they then resume their stories to tell of their marriages, and, finally, in part 3, they reach the text's "present"—a present largely of disappointment and frustration. Although these stories roughly conform to the life stages studied by anthropologists in primitive societies, they are interwoven with other kinds of material designed to illustrate their typicality. This means that there is a constant shifting from the particular to the general, with the gaps between these disparate discourses carefully sutured.[29] For instance, Consuelo comments, "I didn't like this new *vecindad* at all. It had no stairs or windows and the courtyards were long and narrow. We lived in only one room. The electric light almost always had to be on" (p. 93). Here, there is a the slippage between the personal "I" and the communal "we" of the sociological narrative. It is pre-

cisely the ability or inability to occupy the "I" position in the social text that constantly underscores Consuelo's experience, the
problem, of course, being that the "I" can only be comfortably
occupied by the father of the children or the "father" of the text.
One of the most interesting aspects of *The Children of Sánchez* is
the way that the shifts and gaps in the "culture of poverty" narrative suggest, in Consuelo's case, a quite different narrative—that
is, the story of her break with the punitive father and her successful transference.

In the published version, Consuelo's story comes over as one of
failure. Her greatest trauma occurs when her father brings home
her half sister, Antonia, whose existence she had not even sus-
pected, and then shows a marked preference for Antonia's company. Soon after Antonia's mental breakdown, he moves out of
the apartment in Casa Grande and temporarily goes to live with
Antonia's mother. The first part of Consuelo's story ends with the
loss of the father, which coincides with her fifteenth birthday, which
in Mexico marks an important transition for girls, who then become eligible for courtship and matrimony. But Consuelo's fifteenth birthday goes almost unnoticed. In part 2, Consuelo, who
had enjoyed attending school, becomes a young worker, fond of
dancing, with many boyfriends. When her father brings Delila to
live with them, Consuelo runs away with one of her boyfriends,
Mario, and goes to live in Monterey. In part 3 she takes up the
story of her unhappy marriage with Mario, her miscarriage, and
her return to Mexico City and her spasmodic attempts to live in-
dependently and find work. At the end of the published version,
she is once again out of work.

This "failure" is not inherent in the material. On the contrary,
in her autobiography and in many of the themes written for Lewis,
Consuelo speaks in almost religious terms of the change that had
occurred after meeting the Lewises. "Now it is different. I got to
understand a new value in life, that is the value of the person.
Respect, affection, comprehension, guidance, patience, and goodness."[30] In her view, Lewis has performed a talking cure, one which
has given her the power to separate herself from family life. In an
interview that is not included in the published book, she even becomes the voice of Lewis in speaking to her brother, Roberto:

> Whatever do you think the doctor will think of you . . .? I
> say, well probably, they think that it is because of your lack
> of education, your lack of schooling. And he says to me, well,

what should I do now? Well the only thing you can do, I told him, is to find work and show the doctor and everyone else that you are a man whom they can trust.

Consuelo sees her own life in terms of transference not only from one father to another but from one social system to another. In the process of this transference, she comes to want the power of the father, to see herself as the father's rival. What is remarkable about Consuelo's account in *The Sánchez Family,* what makes it different from the stories of the other children, is precisely this self-consciousness, which she relates to social censorship that forces her into the feminine position. For instance, when running about she feels ashamed, "afraid that my dress would fly up" (p. 114), or again, "That year, when I was thirteen, I began to menstruate. It happened one day in school, frightening and embarrassing me terribly" (p. 115). As she grows older, she conforms to what was expected of a *señorita.* "I was a señorita now and I didn't want to play in the courtyard any more. It didn't look right for me to be running about outdoors" (p. 127).

Consuelo recognizes that women gain respect in ways that are different from men, as objects of admiration, and her daydreams reflect this: "I would see myself going to a dance, wearing a blue dress, well-groomed, everybody turning around to look at me. I was the center of attraction. A very serious, good-looking young man would be escorting me. Nobody dared say anything coarse around me; there would be nothing but respect. I would dance in a reserved, dignified way to a slow, smooth tune." She also recognizes that this admiration and respect must come from the father. "I saw my father and brothers in dark suits, and above all, me in a long blue dress, with spangles to make it shine. My little sister would have a long dress, too. And finally, a small orchestra would be playing. How pretty I would look to Fermín. What a couple he and I would make as we danced the waltz, with everybody's eyes on us—my father watching me from the table and thinking that his daughter was now a señorita." Her love of dancing, which could be regarded as shameless, is here turned into an imaginary performance that inspires respect, particularly in her father. Similarly, when she wishes to marry Jaime, Consuelo thinks mainly of her father's role at the wedding; "to enter on my father's arm, in a white dress, and to go up to the altar with him, where the one who was going to give me his name would be waiting for me, to have the bridesmaids all around as I danced the waltz and to see the pleasure my father would feel when the daughter whom he had treated the worst and for whom he had the most contempt, had honored him."

In these daydreams, Consuelo acts out the role of daughter according to the laws of the father's world, although the reality is somewhat different. Jesús shows marked preference for his illegitimate daughter, Antonia, and Consuelo never achieves the recognition she desires. After her marriage and her difficult sexual relationship with Mario, she blames her father for having abandoned her and taken in Dalila. "If you only knew what you have done, Father! you are the one responsible for what happens to me from now on! I continued to cry bitterly. I imagined my papa saw me crying and suffered also. He begged my pardon." The father causes her constant anxiety by refusing to acknowledge her or by treating her as a child. Even when she is an adult, he frequently forces her to leave the family house. In one incident she sees him in the streets and runs after him,

> and he looked me up and down and said go back home, go on, go, go, . . . and then, Yes, dad. I felt ashamed, because, well, I am grown up, aren't I?; and I don't like him to do that to me in the street and now that I have freed myself of him completely, I said, "well if I don't harm him, if I don't ask for anything, if I don't bother him, then why goes he go on eternally telling me that I am this, or that?"

When the school celebrates Mother's Day, a custom imported from the States, Consuelo is struck by the contradictions. To begin with, she had no mother to celebrate, but in any case, "why would there be so much celebration of the mother if fathers are worth more. My father buys everything and never leaves us alone. There ought to be a Father's Day and, if that were the case, I would dress up as a little Indian girl or whatever." Yet retrospectively she would acknowledge that the celebration of Mother's Day was extremely painful to her. As an adult, she thinks of her mother as a star in the sky that she appeals to for help against the father.

Consuelo associates alienation with overcrowded family life. She speaks of the feeling of being constantly constrained by others so that there is no freedom for her true self to emerge:

> I want to say that there is no freedom to develop or at least that is what happened in my family and I have been able to observe that it also happens in other families in the Casa Grande

when one of my friends spends too much time in front of the mirror, the mother, the father or brothers begin to joke about it. Often criticizing her physical defects. All these things mean that one has a constant vision of surveillance. Yes, I mean that often when I am alone and would like to act in all freedom, I cannot.

Significantly, it is the father's voice that symbolizes this constraint:

I am always listening to the voice of my father reining me, forbidding me to do this or that. I sometimes think of other people's jokes and I look in the mirror. Sometimes I manage to overcome that which has been formed in me for many years and I look at myself in the mirror and smile thinking that I have overcome "that" but I nearly always look at my image very rapidly in the mirror.

The biological family and especially the father come between her and her true image.

It is significant, however, that Consuelo never uses the weapon that Marta and the half-sister, Antonia, use so effectively—seduction. Although she occasionally feels the desire to surrender herself, as when she experiences religious ecstasy or when dancing, it is the father's power that truly impresses her. And this is primarily because her main desire is for status and recognition, that is, to be the father's rival. There are many ways in which she tries to get recognition, usually in ways that do not conflict with being a woman—in her schoolwork, as a worker, as a surrogate mother to Manuel's children; she even tries to get into films. In *The Children of Sánchez* she lives as an independent woman in Mexico City, and in *A Death in the Sánchez family* she has taken over the father's role by taking Manuel's children to Nuevo Laredo where she supports them by working as a secretary. But perhaps the most telling expression of her desire is in her use of images.

In her dreams, Consuelo sees woman as mechanical dolls. She dreamed that Marta "was a doll dressed in blue on the top of a white cake."[31] And of her friend Alicia, she writes, "it occurred to me that she was like one of those little tin dolls that you wind up from the back and which move with rapid steps and constantly change direction, left, right, forward, backward, with short steps."

In one of her most imaginative analogies she compares her family to a geometry set.

My father the compass; Roberto a triangle, Manuel the pro-
tractor, the ruler . . . I. Marta seems to be in this set, but she
isn't. She is only there in the squared material, a material that
repels water, that is stuck to the wall with some watery sub-
stance which makes it adhere strongly. This squared material
has only changed color but it stays stuck to that partition or
wall.

It is interesting that Consuelo puts herself here among the geometrical instruments, that is, among the men. Marta as the traditional woman is simply there, like the wall. "Marta seems to be
in this set but she isn't."[32] What is interesting is that both analogies
seem to suggest the rule-bound world of the symbolic, but whereas
Marta cannot be one of the geometrical instruments, Consuelo puts
herself in the instrumental position, appropriating agency for herself.

The irony of Consuelo, however, is that what she has come to
think of as the self is really the other discourse—the discourse of
modernization speaking through her. Asked by Lewis to comment
on proverbs, she discusses those that lock people into accepting
their state in life; for instance, "If you're born a plant pot, you
never get further than the hallway" ("El que nace pa' maceta del
corredor no pasa"). She writes,

> I heard this innumerable times around me—the neighbors,
> friends, my aunt Trinidad, and even my father, . . . even at
> wakes, I have heard this said in other words and afterwards,
> without daring to speak openly of what I was thinking, I ana-
> lyzed it for months, talking to myself. I was afraid of saying
> it openly because I was afraid the majority would crush me
> and that they would say that I was always against the current,
> the current of life and that then "who knows what would
> become of me?"

She similarly mulls over the statement that "it's fate": "With
these proverbs and some others which I analyzed, I reached the
conclusion that "you can't do *anything,* and you shouldn't go against
God's design" (italics in original). Such criticisms are forms of self-
consciousness and indicate a shift from the biological father to a
discourse of modernization. This is also indicated by her many
reflections on slang. She comments:

> In the street, in the patio, in the *vecindad,* in the store, even
> in the cinema and radio, and even close to me, I would hear

my brothers use proverbs and slang, phrases that I did not understand. And although this seems incredible, I would keep those phrases in my head and I analyzed them, trying to discover the relationship between the gramatically incorrect words of the slang expression. So, for example, something as simple as "Guen, mano, a'i nos vidrios" [i.e., a demotic Spanish that roughly translates, "OK, brother, we'll meet there"], I would think and think about it over and over again.

She then goes into a lengthy analysis of why lower-class people pronounce *bueno* as *guen* and astutely recognizes that the vernacular is a form of group bonding. Yet her own self is defined in opposition to this group bonding:

In this way I rejected and resisted their manner of expressing themselves. And as I analyzed this, I "slept," I "was up in the clouds," "I daydreamed," and at these moments I consciously isolated myself from the groups of boys and young men who "threw out" words without realizing that someone was "catching" them.

Another example of this distancing is her dramatization of family scenes such as the following:

(2.30 or 3.00) Manuel comes in. He is wearing his plaid [mezclilla] or khaki pants (ordinary) and his hands are in his pockets, Marta, in the patio playing marbles, Consuelo is listening to Santitos say her prayers, Roberto is hanging from the water pipes on the roof, Santitos is near the brazier [bracero] sitting down wearing her black dress and with her rosary in her hands. Ramón seated at the kitchen table with his face in his hands and laughing away as he reads his comics. As he enters, Manuel looks around the room furtively.

MANUEL: O.K. Santitos, have you eaten already?

SANTITOS: No, son, eat . . . just listen to what I'm telling you son.

MANUEL (*smiling*): OK, we've already eaten, Hi, there, what are you doing?

RAMÓN (*looking up from his reading*): I'm reading Raging Roland (a comic book) and that weak little tick—just look here (*laughter*), he's so skinny and he's fighting. (*Laughter, etc.*)

MANUEL: Yes, these comics are nice. I like reading them too.

Consuelo now goes out to call Marta and finds her sitting on her heels with her legs open and one eye closed ready to shoot the marble which will bring her victory. When Consuelo sees the way her sister is sitting, and when she is near to her, she almost yells: You have to come and eat.

M. (*desperate*): Rotten skinny . . . just because of you, I lost my turn, now I'm not coming.

C: So you're not coming . . . I'll carry you, but you'd better come.

M: OK. Carry me then, you rotten skinny.

C: Come on, they're already serving dinner. If you don't come I'll tell Manuel.

M: Go on, tell him, I suppose you think . . . that I'm scared stiff, scared stiff . . . go on, tell him. (*Her friends are on the alert.*)

C: Come on Marta, I'm telling you to come.

M: I'm not going, I'm not going; you're a real tough guy [*macha*], carry me then.[34]

What is remarkable about such reflections is that the self so constituted is an observing self—a theorist or even an ethnologist. The scene not only distances Consuelo from the vulgarity of her family but shows her ability to represent the family and her own position in the family. She has converted herself into a character in the family drama, the one who stands in for the absent father. Later on in life she not only tries to acquire the father's authority but acts as a more modern and responsible father. It is she who raises bail for Roberto when he lands in jail; she who reports her brother Manuel to the Social Service Office for refusing to support his children. She even dreams of reconstructing a family that never was, of restoring the "lost" community of her brothers and sisters.

Obeying the rules is one way of obliterating the disparity between the self and the social text. There are, however, other ways of overcoming that disparity—by giving up the self altogether. At one point she dreams of entering a convent. And when the disparity becomes intolerable, she dreams of death. This happens when she elopes with Mario and thus becomes a nonperson, someone living outside the accepted social code. Not surprisingly she feels no pleasure, not even guilty pleasure, when she looks back on this incident, but rather remembers it as a period of intense suffering. At a low point, just after a miscarriage, she is ready to die:

My body was free, as if I suddenly became divided in two. One part floated and the other remained in bed. "Finally," I murmured, and felt a smile on my lips. I felt so light, as I had never felt before, and saw Him there, there on the ceiling. There was a luminous cross in a strange shade of green, with a little flame in the center. It seemed as though it were incorporating me into it. I didn't feel my painful body any more. I was a kind of veil that, little by little, rose in the air.

What I felt was so beautiful I cannot find the exact words to describe it. I can only say that with a zigzag I entered nothingness. This was what I had been waiting for all my life.

What she "had been waiting for" all her life was perhaps not exactly death but rather the end of a self-consciousness which can never be anything other for her than a source of suffering and isolation. This is why her happiest moments are those when the self-consciousness disappears—for instance, when she is dancing and "music penetrated so deeply into me that I hardly realized who was dancing with me."

In the modernization narrative, the devaluation of the mother is important not because it makes the girl turn to a man who is like the father but precisely because it makes her conscious of being a decentered subject. If there can be a "better" father, then it is a short step to there being no father at all, perhaps only a machine, a typewriter. The Law is no longer necessarily the Law of a Father but rather is the dispersed flow of the marketplace where sexual identity is never fixed, where one object of desire is quickly replaced by another. Women like Consuelo, who experience their noncoherence within nationalist ideology, may actually feel liberated when they no longer have to answer to an authoritarian father. In Consuelo's case, however, this is a highly ambiguous process, because she puts herself in the place of the ethnographer and learns to scrutinize her own family as if she were an outsider.

Consuelo's story raises questions about subalternity and consciousness. The traditional family was oppressive to someone who knew the realities of a mother's life in the barrio. It was this consciousness of oppression that made her try to acquire the ethnographer's power. When Guadalupe, a woman who had borne some of Consuelo's half-sisters, died, she wrote:

Now my *viejita*, my little old lady, is dead. She had lived in a humble little nest full of lice, rats, filth, and garbage, hidden among the folds of the formal gown of that elegant lady, Mexico City. In that "solid foundation" my aunt ate, slept, loved, and suffered. She gave shelter there for a peso or two to any brother in misery so she could pay her extravagant month's rent of thirty pesos. She swept the yard every day at six in the morning for fifteen pesos a month, unplugged the drains of the *vecindad* for two pesos more, and washed a dozen pieces of laundry for three. For three times eight cents, North American, she knelt at the wash tub from seven in the morning until six at night.[34]

One of the key words here is "North American"; the translation of two pesos into "three times eight cents, North American," devalues Guadalupe and implicitly legitimizes Consuelo's choice of a more "valuable" life. In Freud's account of the little girl's oedipal crisis, she must separate herself from her attachment to the mother and find someone like the father, a husband. Consuelo goes one better. She finds a more powerful figure—the ethnographer. The only snag is that to escape the father, she must become her master's voice.

8

REWRITING THE FAMILY: CONTEMPORARY FEMINISM'S REVISION OF THE PAST

As should now be obvious, women in their struggle for interpretive power have often had to resort to noncanonical genres that are either not within the public sphere (letters, for instance) or their writing has been reappropriated into the public sphere as a "male" text, whether it be hagiography, ethnography, or national allegory. By the late sixties, however, there were other communities competing with the nation and religion for interpretive power. The mass media, particularly radio, television, and comic book literature, "internationalized" culture in ways that were seen as subversive to national ideals and at the same time liberating, in that they often introduced elements in contradiction to the dominant national ideology. This became very clear during 1968 when student demonstrations protesting the Mexican state's intervention in the autonomous university were hailed by prominent intellectuals such as José Revueltas as a new and positive force for change.

Women were eager participants in these movements, which shook the rigid Mexican middle-class family. The army's attack on a peaceful student demonstration on October 2, 1968, the killing of about seven hundred students, and the imprisonment of large numbers of participants restored "law and order," but Mexico would never be quite the same again. For the student movement was symptomatic of the government's inability to control as effectively as before the heterogeneity of Mexican life. Nineteen sixty-eight rightly considered a key moment in Mexican history, a wa-

tershed dividing a period when the nation was considered to be
united in moving toward a common goal of greater equality and
social justice from a "postnational" period when the apparent homogeneity of the state was shown to be mere appearance. In literature this was reflected in the growing strength of regional cultural movements, in the emergence of new forms of urban popular
culture, and in women's movements that developed outside the
official parties.

Two of the symptomatic texts of this period were written by
Elena Poniatowska: *La noche de Tlatelolco* (The Night of Tlatelolco) and *Hasta no verte, Jesús mío* (Till I See the Eyes of the
Lord).[1] The first—the text of a tape-recorded collage of the voices
of participants in the student demonstrations of 1968—was an in-
stant best-seller, an answer to the government's silence on the Tlatelolco massacre. The second is the life story of Jesusa Palancares,
a woman of the popular classes. This text raises important questions about genre and directly challenges the kind of ethnographic
discourse represented by Oscar Lewis' *The Children of Sánchez*.
More importantly, it confronts the deep-rooted assumptions of those
literary and intellectual institutions that had excluded everyday life
as trivial and had insisted on literature's transcendence of social
praxis.

In *El arco y la lira* (The Bow and Lyre), an essay written in the
1950s, Octavio Paz had privileged poetry as the space where fragmented existence could be made whole and where language would
shed its tainted mortality.[2] Everyday life enters into his poetry only
as the fragmentary manifestation of an alienated world. This desire for transcendence also marks the work of the novelist Carlos
Fuentes, particularly the tension in his work between the ephemeral and the archetypal. A short novel, *Aura,* written in 1962, illustrates with extraordinary power how gender metaphors underlie this tension.[3] In this novel, an ambitious though unemployed
historian is given the job of editing the memoirs of a nineteenth-
century general and supporter of the emperor Maximilian. In order to edit the manuscripts, he agrees to live in the house of the
general's aged widow, a house that is itself an anachronistic ram-
bling building now surrounded by a modern city. Inside he finds
an enchanted place utterly closed from the outside world, a place
dominated by the beautiful granddaughter Aura, who, it turns out,
is the double of the general's widow, and the lure who will entrap
the unsuspecting historian in the timeless world of sexuality, which
is also the world of death. When he finally makes love to Aura,

her face and body turn into a skeletal horror. She has become the general's widow and he has replaced the dead general. There is no fixed identity in sex or in death.

Fuentes' enchanted house bears a strange resemblance to literature itself, literature as a timeless confrontation with Eros and Thanatos, which are incarnated in women. Literature belongs to a space outside clock time and outside the everyday life the historian abandoned the moment he stepped over the magic threshold. *Aura* can be read as a story of male fear of loss of boundaries, but it is also, interestingly, the story of a dilemma over the boundaries of discourse. By stepping out of everyday life, which is represented as meaningless and degraded, the protagonist also abandons interpretive power over the public sphere and becomes swallowed in the identityless world of sexuality and death. The dilemma of *Aura's* protagonist depends on the already gendered opposition between the public sphere of history and the private world dominated by nature and the female. History, which is both society's and the social individual's immortality, is threatened both by meaningless routine and by the eternal cycle of sex and death represented by Woman as Vampire. The story simply would not make sense without a male protagonist, since it is the male's public identity that is at stake and his sacrifice of historical self that revitalizes the archetypal springs of literature.

Fuentes' story should not be taken as an isolated example but rather as symptomatic of the gendered constitution of the literary institution, in the light of which *Hasta no verte, Jesús mío* could only be considered an aberration. To begin with, its very genre is problematic, since the text can be classified neither as literature (in Fuentes' sense) nor as ethnography, although it seems to belong to the life stories of the subaltern classes exemplified by Ricardo Pozas' life story of a Chamula, *Juan Pérez Jolote.*[4]

Such life stories are themselves hybrids, often shifting (as I pointed out in the case of Oscar Lewis) between the idiosyncratic and the typical. Elena Poniatowska had briefly helped Oscar Lewis, and in *La noche de Tlatelolco* she would use the tape recorder in a truly innovative fashion to record a collective experience. She has chronicled the socially and politically marginalized and silenced in *Fuerte es el silencio.*[5] Yet *Hasta no verte, Jesús mío* differs from the tape recorded ethnography in an important way, for although Poniatowska interviewed Jesusa Palancares (her real name was Josefa Bórquez), she was not allowed to tape her words.[6] Second, her role as mediator is suppressed; her text includes no explana-

tion of how the material was compiled, and Jesusa's long first person monologue only on rare occasions suggests the presence of a
listener. And even though this is also true of the texts of Ricardo
Pozas and Oscar Lewis, what distinguishes *Hasta no verte, Jesús
mío* is the absence of ethnographic "typicality." Ricardo Pozas'
Chamula and *Juan Pérez Jolote* and Oscar Lewis' *Children of
Sánchez* and *Pedro Martínez* illustrate ways of life. In these texts
the subaltern is shown subordinated to rule and custom. Jesusa,
on the other hand, is highly idiosyncratic. She illustrates nothing,
represents no community. If she represents anything at all it is what
Gayatri Spivak has termed "the loneliness of the gendered subaltern." Poniatowska's "novel" cannot claim the typicality of ethnography, nor does it transcend everyday life in the manner of
history or literature. On the other hand, since the book is not a
transcribed tape recording, but Poniatowska's recreation of Jesusa's
voice, I have chosen to consider it as a compositely authored work,
which, because it is composite, avoids the problem of the hierarchical alignment of writer and informant, writing and voice.

   Elena Poniatowska came across Jesusa when visiting a prison
and was attracted by her extraordinary personality.[7] She wanted
to inscribe the record of this idiosyncratic and "private" life without turning it into allegory or claiming Jesusa to be representative.
Born in the early years of the century in the Isthmus of Tehuantepec, Jesusa was a mestiza. Because of the early death of her mother,
her father reared her, but she was never sure of his affection and
was extremely jealous of his relations with other women. At an
early age she began to work as an unpaid domestic servant. Since
she could neither read nor write, she had no way of communicating with her father when he roamed off in search of work.
However, she did follow him to the front during the Revolution.
There is no explanation for her father's brutal repudiation of her
after she had followed him far from home, though one could spec-
ulate that he feared an incestuous relationship. Rejected by her
father, she had no alternative but to marry Pedro, a revolutionary
officer, though she did not feel any particular affection for him
and, indeed, tried to return to her native Tehuantepec in order to
avoid marrying him. After her marriage, she led the life of a *soldadera,* which meant that along with the other women she went
ahead of the army to prepare food for the soldiers in combat. She
was often in danger, and Pedro was killed in battle, leaving her to
order the company's retreat. Though she could have taken his place
as commander, she refused and made her way to Mexico City.

There she worked at a variety of trades, though she never lost her taste for army life and even returned to the army on one occasion.

It would be erroneous to interpret Jesusa's activities as evidence of "masculine" character traits; rather she does not fit into the conventional gender categories. She is neither María Félix nor Pedro Armendáriz, for while she is courageous in battle, she also tries to "mother" orphans and stray dogs. In Mexico City, she takes whatever work is at hand and picks up whatever friends she can. As an illiterate, her world is always restricted to the immediate. Without a family of her own, she invents grandmothers, brothers, and other relatives out of whoever is at hand. She works in restaurants and factories, cleans houses, and works in a dance saloon. Her isolation is striking. Only once, after the end of the Revolution, does she have some kind of family life when she takes on Perico, the child of a dead friend. She lavishes attention on this child, but Perico takes her money and abandons her. Jesusa is, in fact, a mobile subject, one who says she feels herself to be a stranger wherever she is and who repudiates what is left of her family just as she repudiates her nationality, declaring that she is "not a Mexican." It is this repudiation of family and nation that perhaps explains her bizarre religious convictions. Having narrowly escaped death during a shootout, she becomes convinced that she has a protector and somehow establishes contact with a group known as Obra Espiritual (Spiritual Work). It is a group that believes in resurrection, in purging the sins of former lives in this life, and has adopted as guides Mesmer and Charcot. Her special protector is Luz de Oriente (Light of the Orient), the spirit of a man who had murdered her in a former life and now watches over her.

Jesusa's religion is, of course, not her own invention. Immigration to the cities where the power of Catholic priests was attenuated had encouraged evangelical and Pentecostal sects to take root in Mexico City. But Jesusa's choice of Spiritual Work is significant. Reincarnation undercuts any notion of fixed identity or any humanistic idea of the individual and introduces an idea of immortality quite different from that of Christianity or the secular immortality of great men. At the same time, the importance to her of the historical Mesmer and Charcot, as well as the mythical Light of the Orient, suggest that Jesusa saw herself primarily as a channel through which esoteric knowledge passed.[8]

Hasta no verte, Jesús mío can also be read against the modernization narratives that had begun to dominate the Mexican popular literature market in the sixties. New techniques of mass literature such as the photo novel and the comic strip novel provided models for behavior.[9] Certain genres of comic strip novel, in particular, were openly didactic, offering a moral intended to support a modern style of human relationships compatible with women's incorporation into the work force. But Jesusa, repudiated by old-style patriarchy (the father), cannot plot herself into the modernization narrative—that is, the narrative of transformation from community to the inwardly directed ethic of the capitalist nation state.

Instead, Jesusa creates a transient self, a self that is mobile, uninhibited by constraints of femaleness. The Revolution is a parenthesis of freedom between the old style of patriarchy that has enslaved her mother and the new version in which the need for survival and her own isolation limit her independence. Paradoxically, despite her self-reliance and buoyancy and despite her sense of religious empowerment, she is convinced of the worthlessness of modern life, the degeneration of people in the modern city, and the insignificance of the individual. This is powerfully suggested by the framing of the text between two reflections on death. The epigraph that precedes the text reads:

> One day soon you will not find me: you'll meet with nothing but the wind. That day will come and when it arrives, there will be nobody capable of explaining what happened. And they will think that everything has been a lie. It is true, that it is a lie that we are here, lies that they tell on the radio, lies that the neighbors pass on, and a lie that you will miss me. If I am no longer worth anything, why should anyone miss me? And at work? How could they miss me when they won't even say goodbye?

At the end of the "novel," Jesusa again reminds her listener of her approaching death. But she wants to choose her place of death so as not to die in the city among curious and indifferent neighbors.

> Let God remember me because I would like to lie beneath a tree, far away. Then the buzzards would surround me and that would be it; people may come and look for me, but there I'll be, flying around in the belly of the buzzards. If you die in the city, neighbors come to watch you dying, watch you decomposing, because most people come to laugh at those in agony. That is life. You die to make others laugh. . . .

Wouldn't it be hard to die in such a way? That's why I lock myself in. . . . That's why I don't want to die in the D.F. [Districto Federal, or Greater Mexico City], but there on a hillside or a ravine like my father who died in the open air under a tree. May God give me freedom to walk out of life. It is wonderful to know the hour of one's death. And I ask God to prepare me and to let me walk as far as he will and there leave me as food for the animals of the field, for the coyotes, like Pedro who was my husband. It is not that I don't want to be buried, but who would bury me? They will say, in God's name, this old race has already died.

Jesusa *chooses* to be buried outside the city walls, a prey to birds, to be forgotten by the polis. She will thus share the fate of her husband and her father and all the other anonymous dead of Mexico. The community and family to which Castellanos' and Garro's heroines had stood in such an ambiguous relationship has here disintegrated completely. The important moment of death cannot hold out the promise of the survival of a name even in the limited posterity that is offered by the family. Jesusa's true community is with the unburied dead, not with the unhallowed living. She does not need a Creon to expel her, but goes of her own accord in order to renew her ties with nature and break with the false community of the city.

Jesusa clearly renounces any notion of the significance of one human life and does not set herself apart from nature. What her life reveals is the radical loneliness of the subaltern classes, a loneliness that should not be confused with individualism. The loneliness is related to her being a stranger on earth, on the fact that she belongs to the *vieja raza* that modernization has destroyed. But it is her everyday life experience that establishes the space for this heterogeneity, beyond all the great, overarching, and homogeneous notions such as class, race, and nation. It is also this experience that is linked to the formation of a consciousness, not a consciousness of individuality nor a consciousness of feminine solidarity, but rather a stray consciousness whose solidarity is with the dead, and which leads to her repudiation both of the present and of Poniatowska herself.

Jesusa's story has no moral. It does not lead us to any particular conclusion about the state of the nation or the poor. *Hasta no verte* is not simply a spontaneous life story, but a complex interaction between narrator and listener which ends by affirming the disparity of their projects. Having communicated her last wish to her listener, Jesusa ends her story with the words, "Ahora ya no chingue. Váyase. Déjeme dormir" ("Now stop bothering me [literally, "stop screwing"]. Go away. Let me sleep").

Chingar (fuck)—the most common Mexican insult—is what men invariably do to women. Elena Poniatowska is in the male position, engaging in knowledge retrieval (as Gayatri Spivak puts it) from a "native informant" who wants to sleep. That Jesusa's consciousness has nowhere to go except to sleep leaves us with the giant question, the question not only of how that loneliness can be broken, how Jesusa can commune with someone other than the dead, but also of our own use of her story. Do we allow her to fade back into the ephemerality of oral lore, or do we bring these stories into the public debate by writing them down?

One striking similarity between *The Children of Sánchez* and *Hasta no verte, Jesús mío* deserves comment for its relevance to contemporary writing by women in Mexico. This is the emphasis on the father's power. What inhibits discussion of this is the all-embracing term "patriarchy" used to describe quite different family arrangements. Yet, for Consuelo Sánchez, the patriarchal biological father does not occupy the same position as the paternalistic father of the modernization discourse. There are clearly differences between the position of the father in colonial discourse, that of the ideal father in nationalist discourse, and the position of the father as provider in the subaltern classes. It is true that in each case the father is the source of power and authority, but that authority acquires quite different overtones according to whether that position is identified with a broader social meaning—religious truth, nation, or modernity.

Any attempt to envisage the family other than as patriarchy or as figures in a national allegory must be science fiction or utopian. María Luisa Puga's *Cuando el aire era azul* (When the Air Was Blue),[10] which first appears to be a utopian novel, turns into a dystopia. At the beginning of the novel, the inhabitants of a community, among them Tomás and Marisa, are living in a postrevolutionary society run on egalitarian principles. Tomás is restless with the bureaucracy and the stagnation of society as well as with his relationship with Marisa. Despite the egalitarian relationships between men and women, jealousy and distrust cannot be avoided and both Marisa and Tomás eventually find other partners.

Yet Puga seems to take as a given that all relationships are heterosexual, that youth is less corrupt than age, that it is a man,

Tomás, who will record the history of the utopian society, the society of "blue air," when it has been undermined by the influence
of "a neighboring country" which introduces a consumer society
and insidious forms of oppression. "In the neighboring country,
they were not so much worried about transmitting an ideology as
making acceptable a vision of the world that they believed to be
rational, and in which it [the community] first of all accepted its
own position, a modest dependency and free enterprise" (pp. 329–
330). We can see this as an updating of the national allegory, but
one which leaves unquestioned the constitution of male and female
in either the utopian or the dystopian order.

A rather different attempt to construct a nonauthoritarian father
relationship occurs in the family biography *Las geneologías,* by
Margo Glantz,[11] whose family were Russian Jewish exiles and in
some sense culturally different from her generation, which is in-
tegrated into Mexican culture. Here the dissonance between the
cultures does not allow Glantz to see a unitary self but rather to
recognize her own division as she traces ways of life that both
belong to her and yet are foreign. What Glantz's book demonstrates is how different is the experience of the exile family. Her
father ran a café and was also a literary man and a writer who
wrote in Yiddish, a minority language. Glantz describes herself as
the Telemachus of this Ulysses, an inheritor of a tradition that
came not from a position of power but from exile.[12] The father is
"deterritorialized." He cannot be turned into a metaphor for the
state or for state power since he represents a voice that is outside
the dominant culture. It is through him that Glantz finds the threads
that will lead her to a family history, a history that will always
remain elusive and that can only be grasped through journeys to
already-changed streets, through scraps of writing, and through
stories handed on by older generations. Glantz, though taking a
very different path from Puga, also represents the family as a space
of survival and as a space where the dominant ideological values
are questioned and negated.

But in several contemporary novels, this father position is questioned or undermined. In the enormously popular *Arráncame la
vida* by Angeles Mastreta,[13] set in the 1930s and 1940s, General
Andrés Ascencio, a man who has many women, marries Catalina
when she is less than fifteen, and for years she seems to be the
docile wife, despite the unavoidable evidence of his corruption, his
cruelty, and his inhumanity. But this is the other side of the macho
myth, for the authoritarian personality produces a concealed re-

sentment and a desire for revenge that can only be satisfied when
he is finally dead and buried. At that moment, Catalina feels amused
as she faces her future, "almost happy." This is the antinational
allegory, the moment when woman is liberated because the old
macho order is dead.

Mastreta's novel, written in the first person, presents the other
side of the public allegory—the "private" life that supports the
crumbling national hero whose heroism is mainly displayed in
conquering women and murdering rivals. But there are different
ways of undermining patriarchy. In Carmen Boullosa's *Mejor desaparece* (Better It Vanishes), the patriarchal myth is rewritten as
Gothic fantasy.[14] Described by the author as a story of "parri-
cide," the novel describes a family in which the mother has died.
The girls are all named after flowers, as if they are part of a nature
that is rapidly disappearing. The father, who attempts to assert his
law, can no longer emit a coherent discourse. At one time, he insists on cleanliness; at another, he allows, the house to be invaded
by rats. Indecipherable graffiti appear on the walls of the house,
as incomprehensible as the legal documents that the father sends
to his children. In other words, "father" has become an impossibly
contradictory space, and subjects no longer position themselves
naturally within the symbolic order. At the beginning of the novel,
the father introduces a "thing" into the house, a repugnant object
that can be picked up only by holding it in cardboard and that
appears in unexpected places. The author explains this thing as
the "death of the mother." "For me, as the writer, there is no
doubt that it is the presence of the dead mother who cruelly looks
after her children from the grave."[15] If this is so, then the mother
is the disorder that through the children destroys patriarchal order
and logic and eventually shuts them out of the family house.

A FEMINIST PUBLIC SPHERE

In the light of these recent novels, *Hasta no verte, Jesús mío* perhaps closes rather than opens an epoch. A few years after its publication, in 1975, the International Women's Year celebrations organized by the United Nations were held in Mexico City. At that
conference, prominent and primarily upper-class women from all
over the world met to discuss women's place in society. In the
middle of the proceedings a dissonant note was struck when
Domitila, a Bolivian miner's wife, and other subaltern women tried

to take control of the microphone.[16] This reminder of class and racial differences within the feminist movement was taken to heart by women's movements in Latin America. Thus, when the journal *fem* was founded in Mexico in 1977, it declared itself nonpartisan, open to all opinions, and, at the same time, aligned itself with political struggles, especially those of the subaltern classes. This was emphasized by editorials that positioned the journal with respect to national liberation movements in Latin America, as well as more properly feminist issues. By 1980, when *fem* organized round tables on "Feminism, Culture, and Politics," the editorial collective clearly felt able to outline the requirements of a feminist theory that would be good for Third World countries. And, in one of the debates organized by the journal, Teresa de Barbieri stated as a possible program that of "creating a theory for underdeveloped Latin American capitalism, without which feminism in the metropolis cannot develop."[17]

The emergence of feminism as a force within the public sphere was a symptom of a general realignment of political and social forces during the last two decades. As a prelude, a war was waged all over Latin America to crush the guerrilla movements and to narrow the options on the left. The defeat of the guerrillas (except in Nicaragua and El Salvador) does not mean that there has been democratization but rather that a certain pluralism is permitted (though in some countries scarcely tolerated by the drug mafia or the military).

State terror against the guerrilla movement went far beyond the armed rebels themselves and deeply affected the civilian population, drawing women into the circle of terror. This was tragically demonstrated by the fate of one of the founders of *fem*, Alaíde Foppa, a Guatemalan resident in Mexico who was kidnapped and "disappeared" on a visit to Guatemala at the end of 1980, apparently because her children were involved in the guerrilla movement.[18] Alaíde was a poet and a literary critic, who in relative isolation had grasped the necessity of forming a women's network that could deal with the specific problems of Latin American women. After initiating a series of radio programs, she helped found *fem* along with Margarita García Flores. But as women participated more and more actively in political and guerrilla movements, they also found that they could no longer expect immunity from counterinsurgency. Neither her upper-class origins, her age, nor her status as a mother protected Alaíde. She was not unique, however; in Argentina several members of the Mothers' movement would disappear, and in Chile women students received the same rough treatment from the triumphant military as men.[19]

The stakes for women on the left were thus raised at the very moment when they had begun to emerge as a force in the public sphere. The situation was further complicated by great demographic changes. Massive emigration from rural areas to the city and to the United States altered the balance between country and city; oppressive military regimes in the Southern Cone and Central America not only exterminated political and trade unions and members of the intelligentsia but also sent many others into exile. At the same time, new social forces emerged—indigenous movements protesting the loss of lands, black power movements in Brazil, the Mothers of the Plaza de Mayo, and the base communities associated with liberation theology. New kinds of political movements developed around such everyday life questions as housing, birth control, rape, and human rights. For the first time women's centers began to operate in many major Latin American cities.[20] Thus the rigid homogeneity of modernization, disguised as mass media pluralism and often supported by military governments, confronted new kinds of heterogeneity.

In this environment, the question of where women stand is pertinent. For just at the time when women seem to claim an "identity," they find themselves in a world where identity is challenged, where all "ground" is suspect, and where, moreover, the subaltern classes more and more find their stories told for them by the mass media. In Mexico in particular, mass market literature has developed into a potent force. And comic strip novels and photo novels no longer necessarily feed the masses with romance but even offer images of women who have broken with the traditional family. In other words, emancipation becomes the desirable prerequisite for entry into the work force.[21]

That is why it has been so important for contemporary women novelists not only in Mexico but all over Latin America to move beyond the confines of domesticity. Luisa Valenzuela and Marta Traba of Argentina; Cristina Peri Rossi and Armonía Sommers of Uruguay; the Colombian Albalucía del Angel, and the Puerto Rican Rosario Ferré; Magali García Ramis as well as María Luisa Puga and Elena Poniatowska parody national myths, roam all over the globe, and pronounce the radical exile of women from the traditional family.[22] It is not "daddy, mummy, and me" who dominate their novels, but precarious and often perilous alliances across generations and social classes.[23]

At a congress on women's writing, Elena Poniatowska declared that women's literature is part of the literature of the oppressed.[24] Not all of those present agreed with her. Nevertheless, the tradition of women's movements in Latin America has always been to discuss feminism in relation to other social and political issues. It is not only a question of individual liberation but of social justice and democratization. Since this book has been primarily concerned with representation, and for the most part with representation in narrative, the real struggles of Mexican women have appeared only marginally. It is well to bear in mind, however, that the literary works I have mentioned are both interventions in a new stage of debate and at the same time part of a much broader process of struggle whose outcome is as yet undetermined.

NOTES

INTRODUCTION

1. See Toril Moi, *Sexual/Textual Politics: Feminist Literary Theory* (London and New York: Methuen, 1985); and Gayatri Chakravorty Spivak, "Three Women's Texts and a Critique of Imperialism," in Henry Louis Gates, Jr., ed., *"Race," Writing, and Difference* (Chicago: University of Chicago Press, 1986), pp. 262–282.

2. See Sara Castro-Klarén, "La crítica literaria feminista y la escritora en América Latina," in Patricia Elena González and Eliana Ortega, eds., *La sartén por el mango* (Rio Piedras, Puerto Rico; Ediciones Huracán, 1984), pp. 27–46. But for a discussion of tensions between these different claims, see Cherríe Moraga, "From a Long Line of Vendidas: Chicanas and Feminism," in Teresa de Lauretis, ed., *Feminist Studies: Critical Studies* (Bloomington: Indiana University Press 1986), pp. 173–190.

3. Gayatri Chakravorty Spivak, *In Other Worlds: Essays in Cultural Politics* (New York and London: Methuen, 1987), pp. 179–180.

4. I have found Peter Stallybrass and Allon White, *The Politics and Poetics of Transgression* (Ithaca, N.Y.: Cornell University Press, 1986), particularly suggestive. For an overview of what is often termed the "new historicism," see Jean E. Howard, "The New Historicism in Renaissance Studies," *ELR* (1986), pp. 13–43.

5. Jürgen Habermas touches briefly on this in an interview in which he discusses Southern slave society. See Peter Dews, ed., *Habermas: Autonomy and Solidarity: Interviews with Jürgen Habermas* (London: Verso, 1986), pp. 209–210.

6. Gemelli Carreri, *Viaje a la Nueva España: Mexico a fines del siglo*

XVIII, preface by Fernando B. Sandoval, 2 vols. (Mexico City: Libro-Mex Editores, 1955), 1:45. Quoted in Jacques Lafaye, *Quetzalcóatl and Guadalupe: The Formation of Mexican National Consciousness, 1531–1813,* Benjamin Keen, tr. (Chicago: University of Chicago Press, 1976), p. 13.

7. Quoted in James Lockhart and Enrique Otte, eds., *Letters and People of the Spanish Indies: The Sixteenth Century* (Cambridge: Latin American Studies, 1976), p. 202.

8. For a brief discussion see Lafaye, *Quetzalcóatl and Guadalupe,* especially pp. 18–50.

9. For a discussion of women in colonial society, see Asunción Lavrín, "In Search of the Colonial Woman in Mexico: The Seventeenth and Eighteenth Centuries," in Asunción Lavrín, ed., *Latin American Women: Historical Perspectives* (Westport, Conn., and London: Greenwood Press, 1978), pp. 23–59.

10. See Electa Arenal, "And I Asleep: Where Woman Is Creator of the Wor(l)d, or Sor Juana's Discourses on Method," in Stephanie Merrim, ed., *"Y yo despierta": Towards a Feminist Understanding of Sor Juana Inés de la Cruz* (Ann Arbor: Oxford Books, 1987).

11. Luce Irigaray, "La Mystérique," in *Speculum of the Other Woman,* Gillian C. Gill, tr. (Ithaca, N.Y.: Cornell University Press, 1985), p. 191.

12. Julia Kristeva, "Stabat Mater," in Susan Rubin Suleiman, ed., *The Female Body in Western Culture* (Cambridge: Harvard University Press, 1986).

13. Michel de Certeau, who attempted an account of mystical discourse in relation to the intellectual tradition of Catholicism, unfortunately completed only one volume of his work. See *La Fable mystique: XVI–XVIIe siècle* (Paris: Gallimard, 1982).

14. Michel Foucault, "Two Lectures," in *Power/Knowledge: Selected Interviews and Other Writings, 1972–1977,* Colin Gordon, ed. (New York: Pantheon Books, 1980), p. 83.

15. Juan Pedro Viqueira Albán, "Relajados o reprimidos?" Supplement to *La Jornada* (January 3, 1988), no. 155, pp. 5–6.

16. Much depended on social class. Women worked as seamstresses, spinners, weavers, and hatters. See Julia Tuñón Pablos, *Mujeres en México: Una historia olvidada* (Mexico City: Planeta, 1987), p. 56.

17. For an extensive discussion of the constitution of the intelligentsia in Latin America from colonial times, see Angel Rama, *La ciudad letrada* (Hanover, N.H.: Ediciones del Norte, 1984).

18. See Lafaye, *Quetzalcóatl and Guadalupe.*

19. Quoted in Rachel Phillips, "Marina/Malinche," in Beth Miller, ed., *Women in Hispanic Literature: Icons and Fallen Idols* (Berkeley: University of California Press, 1983), pp. 97–114.

20. Octavio Paz, *The Labyrinth of Solitude,* Lysander Kemp, tr. (New York: Grove Press, 1961), p. 72.

21. See Anna Macías, "Yucatán and the Women's Movement," in *Against All Odds: The Feminist Movement in Mexico to 1940* (Westport, Conn.: Greenwood Press, 1982), pp. 59–86.

22. For a literary account of this trial, see Vicente Leñero's play *El juicio* (Mexico City: Joaquín Mortíz, 1972).

23. See Jean Franco, "The Incorporation of Women: A Comparison of North American and Mexican Popular Narrative," in Tania Modleski, ed., *Studies in Entertainment: Critical Approaches to Mass Culture* (Bloomington: Indiana University Press, 1986), pp. 119–138.

24. Stallybrass and White's *The Politics and Poetics of Transgression* begins with a critique of Bakhtin's overly celebratory view of carnival. They then draw on anthropological theory in their discussion of symbolic systems. What is perhaps important in Bakhtin is his insistence on the always unfinished and heterogeneous nature of social processes and the dialogic character of texts. See Katerina Clark and Michael Holquist, *Mikhail Bakhtin* (Cambridge: Harvard University Press, 1984).

25. The relevant text is Michel Foucault, *History of Sexuality*, vol. 1, Robert Hurley, tr. (New York: Pantheon Books, 1978).

26. See Dews, ed., *Habermas: Autonomy and Solidarity;* and Raymond Williams, *Marxism and Literature* (New York: Oxford University Press, 1977), pp. 128–155. There are many overlapping terms used to describe the dispositions and attitudes that are crystallized by life experience. Theorists reject "experience" for various reasons, and use a variety of terms to suggest a combination of the personal and social lived experience. The feminist critic Teresa de Lauretis has opted for a redefinition of experience based on Peircian semiotics; see Teresa de Lauretis, *Alice Doesn't: Feminism, Semiotics, Cinema* (Bloomington: Indiana University Press, 1984). A more sociological definition is Pierre Bourdieu's "habitus," in *Outline of a Theory of Practice,* Richard Nice, tr. (Cambridge: Cambridge University Press, 1977), pp. 76–78. See also Jean-Paul Sartre, *Critique of Dialectical Reason,* Alan Sheridan Smith, tr. (London: New Left Books, 1976), where Sartre posits the field of the "practico-inert *as the no longer dynamic remains of past praxis."*

27. Quoted in John Rajchman, *Michel Foucault: The Freedom of Philosophy* (New York: Columbia University Press, 1985), pp. 35–36.

28. "Serialization" is a term used by Sartre in *Critique of Dialectical Reason,* pp. 256–306. Sartre's examples of serial forms of collectivity include the bus line, radio listening, and the free market.

29. See Toril Moi's critique of feminist criticism in the United States in *Sexual/Textual Politics.*

30. See Michèle Barrett, *Women's Oppression Today* (London: Verso, 1980); Moi, *Sexual/Textual Politics;* Alice A. Jardine, *Gynesis: Configurations of Woman and Modernity* (Ithaca, N.Y.: Cornell University Press, 1985).

31. See Teresa de Lauretis, "Issues, Terms and Contexts," introductory

essay in Teresa de Lauretis, ed., *Feminist Studies: Critical Studies*, pp. 1–19. See also her *Alice Doesn't: Feminism, Semiotics, Cinema*. Two critics writing in *Feminist Studies: Critical Studies* specifically urge women to struggle for the power of interpretation and authorship. See Tania Modleski, "Feminism and the Power of Interpretation," pp. 121–138, and Nancy K. Miller, "Changing the Subject: Authorship, Writing and the Reader," pp. 102–120.

32. See *I . . . Rigoberta Menchú: An Indian Woman in Guatemala*, Elisabeth Burgos-Debray, ed., Ann Wright, tr. (London: Verso Editions, 1983). For the personal story of one of the Mothers of the Plaza de Mayo in Argentina, see Hebe de Bonafini, *Historias de vida*, Matilde Sánchez, ed. (Buenos Aires: Fraternal/Del Nuevo Extremo, 1985). In Mexico as in other parts of Latin America, political parties have tended to subordinate women's issues. For some interesting reflections on this, see Sol Arguedas, *Parientes pobres* (Mexico City: Ediciones de Cultura Popular, 1973).

33. James Clifford, *The Predicament of Culture: Twentieth-Century Ethnography, Literature, and Art* (Cambridge: Harvard University Press, 1988).

1: WRITERS IN SPITE OF THEMSELVES

1. María de San Joseph, quoted in Fray Sebastián de Santander y Torres, *Vida de la Benerable Madre María de S. Joseph, Religiosa Augustina Recoleta: Fundadora en los conventos de Santa Mónica de la Ciudad de la Puebla y después en el de la Soledad de Oaxaca* (Seville: 1725), p. 164. (Unless otherwise indicated, all translations are my own.) María de San Joseph lived between 1656 and 1719. Some of María de San Joseph's notes on which this biography was based have been transcribed by Kathleen Ann Myers in "Becoming a Nun in Seventeenth-Century Mexico: An Edition of the Spiritual Autobiography of María de San Joseph," vol. 1, (Ph.D. dissertation, Brown University, 1986). I am also indebted to Josefina Muriel's book *Cultura femenina novohispana* (Mexico City: UNAM, 1982), pp. 320–321, for drawing my attention to this material. See also Electa Arenal and Stacey Schlau's anthology of Hispanic nuns' writings, *Untold Sisters* (Albuquerque: University of New Mexico Press, in press); Julia Tuñón Pablos, *Mujeres en México: Una historia olvidada* (Mexico City: Planeta, 1987); and Pilar Gonzalbo Aizpuru, *Las mujeres en la Nueva España. Educación y vida cotidiana* (Mexico City: Colegio de México, 1987).

2. See Michel de Certeau, *Heterologies: Discourse on the Other*, Brian Massumi, tr., vol. 17 of *Theory and History of Literature* (Minneapolis: University of Minnesota Press, 1986).

3. The practice of making notes on the experiences of holy women and

then using them as the basis for a saintly life goes back to the Middle Ages. See Rudolph M. Bell, *Holy Anorexia* (Chicago: University of Chicago Press, 1985), p. 24. The note-taking was related to the practice of the confessional. See Michel Foucault, *History of Sexuality,* vol. 1, Robert Hurley, tr. (New York: Pantheon Books, 1978), pp. 58–59. For the development of high style by the bureaucracy of what he calls the "lettered city," see Angel Rama, *La ciudad letrada* (Hanover, N.H.: Ediciones del Norte, 1984).

4. Diego de Lemus, *Vida, virtudes, trabajos, favores y milagros de la Venerable madre Sor María de Jesús, angelopolitana religiosa, en el insigne convento de la Limpia Concepción de la Ciudad de los Angeles en la Nueva España y natural de ella* (León, 1683). The pages of the preface are unnumbered. Don Diego de Victoria Salazar wrote the "approval" which prefaces the Life.

5. See Fernando Benítez, *Los demonios en el convento: Sexo y religión en la Nueva España* (Mexico City: Ediciones Era, 1985), pp. 107–110.

6. See Muriel, *Cultura femenina novohispana,* p. 21. On the censorship of novels, see Irving A. Leonard, *Books of the Brave: Being an Account of Books and of Men in the Spanish Conquest and Settlement of the Sixteenth-Century New World* (Cambridge: Harvard University Press, 1949).

7. On the fate of some Spanish women mystics, see Claire Guilhem, "La Inquisición y la devaluación del verbo femenino," in Bartolomé Bennassar, ed., *Inquisición española: Poder político y control social,* 2d ed. (Barcelona: Editorial Crítica, 1984), pp. 171–207.

8. See Miguel Godínez (Godínes or Wadding), *Práctica de la Theología Mystica* (Seville, 1682), printed under the patronage of Manuel Fernández de Santa Cruz. Godínez is the Hispanicized name of an Irish Jesuit, Father Michael Wadding, who taught theology in the college of San Pedro and San Pablo in Mexico City. He devoted an entire chapter of his book (pp. 327–331) to the heretical beliefs of the *alumbrados.* He was also author of notes on the life of Madre María de Jesús, which were used by Father Félix de Jesús María, in *Vida, virtudes y dones sobrenaturales de la Venerable sierva de Dios la madre María de Jesús, religiosa profesa en el monasterio de la Puebla de los Angeles, en las Indias Occidentales* (Rome, 1756).

9. Antonio Núñez de Miranda, *Distribución de las Obras Ordinarias y Extraordinarias del día, para hazerlas perfectamente, conforme al Estado de las Señoras Religiosas: Instruída con doce máximas substanciales, para la vida Regular y Espiritual, que deben seguir* (Mexico City: viuda de Miguel Ribera de Calderón, 1712), p. 20.

10. José de Lezamis, *Breve relación de la vida y muerte del Ilmo. y Revmo. Señor Doctor Don Francisco Aguiar y Seijas* (Mexico City, 1699).

11. J. Eric S. Thompson, ed., *Thomas Gage's Travels in the New World* (Norman: University of Oklahoma Press, 1958), p. 73.

12. Godínez, *Práctica de la Theología Mystica,* pp. 92–98. In his book,

Godínez has questions and answers on mysticism. Here the question is why women who are naturally less saintly than men receive more favors. Godínez gives a number of answers: 1) their soft nature, which accommodates the spirit more easily; 2) because they are weaker, they need this carriage or stretcher to help them over the difficult work of spiritual life— "porque como las mujeres en lo temporal, aunque sean muy pobres, gastan de ordinario más galas que los hombres, lo mismo sucede a veces con lo espiritual donde las mujeres se llevan la gala; y como Dios es tan amigo de honrar a sus amigas, siendo las mujeres incapaces del sacerdocio, predicación apostólica y otros semejantes favores, las honra con estas favores de las visiones, raptos y revelaciones."

13. Irigaray, "La Mystérique," in *Speculum of the Other Woman*, Gillian C. Gill, tr. (Ithaca, N.Y.: Cornell University Press, 1985), pp. 191–202. See also de Certeau, *La Fable mystique: XVIᵉ–XVIIᵉ siècle* (Paris: Gallimard, 1982), p. 24.

14. Núñez de Miranda, *Distribución*, p. 55. This is obviously the case with the rules for religious orders which also emphasized obedience. See, for instance, *Regla dada por nuestro padre San Agustín a sus monjas: Constituciones que han de guardar las religiosas agustinas recoletas de Santa Mónica de la Ciudad de la Puebla: Aprobadas por los M.SS.PP. Paulo V y Urbano VIII y ampliadas por el Illmo. Señor Doctor D. Manuel Fernández de Santa Cruz*, 2d ed. (Puebla, Mexico: 1753). The influence of the *Regla* on María de San Joseph is discussed by Myers, "Becoming a Nun," pp. 25–27.

15. "Parecer del doctor Don Luis de la Peña, Juez Comissario de la nueva información para la Curia Romana, sobre la Aparición de la Milagrosa Imagen de nuestra Señora de Guadalupe de México, Rector del Apostólico Colegio de N.S. Pedro, y Calificador (con exercicio) del Santo Tribunal de la Inquisición de esta Nueva España," in unnumbered prefatory pages of Santander y Torres, *Vida*.

16. Santander y Torres, *Vida*, "Prólogo al Lector" (pages unnumbered). "Porque como buen Pastor quería reconocer muy de espacio los passos, y sendas por donde caminaba esta Oveja; porque no es fácil reduzir a la que anda descarriada, o perdida, si el Pastor no se haze Argos para observarle los movimientos."

17. Serge Gruzinski, "La 'conquista de los cuerpos' " in *Familia y Sexualidad en Nueva España* (Mexico City: Fondo de Cultura Económica, 1982), pp. 177–206.

18. Lemus, *Vida*, p. 79.

19. Thompson, ed., *Thomas Gage's Travels in the New World*, p. 71.

20. Myers, "Becoming a Nun," pp. 155–156.

21. De Certeau, *La Fable mystique*, p. 248.

22. Irigaray, "La Mystérique," in *Speculum of the Other Woman*, p. 193.

23. María de San Joseph wrote several versions of her own life at the request of different confessors. The most complete is a two-volume life

written for Fray Plácido after she had been in the convent for fourteen years. See Kathleen Myers, "Becoming a Nun," pp. 21–24.

24. Lemus, *Vida*, p. 26: "Llegando a sacar la daga, y correr tras ella."

25. María de San Joseph, quoted in Myers, "Becoming a Nun," pp. 104–105. Myers draws attention in her introduction to the influence of exemplary lives on María de San Joseph, especially that of the austere San Pedro de Alcántara.

26. Santander y Torres, *Vida*, p. 113: "Quítase de aquí, ¿no le he dicho ya, que no tiene lugar?"

27. Lemus, *Vida*, p. 10.

28. Santander y Torres, *Vida*, pp. 130–131.

29. Lemus, *Vida*, p. 334: "el qual aviéndole advertido una de aquel convento, digno de todo crédito, como nuestro Señor le comunicaba a la vener. Madre muchos secretos, y particulares fabores: juzgo que era conveniente que se conservasse alguna memoria de ellos para lo que su majestad dispusiesse en adelante."

30. Lemus, *Vida*, p. 112. Godínez presented written questions which were answered both orally and in writing. According to Lemus, he found María de Jesús one of the most perfect in matters of prayer.

31. Lemus, *Vida*, p. 336: "No quedaba satisfecha de lo que avía escrito, y lo borrava, y rompía, pareciendole que no iba con el acierto que deseaba."

32. Lemus, *Vida*, p. 337: "Ambas, hija, cumplimos con la obediencia; tu con la del Prelado que te manda que no me manifiestes nada y yo con la de Dios que gusta, que se escrivan las maravillas que por su bondad infinita ha obrado, y obra en esta vil criatura: y así bien puedes proseguir de aquí adelante sin rezelo, pues es voluntad de Dios que yo te descubra a ti las mercedes que el ha hecho, y haze, para que tu las escrivas."

33. Lemus, *Vida*, p. 336: "Ha de ser mi obra, y sobre todo el: ya ha de escrivir en honra, y gloria mia, el amor, y llaneza con que me comunico a las almas por la intercesión de mi santísima Madre."

34. Lemus, *Vida*, p. 338: "Porque el velo es significación de que han de querer obscurecer estos escritos, pero no podran; porque el Señor los defenderá, y assi repara como ves las letras, aunque un poco obscuras."

35. Lemus, *Vida*, p. 394: "Sello este libro en que estan escritos tus trabajos, y yo soi el sello."

36. Santander y Torres, in his preface to the *Vida* addressed "Al Lector," quotes these words from a letter of Fernández de la Cruz: "Apurela mas en que diga lo demás que le passó en los veinte años del Siglo, pues no es posible, que no tenga más; y con ocasión de que refiere, si tuvo tentaciones, o otros trabajos interiores, y socorros espirituales de Dios, se acordará para dezirlos. Guarde V. md. con cuydado los papeles, y embieme los de essa otra con don Ignacio."

37. Santander y Torres, *Vida*, p. 164. For a complete list of the confessors for whom María de San Joseph wrote, see Myers, "Becoming a Nun." In the appendix to her edition of part of the nun's writing, Myers

lists the contents of the different volumes and the confessors to whom they were addressed. María de San Joseph wrote for no less than seven confessors in all.

38. Santander y Torres, *Vida,* p. 165: "Porque si escribes con facilidad, has de tener mucho desahogo, y consuelo, y no nasciste para tener descanso en esta vida."

39. Santander y Torres, *Vida,* p. 225: "y di à tu Padre, mire como dispone los papeles que le vas escribiendo, porque han de servir de aviso, y de mucho provecho à las almas."

40. Santander y Torres, *Vida,* p. 358: "Mira que yo te assisto, y no te falto; escribelo, que todo es de mi, y nada de ti; y si no, mira si por ti sola huvieras podido dar un solo passo y hecho lo que has hecho?"

41. Myers, "Becoming a Nun," p. 198.

42. There are three biographies of Sor María de Jesús Tomelín. Besides the two by Father Lemus and Félix de Santa María already mentioned, there is a biography by Francisco Pardo, *Vida y virtudes heroicas de la Madre María de Jesús, religiosa profesa en el Convento de la Limpia Concepción de la Virgen María en la ciudad de Los Angeles* (Mexico City, 1676). The canonization was begun soon after her death and then taken up in 1696 by the Bishop of Puebla, Manuel Fernández de Santa Cruz.

43. Lemus, *Vida,* pp. 337–338. One chaplain, Don Gutierre Bernardo de Queiros, threatened to have Sor Agustina's notes on María de Jesús burned.

44. Lemus, *Vida,* "Al Lector" (pages unnumbered).

45. See Muriel, *Cultura femenina novohispana,* p. 331. Muriel herself traced Agustina's manuscript between the lines of these hagiographies.

46. Santander y Torres, *Oración funebre que predicó el M.P. P. M. Fr Sebastian de Santander, del Orden de Predicadores de N.P. Santo Domingo en las Honras de la V.M. Maria de San Joseph, Religiosa Recoleta augustina, en la ciudad de Antequera,* (Puebla, 1719).

47. Myers, "Becoming a Nun," p. 225: "Entró mi hermana Ana en el tal aposento a sacar no se qué. Llevava una mosa consigo, que le iva alumbrando, i al entrar por la puerta, vido mi hermana bajar del techo de arriva a el enemigo, con gran estruendo, en forma de un negrillo mui atesado. La mosa, con el espanto i gritos que dio, apagó la lus que llevava en gran aprieto."

48. Santander y Torres, *Vida,* p. 277: "¡Qué padecerá su cuerpo hallándose tan apretado y oprimido en brazos de un Demonio!"

49. Santander y Torres, *Vida,* p. 170.

50. Myers, introduction, "Becoming a Nun," p. 27. Myers' introduction gives an excellent account of the possibilities and limitations of autobiography written under these circumstances.

51. Santander y Torres, *Vida,* p. 256: "Es quando Dios dà à el entendimiento una subidisima inteligencia, y a la voluntad un fervor intensissimo; lo qual no da, ni comunica, sino à aquellas almas que estan yà muy purgadas, y puras." He is paraphrasing Saint John of the Cross.

52. Quoted in Muriel, *Cultura femenina novohispana,* p. 328.

53. Lemus, *Vida.* See especially book 3, "Del espíritú prophético de la M. María de Jesús," pp. 325–331.

54. Santander y Torres, *Vida,* pp. 147–149.

55. Santander y Torres, *Vida,* p. 170.

56. Santander y Torres, *Vida,* p. 194: "O qué buen dia hemos de tener, quando conociendo la burla el Obispo y su Confessor, la declaren por ilusa, por hypocrita, por embustera, y por endemoniada! Entonces si, que la pondrán en una Cárcel, separada de las demás, y de darán el premio, que sus Revelaciones merecen: alli tendrá el pago à el tamaño de sus Profecías, en disciplinas, en ayunos, y en correcciones."

57. Santander y Torres, *Vida,* p. 176. "Puedo assegurar, que para cada virtud de las que debo, y quiero exercitar, tengo un Demonio, que me la contradize, y en esto no tengo duda; porque tengo claridad de que es assí, y me fuerzan a dezir tantas, y tan terribles blasfemias, contra nuestro Señor, que solo en la iniquidad horrorosa, de que me fuerza a dezirlas, pueden caber, y esto con tan gran violencia, que aprieto los dientes con mucha fuerza; porque parece segun lo que siento, que las pronuncia la lengua, y assi padezco congoxas mortales, para resistir."

58. Santander y Torres, *Vida,* pp. 279–280: "Poniendo a sus ojos diferentes torpezas, como por todo el cuerpo, encendiendo en todo él aquella llama con que se abrasaba. . . . Se ponian a mofar, y a hazer burlar de la Sierva de Dios, celebrando, que los compañeros avian ya conseguido de ella el triunfo, porque la avian ya obligado a consentir, y deleytarse en las tentaciones, y representaciones impuras."

59. Santander y Torres, *Vida,* p. 240. "Que cada palabra que pronunciaba, veía salir de mis labios una luz muy resplandenciente, en forma de una Estrella; esta la veía subir a lo alto, hasta entrar en el Cielo, y llegar ante el Trono de su Divina Magestad. Allí paraba, y de esta manera veía ir subiendo todas las palabras, que iba diziendo, hasta que acabé de rezar las Vísperas."

60. Santander y Torres, *Vida,* p. 172.

61. Santander y Torres, *Vida,* p. 340: "Esso, y mucho mas haré por tí, y aora ensancha tu corazón, para recibir las mercedes que estoy para hazerte. Luego ví, y senti como se entró el Señor en mí corazón en forma de una llama de fuego, de tal suerte, que parecia se avia unido conmigo, y hecho una misma cosa."

62. Santander y Torres, *Vida,* p. 354: "Veía los labios de mi alma metidos dentro de la Llaga de mi Señor, y tragaba a boca llena la Sangre caliente." In an extensive study of medieval women, Caroline Walker Bynum suggests that it was through food that women's piety was expressed. See *Holy Feast and Holy Fast: The Religious Significance of Food to Medieval Women* (Berkeley: University of California Press, 1987). But food itself is also a metaphor for knowledge which we "imbibe" and "digest," even "chew over." The Mexican nuns expressed through these metaphors their direct relation to the source of knowledge.

63. Santander y Torres, *Vida*, p. 353: "Hija querida de mi corazón, y mi María, descansa en mi, y yo en ti; que pues participas de mis penas, y amarguras, razón es, que yo te participe de mis gustos, y glorias. Bebe, hija, bebe a boca llena de el rio de mis dulzuras, y amor; descansa en mis brazos, pues tan trabajada estás."

64. Santander y Torres, *Vida*, p. 352: "Lo que aqui sentí, no halló términos para explicarlo; porque según sentí, me participo su Magestad de sus penas, y sus dolores."

65. Santander y Torres, *Vida*, pp. 255–256.

66. Lemus, *Vida*, pp. 412–413.

67. See especially "The Practice of Joy Before Death," in Georges Bataille, *Visions of Excess: Selected Writings, 1927–1939,* Allan Stoekl, ed.; Carl R. Lovitt, Donald M. Leslie, Jr., and Allan Stoekl, trs., vol. 14 of *Theory and History of Literature* (Minneapolis: University of Minnesota Press, 1985), pp. 235–239.

68. Santander y Torres, *Vida*, p. 363: "Los cabellos parecian hebras de oro fino, los ojos bellisimos, el color mas que la nieve, las mexillas rosadas; traía puestas unas como vandas encarnadas."

69. Santander y Torres, *Vida*, p. 175: "vi la celda llena de demonios en figura humana, como unos mulatos muy feos, desnudos."

70. Muriel, *Cultura femenina novohispana*, pp. 337–341.

71. Muriel, *Cultura femenina novohispana*, p. 341.

72. Caroline Walker Bynum, in *Holy Feast and Holy Fast*, p. 296, argues that "women saw themselves not as flesh opposed to spirit, female opposed to male, nurture opposed to authority: they saw themselves as human beings—fully spirit and fully flesh." Much the same could be said of these seventeenth-century Mexican nuns, except that clearly the relationship to writing was one form in which they lived their oppression.

2 : SOR JUANA EXPLORES SPACE

1. In an epistolary poem to an admirer, "newly arrived in New Spain," who had addressed her as "the phoenix," Sor Juana jokes that he came with a command from Apollo and the description of the "rara avis." See "Que respondió nuestra Poetisa al Caballero recién llegado a Nueva España. . . ." in Sor Juana Inés de la Cruz, *Obras completas*, 4 vols. (Mexico City: Fondo de Cultura Económica, 1951), 1:143–148. The four volumes were edited by Alfonso Méndez Plancarte and Alberto G. Salceda. In subsequent citations, this edition will be abbreviated *OC*.

2. See Francisco de la Maza, *El guadalupanismo mexicano* (Mexico City: Fondo de Cultura Económica, 1981). For the cult of Sor Juana and its relation to criollo nationalism, see Jacques Lafaye, *Quetzalcóatl and Guadalupe: The Formation of Mexican National Consciousness 1531–1813*, Benjamin Keen, tr. (Chicago: University of Chicago Press, 1974), pp. 68–76.

3. "Dexando mas edificada con su resolución heroica, y exemplos singulares de virtud a toda esta Ciudad, de lo que la avia admirado con su ingenio, escritos, y talentos." Juan de Oviedo, *Vida ejemplar, heroicas virtudes y apostólico ministerio del venerable padre Antonio Núñez de Miranda de la Compañía de Jesus* (Mexico City, 1702). His Sor Juana chapter is reproduced in Marie-Cécile Benassy-Berling, *Humanisme et religion chez Sor Juana Inés de la Cruz: La femme et la culture au XVIIe siècle* (Paris: Sorbonne, Éditions hispaniques, 1982), annexe no. 5, pp. 434–437. The quotation is on page 437.

4. *Inundación Castálida de la única poetisa, musa dézima: Soror Juana Inés de la Cruz, religosa professa en el Monasterio de San Gerónimo de la Imperial Ciudad de México que en varios metros, idiomas, y estilos, fertiliza varios assumptos con elegantes, sutiles, claros, ingeniosos, útiles versos para enseñanza, recreo, y admiración dedícalos a la excelentisima Señora D. María Luisa Gonçaga Manrique de Lara, Condesa de Paredes, Marquesa de la Laguna, y los saca a luz d. Juan Camacho y Gayna, Cavallero del Orden de Santiago, Mayordomo, y Cavallerizo que fue de su Excelencia, Governador actual de la Ciudad del Puerto de Santa María* (Madrid, 1689). A second edition was published as *Poemas* (Madrid, 1690), followed by editions published in Barcelona, 1691, and in Zaragoza, 1692. The second volume of the *Obras* was published in Seville, 1692 (with additions by Sor Juana), and Barcelona, 1693, with the title *Obras poéticas*. After her death, her complete works were published in three volumes as *Fama y Obras póstumas* (Madrid, 1700).

5. Father Diego Calleja included the biographical essay in the third volume of Sor Juana's collected works, *Fama y obras póstumas del Fénix de México, Décima Musa, poetisa americana etc.* (Madrid, 1700). It was published by Amado Nervo in 1910 as an appendix to his biography, *Juana de Asbaje*. Octavio Paz summarizes recent research on Sor Juana's family in the chapter "La familia Ramírez" in *Sor Juana Inés de la Cruz o Las trampas de la fe*, 3d ed. (Mexico City: Fondo de cultura económica, 1983), pp. 89–107; in English, *Sor Juana, or, the Traps of Faith* (Cambridge: Harvard University Press, 1988). That Sor Juana's mother, Isabel Ramírez, was not married to Pedro Manuel de Asbaje by whom she had Juan Inés and two other daughters was established by Guillermo Ramírez España, *La familia de Sor Juana* (documentos inéditos) (Mexico City: Imprenta Universitaria, 1947); and by Enrique A. Cervantes, *El testamento de Sor Juana Inés de la Cruz y otros documentos* (Mexico City, 1949). Isabel Ramírez had three other children by Diego Ruiz Lozano. One of Sor Juana's sisters, María, also apparently had three children out of wedlock. It should be noted, however, that this was a period of considerable flux in matrimonial arrangements, and promises to marry were frequently only verbal, thus making it easy to evade them.

6. "He intentado sepultar con mi nombre mi entendimiento y sacrificarsela sólo a quien me le dio," in *Respuesta a Sor Filotea de la Cruz*, in *OC*, 4:444–445.

7. The best-known version of the "repression hypothesis" applied to Sor Juana is the book by Ludwig Pfandl, *Sor Juana Inés de la Cruz, la Décima Musa de México: Su vida, su poesía, su psique,* Juan Antonio Ortega Medina, tr. (Mexico City: UNAM, 1963). It also resurfaces in more recent studies; for example, Fernando Benítez, *Los demonios en el convento: Sexo y religión en la Nueva España* (Mexico City: Era, 1985). Much discussion has also centered on Sor Juana's religious orthodoxy. Defenders of her orthodoxy include the erudite Alfonso Méndez Plancarte, editor of San Juana's complete works, and the pioneer Sor Juanista Dorothy Schons, in "Some Obscure Points in the Life of Sor Juana," *Modern Philology* (November 1926), pp. 141–162. There is a well-argued and well-documented discussion of Sor Juana's religious convictions in Benassy-Berling, *Humanisme et religion chez Sor Juana Inés de la Cruz.* The author takes a middle ground between the orthodox and those who stress potentially heretical elements in Sor Juana's work; among them are Paz, in *Sor Juana Inés de la Cruz,* who examines evidence of the influence of hermetic writings on Sor Juana, and José Pascual Buxó, "El Sueño de Sor Juana: Alegoría y modelo del mundo," *Las figuraciones del sentido: Ensayos de poética semiológica* (Mexico City: Fondo de Cultura Económica, 1984), pp. 235–262. Buxó argues for the Neoplatonism of *El Sueño.* See also Manuel Durán, "Hermetic Traditions in Sor Juana's *Primero Sueño,*" *University of Dayton Review* (Spring 1984), pp. 107–115.

8. Ludwig Wittgenstein, *Philosophical Investigations,* the English text of the 3d edition, G. E. M. Anscombe, tr. (New York: Macmillan, 1958).

9. Michel Foucault uses the term "domain of discourse" in *History of Sexuality* (New York: Pantheon, 1978). It is given Bakhtinian connotations by Peter Stallybrass and Allon White, *The Politics and Poetics of Transgression* (Ithaca, N.Y.: Cornell University Press, 1986).

10. This is the topic of Father Vieira's sermon and Sor Juana's famous refutation, published as the *Carta Atenagórica.* The *Carta* is included in *OC,* 4:412–439; the sermon in the appendix, 4:673–694.

11. See Stallybrass and White, *The Politics and Poetics of Transgression,* especially the introduction, pp. 1–26.

12. Sor Juana Inés de la Cruz, "Los empeños de una casa," *OC,* 4:3–184; "Amor es más laberinto," *OC,* 4:185–352.

13. See Asunción Lavrín, "In Search of the Colonial Woman in Mexico: The Seventeenth and Eighteenth Centuries," in Lavrín, ed., *Latin American Women: Historial Perspectives* (Westport, Conn. and London: Greenwood Press, 1978), pp. 23–59.

14. See especially sonnet no. 149, "Si los riesgos del mar considerara," *OC,* 1:279, in which Phaeton is the mythological character who enables the figuration of this mortal leap. In the love sonnets, for example no. 168, *OC,* 1:289, the choice between the desired but disdainful lover and the undesired but persistent lover is arbitrarily resolved in favor of the former.

15. These aristocratic values appear as allegorical figures in some of the *loas*. See for instance the introductory *loa* to "Los empeños de una casa," *OC*, 4:3–25. For a discussion of correct courtly behavior, see Antonio Maravall, *Culture of the Baroque: Analysis of a Historical Structure*, Terry Cochran, tr., vol. 25 of *Theory and History of Literature* (Minneapolis: University of Minnesota Press, 1986), especially ch. 2, "A Guided Culture," pp. 57–78. See also the interesting discussion of Spanish court behavior by Alberto G. Salceda in the introduction to *OC*, 4:xxiii–xix.

16. María de Jesús de Agreda published her well-known life of the Virgin, *Ciudad mystica de Dios* (Madrid, 1668), saying that it had been dictated to her by the Virgin herself. References to this work are from the abbreviated *Vida de la Virgen María*, with a prologue by the nineteenth-century Spanish Catholic feminist, Emilia Pardo Bazán (Barcelona: Montaner editores, 1899).

17. See Juan Díaz de Arce, *Compendium Operis de studioso sacrorum Bibliorum, ad opportunitatem causae venerabilis servi Dei*, Gregorii López exaratus a reverindissimo patre Fr. Bernardino Membrive (Rome: A. de Rubens, 1751). This was first published in Mexico in 1648.

18. Antonio Núñez de Miranda, *Distribución de las Obras Ordinarias y Extraordinarias del día, para hazerlas perfectamente, conforme al Estado de las Señoras Religiosas* (Mexico City: viuda de Miguel Ribera de Calderón, 1712), p. 74. In the preface to *Distribución*, Juan de Torres described nuns as the teeth in the Church, and remarked that they could be kept white only by closing the lips.

19. Juan Díaz de Arce, "An liceat feminis Sacrorum Bibliorum studio incumbere, eoque interpretari?" *Compendium Operis*, pp. 21–30, summarizes different interpretations of Saint Paul and others.

20. *Respuesta a Sor Filotea de la Cruz*, in *OC*, 4:440–475, the quoted remark is on p. 458.

21. Such criticism is mentioned in the recently discovered *Carta de Sor Juana Inés de la Cruz a su Confesor: Autodefensa espiritual*, published by Aureliano Tapia Méndez (the discoverer of the letter) in his own edition (Monterrey, Mexico, 1986), p. 17. The letter is also included in Paz, *Sor Juana Inés de la Cruz*, 3rd ed. (1983), pp. 638–646.

22. For instance, she writes from the point of view of a woman who has suffered the death of her husband, *OC*, 1:204–206. But in some of her sonnets, e.g., no. 178, the poetic voice is explicitly masculine. "Yo no dudo, Lisarda, que te quiero / aunque se que me tienes agraviado." See also Emilie Bergmann, "Sor Juana Inés de la Cruz: Dreaming in a Double Voice," in Seminar on Feminism and Culture in Latin America, ed., *Women, Culture, and Politics in Latin America* (Berkeley: University of California Press, 1990), pp. 151–172.

23. These works include not only direct quotations from the Apostles but also the translation of a hymn by Saint Thomas. See notes by Méndez Plancarte, *OC*, 3:554.

24. Luce Irigaray, *This Sex Which Is Not One,* Catherine Porter, tr. (Ithaca, N.Y.: Cornell University Press, 1985), p. 76.

25. See her "Neptuno Alegórico," *OC,* 4:353–411, especially p. 356. The work is extensively discussed by Paz in *Sor Juana Inés de la Cruz,* pp. 212–241, and by Georgina Sabat de Rivers, "El Neptuno de Sor Juana: Fiesta barroca y programa político," *University of Dayton Review* (Spring 1983), 16(2):63–73.

26. For a discussion of allegory that stresses the act of understanding, see Angus Fletcher, *Allegory: The Theory of a Symbolic Mode* (Ithaca, N.Y.: Cornell University Press, 1964).

27. See for instance the *loa* for *El Divino Narciso, OC,* 4:20, in which she explains that the characters are only "abstract ones which paint what it is intended to say."

28. Sor Juana included this explanation of her methodology in the *Respuesta a Sor Filotea, OC,* 4:450.

29. Paz, *Sor Juana: Las trampas de la fe,* makes much of the hermetic influences on Kircher and reproduces several fascinating illustrations from his books. However, Kircher can be seen in another light as an infatigable retriever of information in the service of the Church.

30. Athanasius Kircher, *Itinerarium Exstaticum coeleste quo Mundi opificium, id est, Coelestis Expansi, siderumque tam errantium, quam fixorum natura, vires, propietatis, singulorumque compositio et structura ab infimo Telluris globo, usque ad ultime Mundi confinia per ficti raptus integumentum explorata, nova hypothesi exponitur ad veritatem. Interlocutoribus Cosmiele et Theodidacto* (Rome: Vitalis Mascardi, 1656), pp. 136–137. This work relates an imaginary journey through the cosmos which is entirely structured by these laws of resemblance. For a discussion of Kircher's philosophy, see Dino Pastine, *La Nascità dell' Idolatria: L'Oriente religiosa di Athanasius Kircher* (Florence: La nuova Italia, 1978). Pastine's book recognizes that Kircher's draws on hermetic philosophy but sees this as part of the missionary zeal and the wealth of information that had to be synthesized and which came from far-flung Jesuit missions in China and the New World. Kircher does not merely continue hermetic philosophy but appropriates it for the Church.

31. See Michel Foucault, *The Order of Things: An Archaeology of the Human Sciences* (New York: Vintage, 1973), pp. 17–44.

32. Gracián describes the conceit as "an act of understanding which expresses the correspondence that is found between objects." *Agudeza y arte de ingenio, en que se explican todos los modos y diferencias de concetos, con ejemplares escogidos de todo lo mas bien dicho, assí sacros como humano,* tercera impresión aumentada (Antwerp, 1669), p. 7.

33. For a discussion of Góngora and Sor Juana, see Alfonso Méndez Plancarte's introduction to *OC,* vol. 1. For an analysis of Góngora's poems, see John R. Beverley, *Aspects of Góngora's "Soledades"* (Amsterdam: Purdue University Monographs in Romance Languages, 1980). The poem,

which Sor Juana herself refers to as *Sueño,* was given the title *Primero Sueño* when published and was described as written "imitando a Góngora" in the Seville, 1692, edition of her works. Góngora's poem consists of two *Soledades* and is incomplete.

34. Lines from the ballad "Lo atrevido de un pincel," *OC,* 1:57, and from the ballad, "Señor: para responderos," *OC,* 1:138.

35. From John Milton, "Il Penseroso." However, Sor Juana's poem could not be more distant from Miltonian melancholy.

36. For the use of Greek allegory in the baroque, see Walter Benjamin, *The Origin of German Tragic Drama,* John Osborne, tr. (London: NLB, 1977), p. 223. Dario Puccini discusses allegory in Sor Juana's poetry in "Allegoria profonda e allegoria diffusa nella poesia di Sor Juana," in *Sor Juana Inés de la Cruz: Studio d'una personnalità del barroco messicano* (Rome: Edizione dell' Alenco, 1967), pp. 89–144; and Rafael Catalá, *Para una lectura americana del barroco mexicano: Sor Juana Inés de la Cruz y Siguenza y Góngora* (Minneapolis: Prisma Institute and Institute for the Study of Ideologies and Literature, 1987), pp. 99–148, discusses the bird images in the light of the poetic tradition of Mexico and as evidence of the syncretism of indigenous with classical culture.

37. As Paz and Sabat de Rivers have shown (see n. 25), Sor Juana was quite capable of the most recondite allusions to ancient deities. Catalá, *Para una lectura americana,* regards this as part of the syncretic culture of the New World. But, as Walter Benjamin points out in *The Origin of German Tragic Drama,* p. 223, these ancient gods were no longer dangerous and could now be recuperated as signs in the baroque system.

38. See Beverley, *Aspects of Góngora's Soledades,* p. 113.

39. For a discussion of Juan de Tarsis, Conde de Villamediana's *Fabula de Faetón,* see José María de Cossío, *Fábulas mitológicas en España* (Madrid: Espasa Calpe, 1952), pp. 429–438.

40. The cycle not only suggests that the poem is complete and that the idea that she planned a second poem is simply a red herring, but it also underlines her difference from the mystics. For discussions of Sor Juana and mysticism, see Asunción Lavrín, "Unlike Sor Juana? The Model Nun in the Religious Literature of Colonial Mexico," *University of Dayton Review* (Spring, 1983), 16(2):75–92.

41. Benjamin, *The Origin of German Tragic Drama,* p. 235.

42. "Al lector," *OC,* 1:4; not included in the first edition of the *Inundación Castálida.*

43. "Neptuno Alegórico," *OC,* 4:358.

44. *Carta de Sor Juana Inés de la Cruz a su Confesor: Autodefensa espiritual* (see n. 21).

45. Michel de Certeau, *Heterologies: Discourse on the Other,* Brian Massumi, tr., vol. 17 of *Theory and History of Literature* (Minneapolis: University of Minnesota Press, 1986), p. 206. De Certeau is comparing the news media with older versions of divine truth.

46. The sermon of Father Vieira is included in the appendix to *OC*, 4:673–694. According to Puccini, *Sor Juana Inés de la Cruz*, pp. 60–63, two volumes of Vieira's sermon's appeared in Spain in 1678 and were dedicated to Aguiar y Seijas, who was then Bishop of Michoacán. One of his sermons was published in Mexico on the suggestion of Aguiar y Seijas, and a sermon preached in San Jerónimo by Lic. Francisco Xavier Palavicino may well have been an answer to Sor Juana's refutation.

47. Raymond Cantil, *Prophétisme et messianisme dans l'oeuvre d'Antonio Vieira* (Paris: Ediciones hispanoamericanas, 1960).

48. Miguel de Torres, *Dechado de príncipes eclesiásticas que dibujó con su ejemplar y virtuosa vida el Ilmo. y Excmo. Sr. D. Manuel Fernández de Santa Cruz* (Madrid, 1722), p. 380, mentions the Archbishop's devotion to this saint who advocated practical piety in the world. Torres also claims that it was the Archbishop's letter that reformed Sor Juana so that she died in exemplary fashion (p. 421). Antonio Oviedo, however, would give Núñez de Miranda credit for this "miracle."

49. On the investment of authority and its relation to speech acts, see Pierre Bourdieu, *Ce que parler veût dire* (Paris: Fayard, 1982).

50. See Josefina Ludmer, "Las tretas del débil," in *La sartén por el mango,* Patricia Elena González and Eliana Ortega, eds. (Rio Piedras: Huracán, 1984), pp. 47–54.

51. Juan Díaz de Arce, *Compendium Operis*, pp. 21–30.

52. See Luis Martín, *Daughters of the Conquistadores: Women of the Viceroyalty of Peru* (Albuquerque: University of New Mexico Press, 1983), pp. 282–294.

53. Sor María Magdalena de Lorravaquio Muñoz, quoted in Muriel, *Cultura femenina novohispana*, pp. 320–321.

54. Michel de Certeau, *L'Ecriture de l'histoire* (Paris: Gallimard, 1975), pp. 284–287.

55. Josefina Ludmer, "Las tretas del débil," pp. 53–54.

56. Fray Luis Tineo de Morales, Aprobación, *Inundación Castálida,* pages unnumbered.

57. In a ballad in which she mocks the "Pens of Europe" who have praised her talents, Sor Juana marvels that they would direct their praises to an ignorant woman, "to an almost rustic abortion [*aborto*] of sterile fields which were made even more infertile by the fact that I was born there." The word "abortion" or "fetus" was commonly used, however, as an analogy for something incomplete. See *OC,* 1:159.

58. See Maravall, *Culture of the Baroque*; and Richard Morse, *El espejo de Próspero: Un estudio de la dialéctica del nuevo mundo* (Mexico City: Siglo XXI, 1982).

59. Benedict Anderson, *Imagined Communities: Reflections on the Origin and Spread of Nationalism* (London: Verso, 1986), p. 22.

60. "Sin tí, hasta mis discursos/parece que son ajenos," "Darte, Señora, las Pascuas," *OC,* 1:82.

61. See "Darte, Señora, las Pascuas," *OC*, 1:82. The standard gesture of obeisance—kissing the feet of those in power—always becomes an ingenious trope which draws attention to the skill of the poet. See, for example, *OC*, 1:70, which ends, "Doyle por ella a tus pies/mil besos en recompensa,/sin que parezca delito/pues quien da y besa, no peca."

62. "Lámina sirva el Cielo," *OC*, 1:171: "cálamos forme el Sol de sus luces;/ sílabas las Estrellas compongan."

63. See "Sor Juana et les Indiens" in Marie-Cécile Benassy-Berling, *Humanisme et religion chez Sor Juana Inés de la Cruz*, pp. 317–335.

64. See *OC*, vol. 4. Each group of villancicos included lyrics in a different style on the subject of the particular feast day, for instance, the Assumption. The "languages" Sor Juana used ranged from Latin verse to black and regional Spanish dialects and to poems in Nahuatl. These villancicos also included a mixture of high and low styles, verse that places the emphasis on word play, and praise poems. It is this very variety that is made possible by the ecumenical Church. See Elias L. Rivers, "Diglossia in New Spain," *University of Dayton Review* (Spring 1983) 16(2):5–7.

65. Marina Warner, *Alone of All Her Sex: The Cult of the Virgin Mary* (London: Pan Books, 1985), p. 254.

66. "Yo de mí sé decir que si fuera posible comutar las miserias de mi naturaleza humana con los privilegios y perfecciones de la angélica, perdiendo la relación que tenemos de parentesco con María Santísima, no lo admitiera, aunque pudiera, atento a este respeto y a lo que estimo y aprecio en toda mi alma el ser de su linaje." "Ejercicios de la Encarnación," *OC*, 4:500. Electa Arenal draws attention to this remarkable sentence in "Sor Juana Inés de la Cruz: Speaking the Mother Tongue," in *University of Dayton Review* (Spring 1983), 16(2):93–105.

67. María de Jesús de Agreda, *Vida de la Virgen María*, pp. 68–69.

68. Villancico 3, for the feast of the Assumption, 1676, 2:6: "La soberana Doctora/de las Escuelas divinas,/de que los Ángeles todos/deprenden sabiduría."

69. Villancico on the theme of the Incarnation, *OC*, 2:221. "¿Qué bien al mundo no ha dado / la Encarnación amorosa, / si aun la culpa fue dichosa / por haberla ocasionado.?"

70. "Ciñéndose al tálamo virginal de vuestras purísimas entrañas el que no cabe en la portentosa máquina de los Cielos" "Ejercicios de la Encarnación," *OC*, 4:505.

71. Paz, *Sor Juana Inés de la Cruz*, pp. 524–533, following Puccini, "Dalla crisi di Sor Juana alla crisi dell'ordine coloniale," *Sor Juana Inés de la Cruz*, pp. 49–69.

72. Warner, *Alone of All Her Sex*, p. 337. Julia Kristeva, in her article "Stabat Mater," in Susan Rubin Suleiman, ed., *The Female Body in Western Culture* (Cambridge: Harvard University Press, 1986), draws heavily on Warner, but uses the material to argue for a contemporary ethics appropriate to the second sex and based on motherhood.

3: THE POWER OF THE SPIDER WOMAN

1. See Josefina Muriel, *Los recogimientos de mujeres, respuesta a una problemática social novohispana* (Mexico City: UNAM, 1974).

2. John Frow, *Marxism and Literary History* (Cambridge: Harvard University Press, 1986), p. 178.

3. For some thoughts on this topic, see Gayatri Chakravorty Spivak, "A Literary Representation of the Subaltern: A Woman's Text from the Third World," *In Other Worlds: Essays in Cultural Politics* (New York and London: Methuen, 1987), pp. 241–268.

4. *Ana Rodríguez de Castro y Aramburu, Ilusa, Afectadora de Santos, Falsos Milagros y Revelaciones Divinas: Proceso Inquisitorial en la Nueva España (Siglos* XVIII Y XIX), prólogo de Dolores Bravo, transcripción de Alejandra Herrera (Mexico City: Universidad Autonoma Metropolitana, 1984). This is a selection of documents from the trial, and page numbers given parenthetically in text refer to this published edition. At one or two points in the argument, I have quoted from documents not included in the selection. These documents are in the Archivo General de la Nación (AGN, Ramo Inquisición, vol. 1358, exp. 14 o 16).

5. John Rajchman, *Michel Foucault: The Freedom of Philosophy* (New York: Columbia University Press, 1985), p. 70.

6. This is clear from the summary of the proceedings, which refer specifically to hysteria, to which Mexican women are said to be extremely prone. See *Ana Rodríguez de Castro*, p. 121.

7. María Dolores Bravo, "Del espacio de la historia al espacio de la ficción," preface to the published version of the trial, *Ana Rodríguez de Castro*, pp. 7–18. There is some confusion in this preface between rhetoric and literature. But, of course, precisely the point of discussing the trial is that it is not generically marked, although it does shed light on the way that subaltern cultures are formed.

8. One of the classical accounts of the symbolism of the pure and the impure is to be found in Mary Douglas, *Purity and Danger: An Analysis of Concepts of Pollution and Taboo* (London: Routledge and Kegan Paul, 1966). Obviously Ana contaminates and thus undermines the boundaries that determine identity.

9. Douglas, *Purity and Danger*, p. 145.

10. Juan Pedro Viqueira Albán, "Relajados o reprimidos?," book supplement to *La Jornada*, January 3, 1988, no. 155, pp. 5–6.

11. See Toribio Medina, *Historia del Santo Oficio de la Inquisición en México*, 2d ed., ampliada por Julio Jiménez Rueda (Mexico City: Ediciones Fuente Cultural, 1952). This book originally appeared in Santiago, Chile, in 1905 and was dedicated to Porfirio Díaz. See also Solange Alberro, "Herejes, Brujas y Beatas: Mujeres ante el Tribunal del Santo Oficio de la Inquisición en la Nueva España," included in *Presencia y transparencia: La mujer en la historia de México* (Mexico City: Colegio de

México, 1987), pp. 79–94, and by the same author, "La sexualidad manipulada en Nueva España: modalidades de recuperación y de adaptación frente a los Tribunales Eclesiásticos," in proceedings of the first symposium of Historia de Mentalidades, *Familia y Sexualidad en Nueva España* (Mexico City: Colegio de México, 1982), pp. 238–257.

12. There is an interesting account of the auto de fe of 1659, describing the procession and the officiants. See *Auto General de la Fe a que asistió presidiendo en nombre y representación de la Cathólica Magestad del Rey N. Señor Felipe Quarto (que Dios guarde) con singulares demostraciones de Religiosa y Christiana piedad, y ostentaciones de grandeza, su Virrey Governador, y Capitán General de esta Nueva España, el excellentíssimo Señor D. Francisco Fernández de la Cueva, celebrado en la Plaza mayor de la muy noble, y muy leal ciudad de México a lo 19 de noviembre de 1659 años.*

13. See Claire Guilhem, "La Inquisición y la devaluación del verbo femenino," pp. 171–207, in Bartolomé Bennassar, ed., *Inquisición española,* 2d ed. (Barcelona: Editorial Crítica, 1984). Guilhem points out that ilusas were women, that it was a category constituted for women who were described as *iludentes* ("illusioning" and ilusas or deluded). In Peru there was a veritable outbreak of "delusion," the most famous case being that of Angela de Carranza, who preached in friar's robes on the steps of the Cathedral. She is mentioned briefly by Luis Martín, *Daughters of the Conquistadores: Women of the Viceroyalty of Peru* (Albuquerque: University of New Mexico Press, 1983), pp. 298–299.

14. See Guilhem, "La Inquisición y la devaluación del verbo femenino," p. 194, where she states that what makes the "madness" of the ilusa dangerous is that people listen to her.

15. Guilhem, "La Inquisición y la devaluación del verbo femenino," p. 191.

16. The trial of Teresa Romero, who called herself Teresa de Jesús, has been transcribed as "El proceso de una seudo iluminada," *Boletín del Archivo General de la Nación,* 17 vols. (1649), 1:35–72, 2:217–242, 3:387–442. For the story of the child who seems to have been reared with her in prison, see 2:218–219.

17. "El proceso de un seudo iluminada," 3:411.

18. Marina Warner, *Alone of All Her Sex: The Cult of the Virgin Mary* (London: Pan Books, 1985).

19. "El proceso de una seudo iluminada," 1:65. Teresa was said to have played obscene games with an image of Christ and also to have pretended to be maimed.

20. AGN, vol. 1358, fol. 272.

21. AGN, vol. 1358, fol. 365.

22. AGN, vol. 1358, fol. 272.

23. AGN, vol. 1358, fol. 435. The Marqués de Castañiza declares that he has noted "un no sé qué, que me hace dudar de la verdad de lo mismo que se refiere." He shows himself to be an acute judge of character and

also not to be anxious to respond to Father Ynfantas' witch-hunting zeal: "En la Declarante he notado artificio y ficción en el modo de producirse, fingiendo por una parte mucho rubor y por otra descaro y desemboltura contraria a la verguenza que se aparentaba."

24. AGN, vol. 1358, fol. 436.

25. AGN, vol. 1358, fol. 436.

26. AGN, vol. 1358, fol. 279.

27. Serruto, described as "doctor and master," was one of those who had denounced her as an ilusa. According to Ana María de la Colina, he had spent fourteen days in purgatory for this before being taken out because of her prayers, and his ghost also haunted Licenciado Esquivel's house, asking her pardon while she was living there (p. 83).

28. The mention of *nahualismo* comes from the suspect evidence of María Encarnación Mora (p. 155). What is interesting is that it demonstrates the fear of popular indigenous lore filtering upward into the criollo population.

29. AGN, vol. 1358, fol. 119.

30. Ana's is a performance of which the script is the mystical fable now transposed from the inner theater of the self to the public theater of the streets.

31. Sor María de Jesús de Agreda, *Vida de la Virgen María* (Barcelona: Montaner Editores, 1899), pp. 75–85.

32. Michel Pêcheux, *Les Vérités de la Palice* (Paris: Maspero, 1975), pp. 144–145, offers the useful notion of "discursive formation" to demonstrate the investment of class power in language: "Nous apellerons des lors *formation discursive* ce qui, dans une formation idéologique donnée, c'est-à-dire a partir d'une position donnée une conjoncture donnee determinée par l'état de la lutte des classes, determiné *ce que peut et doit être dit* (articulé sous la forme d'une harangue, d'un sermon, d'un pamphlet, d'un exposé, d'un programme, etc.)." For a sociological definition of the investment of power in certain forms of address see Pierre Bourdieu, *Ce que parler veût dire* (Paris: Fayard, 1982).

33. See for instance AGN, vol. 1358, fol. 315. Juana Francisca López reports having seen Arumbura vomit blood with water which she said was Divine Blood.

34. Gabriel García Márquez, "Blacamán el bueno, vendedor de milagros," in *La increíble y triste historia de la cándida Erendira y de su abuela desalmada, Siete cuentos*, 4th ed. (Barcelona, Bruguera, 1981).

35. Esquivel, for instance, cites Le Brun, *Histoire critique des pratiques superstitieuses qui ont séduit les peuples et embarassé les scavans, avec la méthode et les principes pour discerner les effets naturels d'avec ceux qui ne sont pas* (Paris, 1702). Le Brun is anxious to show that there are physical causes for apparent supernatural phenomena. Esquivel's attempted physical explanations of Ana's "infirmity" reveal that demonic explanations were no longer convicing even to the clergy.

36. On the world turned upside down, see Peter Stallybrass and Allon White, *The Politics and Poetics of Transgression* (Ithaca, N.Y.: Cornell University Press, 1986), pp. 183–187.

4: SENSE AND SENSUALITY

1. Benedict Anderson, *Imagined Communities* (London: Verso, 1983), p. 19.

2. For a discussion of the role of the coffee house in the formation of bourgeois manners, see Peter Stallybrass and Allon White, *The Politics and Poetics of Transgression* (Ithaca, N.Y.: Cornell University Press, 1986), pp. 95–100.

3. Juan Rulfo, "Luvina," is included in the collection *El llano en llamas* (Mexico City: Fondo de Cultura Económica, 1953). An English translation is included in Juan Rulfo, *The Burning Plain and Other Stories*, George D. Schade, tr. (Austin: University of Texas Press, 1967), pp. 111–121. The story describes a government-appointed teacher going to a bleak town inhabited only by black-robed women for whom the idea of government is totally mysterious.

4. There are two useful articles on women in the nineteenth and early twentieth centuries: Françoise Carner, "Estereotipos femeninos en el siglo XIX," *Presencia y transparencia: La mujer en la historia de México* (Mexico City: El Colegio de México, 1987), pp. 95–109, which deals with the problem of periodization, and in the same volume, Carmen Ramos Escandón, "Señoritas Porfirianas: Mujer e ideología en el México progresista, 1880–1910," pp. 143–161. Nestor García Canclini, in *Culturas populares en el capitalismo* (Mexico City: Editorial Nueva Imagen, 1982), shows the disintegration of indigenous family arrangements in recent times.

5. One way of registering this is in the changing language and educational policies in Mexico as described by Shirley Brice Heath, *Telling Tongues: Language Policy in Mexico: Colony to Nation* (New York: Teacher's College Press, 1972). As Brice Heath shows, there was almost constant concern throughout the nineteenth century for the education of the Indian, yet very little in the way of concrete results before the Revolution of 1910.

6. Jean Franco, "En espera de una burguesía: La formación de la intelligentsia mexicana en la época de la Independencia," *Actas del VIII Congreso de la Asociación Internacional de Hispanistas* (Madrid: Istmo, 1986), pp. 1253–1268. See, for example, Charles A. Hale, *El liberalismo mexicano en la época de Mora, 1821–1853*, 3d ed. (Mexico City: Siglo XXI, 1978), p. 282, on the efforts of Estevan Antunano to instill the industrial spirit in Mexico.

7. This new interest in early childhood is registered in the many articles on the same subject that appeared in the *Diario de México*, which had

been founded with Viceregal approval in 1805. For a discussion of the situation of women at this time, see Silvia Marina Arrom, *The Women of Mexico City, 1790–1857* (Stanford: Stanford University Press, 1985), pp. 32–43. Arrom goes into the difference between the prescriptive literature mentioned in the first part of this chapter and the actual situation of women. See also Johanna S. R. Mendelson, "The Feminine Press: The View of Women in the Colonial Journals of Spanish America, 1790–1810," in Asunción Lavrín, ed., *Latin American Women: Historical Perspectives* (Westport, Conn.: Greenwood Press, 1978), pp. 198–218; and Jane Herrick, "Periodicals for Women in Mexico During the Nineteenth Century," *The Americas* (October 1957), 14(2):135–144.

8. It should be noted, however, that the number of subscribers was very small. The *Diario de México* is interesting because, along with reports of robberies and lost items, political articles, and letters from subscribers, the journal gave information on phases of the moon, the weather, and the major events of the liturgical calendar. See Ruth Wold, *El Diario de México: Primer cotidiano de Nueva España* (Madrid: Editorial Gredos, 1970).

9. See, for instance, "Diálogo entre la Coquetilla y su Doncella," *Diario de México*, January 3, 1806, no. 95. Many letters and articles were signed with pseudonyms so that it cannot be assumed that letters signed, for instance, "a widow from Querétero" were actually written by women, although in an article on this correspondent I worked on the assumption that the writer was a woman. See Jean Franco, "Cartas querentanas," *fem*, año 8 (Oct.–Nov. 1984), no. 36.

10. See, for instance, the preface to Lizardi, *El Periquillo Sarniento*, in which he registers the shift from aristocratic patronage to a market economy in which the moral integrity or nobility of the readership cannot be taken for granted. For a discussion of his readership, see Nancy Vogeley, "Defining the Colonial Reader: *El Periquillo Sarniento*," *PMLA* (October 1987): 102(5):784–800.

11. Quotations are from the edition *La educación de las mujeres o La Quijotita y su prima* (Mexico City: Feria del libro, 1942). The first volume of *La Quijotita* was sold by subscription and in *pliegos sueltos* (broadsheets) in 1818. A second volume appeared in 1819, but the third was not published in Lizardi's lifetime. The second edition, of 1832, was the first complete edition. See María del Carmen Ruíz Castañeda, who wrote the introduction to the edition published by Editorial Porrúa in 1967 and who argues that *La Quijotita* was based on the "Diálogo entre Cecilia y Feliciano sobre la educación de las niñas," which appeared in the *Semanario Económico de México*, January 1810, and was probably written by Juan Wenceslao Sánchez de la Barquera.

12. François de la Motte Fénélon, *Éducation des filles* (Paris, 1687).

13. Leonard Thomas, *Essai sur le caractère, les moeurs et l'esprit des femmes dans les differents siècles* (Paris, 1772), and Jean Baptiste

Blanchard, *L'École des Moeurs* (1775), translated into Spanish in 1797.

14. See Jean Bethke Elshtain, *Public Man, Private Woman: Women in Social and Political Thought* (Princeton, N.J: Princeton University Press, 1981) on Rousseau, especially pp. 148–170.

15. Fray Luis de León, *La perfecta casada,* first published in 1584, was translated into English by Alice Philena Hubbard as *The Perfect Wife* (Denton, Texas: The College Press, 1943).

16. Phillipe Ariès, *Centuries of Childhood: A Social History of Family Life,* R. Baldick, tr. (New York: Vintage Books, 1962).

17. Nicolás Pizarro Suárez, *La coqueta* (Mexico City: Premiá, 1982); and José Tomás Cuellar, *La linterna mágica,* ed. and prologue by Mauricio Magdaleno, 3d ed. (Mexico City: UNAM, 1973).

18. Mariano Azuela, *La mujer domada* (Mexico City: El Colegio Nacional, 1946).

19. *El Semanario de las Señoritas Mejicanas,* 3 vols. (Mexico City, 1841– 42) was described as being dedicated to the "scientific, moral, and literary education of the Fair Sex." The director of the National Museum, Isidro Rafael Gondra, was editor and wrote many of the articles as "I. G." The first issue appeared in 1841 in Mexico City, published by Vicente García Torres. *Panorama de las Señoritas* (Mexico City: Vicente García Torres, 1842), described itself as a "picturesque, scientific, and literary periodical." *La Semana de las Señoritas mexicanas,* was published by Juan R. Navarro in Mexico City, 1851–1852. All of them were short-lived. Much of the material was translated. For a survey of these and other women's periodicals, see Herrick, "Periodicals for Women in Mexico."

20. "De las facultades intelectuales," *Semanario de las Señoritas,* 3:164– 168. Women were warned not to be opinionated. Although I. G. addresses his subscribers in this article, many of the essays dealt with women as objects to be studied. In the *Calendario de las Señoritas Mejicanas* for 1840 and 1841 (Librería de Mariano Galván) that I studied, Mariano Galván repeatedly refers to women as "the fair sex" and urges that they should educate themselves. It is interesting that the only women whose accomplishments are reviewed in the *calendarios* are performers. Galván does not hesitate to recommend certain fashions as being in good taste.

21. *Semanario de las Señoritas Mejicanas,* 1:14–15. This first volume supposedly describes how the journal began after a discussion (between men) in a *tertulia.*

22. Frances Calderón de la Barca, *Life in Mexico,* Howard T. and Marion Hall Fisher, eds. (New York: Doubleday, 1966), p. 287.

23. The style of writing that was closely related to travel literature was *costumbrismo*—sketches of "manners" in which the subjects described were often members of the lower classes. In mid-century this was a genre frequently found in newspapers, and one of its exponents was Guillermo Prieto, who wrote under the pseudonym "Fidel." Mexican *costumbristas* imitated the style of the famous Spanish writer Mariano Larra, one of

the first in the Hispanic world to establish himself primarily through the periodical press. On the relation of travel writing to ethnography, see Mary Louise Pratt, "Field Work in Common Places," in James Clifford and George E. Marcus, eds., *Writing Culture: The Poetics and Politics of Ethnography* (Berkeley: University of California Press, 1986), pp. 27–50.

24. An anthology of Prieto's texts on love and marriage has been published as Guillermo Prieto, *El placer conyugal y otros textos similares,* Matraca, 2d series (Mexico City: Premiá, 1984), no. 6. An anthology of Payno's texts on women, love, and matrimony has been published as Manuel Payno, *Sobre mujeres, amores y matrimonios,* Matraca, 2d series (Mexico City: Premiá, 1984), no. 3.

25. See Concepción Lombardo de Miramón, *Memorias,* Felipe Teixidor, ed., 2 vols. (Mexico City: Porrúa, 1980).

26. Peter Bürger, *Theory of the Avant-Garde,* Michael Shaw, tr. (Minneapolis: University of Minnesota Press, 1984).

27. See Angel Rama, *Rubén Darío y el Modernismo* (Caracas: Biblioteca de la Universidad Nacional de Venezuela, 1970); Françoise Perús, *Literatura y Sociedad* (Mexico City: Siglo XXI, 1976).

28. On the relationship between Mexican and other Latin American Modernismos, see José Emilio Pacheco, introduction to *Antología del Modernismo, 1884–1921,* 2 vols. (Mexico City: UNAM, Biblioteca del estudiante universitario, 1970).

29. Gertrudis Gómez de Avellaneda (1814–1873), though born in Cuba, lived for most of her life in Spain. Her antislavery novel *Sab,* published in Spain, was not included in her complete works, since its antislavery message would have made her *persona non grata* in Cuba. For an overview, see Beth Miller, "Gertrude the Great," in Beth Miller, ed., *Women in Hispanic Literature: Icons and Fallen Idols* (Berkeley: University of California Press, 1976), pp. 201–214.

30. Juárez owed his education to Jesuits. He initiated a program of secular and free education, and at least one member of his cabinet, Ignacio Ramírez, urged bilingual education as a means of drawing the indigenous into political life. See Brice Heath, *Telling Tongues,* pp. 69–71.

31. Alicia Peralta de Mercado, "Asociaciones literarias en la época," *La vida y la cultura en Mexico al triunfo de la República en 1867* (Mexico City: Institución Nacional de Bellas Artes, 1968), pp. 105–168, gives an exhaustive list of literary associations from 1867 onward. One of the women who participated most actively in literary associations was Laureana Wright de Kleinhaus, who wrote a patriotic poem against the French occupation, "El 5 de mayo de 1862," included in José María Vigil, ed., *Poetisas mexicanas: Siglos XVI, XVII, XVIII y XIX* (Mexico City: UNAM, 1977), pp. 104–106. Peralta de Mercado quotes Altamirano's description of the spirit that prevailed in these meetings. It was like a "family party in which, intimate as brothers, poets try out their favorite songs. . . . The soldier remem-

bers his campaigns, the traveler his journeys and the exile returns with emotion to visit the tomb of his ancestors" (p. 111). On literary associations and cultural nationalism, see also José Luis Martínez, "México en busca de su expresión," in *Historia General de México* (Mexico City: El Colegio de México, 1976), 3:285–337.

32. Francisco Zarco, "Discurso sobre el objeto de la literatura," *Escritos Literarios,* René Avilés, ed. (Mexico City: Porrúa, 1980), p. 233.

33. Ignacio M. Altamirano, "Las veladas literarias," in *La literatura nacional,* José Luis Martínez, ed. (Mexico City: Porrúa, 1949) 1:16–18.

34. Ignacio Altamirano, "Carta a una poetisa," *Obras literarias completas* (Mexico City: Oasis, 1959), pp. 653–673. See especially pp. 672–673.

35. In his essays, "Las veladas literarias," for instance, Altamirano clearly favors the novel over other literary genres and "public" over private themes. The novel has a social role to fill since it bridges the gulf between the intellectual and the masses (p. 40). Love stories he finds potentially corrupting to youth (p. 37). In effect, no nineteenth-century novelist could possibly aspire to become a popular novelist given the enormously high rate of illiteracy.

36. José María Vigil, "La mujer mexicana," in *Poetisas mexicanas,* pp. lxviii–lxxviii. See especially pp. lxxiv–lxxv.

37. José María Vigil, *La Señora, Doña Isabel Prieto de Landázurri* (Mexico City, 1882). This was a published version of a paper read in the Mexican Academy. See especially pp. 102–103.

38. Luis Lara y Prado, *La prostitución en México* (Paris, Mexico City: Librería de la viuda de Ch. Bouret, 1908), pp. 252–253; and Ramón López Velarde, "Hormigas," *Zozobra* (1919), in *Poesía completa y el Minutero,* 2d ed. (Mexico City: Porrúa, 1957), pp. 185–186.

39. Stallybrass and White, *The Politics and Poetics of Transgression,* p. 145.

40. Federico Gamboa, *Santa* (Barcelona: Araluce, 1903). For a comment on this novel, see Margo Glantz, "*Santa* y la carne," in *La lengua en la mano* (Mexico City: Premiá, 1983), pp. 42–49.

41. Federico Gamboa, *Mi Diario,* 1st series (Mexico City: Eusebio Gómez de la Puente, Editor, 1910), p. 15.

42. Manuel Gutiérrez Nájera, "La novela de tranvía," *Cuentos frágiles* (Mexico City: Libro-Mex, Costa-Amic, 1955).

43. Manuel Gutiérrez Nájera, "En hora de calor," in *Cuentos completos* (Mexico City: Fondo de Cultura Económica, 1958), pp. 301–303. Margo Glantz, in "Cuerpo y clase," *La lengua en la mano,* pp. 37–41, has some amusing reflections on Manuel Payno's representation of the clothed and semiclothed female body according to social class.

44. Sylvia Molloy, "Dos lecturas del cisne: Rubén Darío y Delmira Agustini," pp. 57–69 in Patricia Elena González and Eliana Ortega, eds., *La sartén por el mango* (Rio Piedras, Puerto Rico: Ediciones Huracán, 1984).

45. María Enriqueta, a pen name. Her complete name is María Enriqueta Camarillo de Pereyra. See "Aspiración sencilla," *Album sentimental,* (Madrid: Espasa Calpe, 1926).

46. Laura Méndez de Cuenca, *Simplezas* (Mexico City: Premiá, 1982).

47. Gonzalo de Quesada, "En La exposición de Chicago. La mujer de México," originally published in *El Partido Liberal,* Mexico, September 13, 1893, and reprinted in Vigil, *Poetisas mexicanas,* pp. lxi–lxvii; see especially p. lxvi.

48. Ester Tapia, "Dos Almas," in Vigil, *Poetisas mexicanas,* pp. 93–96.

49. See Frank Bishop Putnam, "Teresa Urrea, 'The Saint of Cabora,' *Southern California Quarterly* (September 1963), 45(3):245–264.

50. Vicente Leñero's play *El juicio: El jurado de León Toral y la Madre Conchita* (Mexico City: Joaquín Mortíz, 1972) is based on the record of the trial of Obregón's assassin, José de León Toral, in which she was also accused as the intellectual author of the deed. Toral was executed and Madre Concha sent to prison where she married. She was released after twelve years, in 1940.

51. Octavio Paz, *The Labyrinth of Solitude,* Lysander Kemp, tr. (New York: Grove Press, 1961). A long-standing tradition of feminine struggle is outlined by Anna Macías, *Against All Odds: The Feminist Movement in Mexico to 1940* (Westport, Conn.: Greenwood Press, 1982).

52. See Angeles Mendieta Alatorre, *La mujer en la Revolución Mexicana* (Mexico City: Biblioteca Nacional de Estudios Históricos de la Revolución Mexicana, 1961), no. 25; and Shirlene Ann Soto, *The Mexican Woman: A Study of Her Participation in the Revolution, 1910–1940* (Palo Alto: R&E Research Associates, 1970).

5: BODY AND SOUL

1. See Angeles Mendieta Alatorre, *La mujer en la Revolución Mexicana* (Mexico City: Biblioteca Nacional de Estudios Históricos de la Revolución Mexicana, 1961), no. 25; and Shirlene Ann Soto, *The Mexican Woman: A Study of Her Participation in the Revolution, 1910–1940* (Palo Alto: R&E Research Associates, 1979).

2. See Anna Macías, *Against All Odds: The Feminist Movement in Mexico to 1940* (Westport, Conn.: Greenwood, 1982). For a tradition of feminist militancy, see "Feminismo en México: Antecedentes," *fem* (Oct.–Nov. 1983), vol. 8, no. 30.

3. See José Joaquín Blanco, *Se llamaba Vasconcelos: Una evocación crítica* (Mexico City: Fondo de Cultura Económica, 1977), pp. 98–102.

4. Quoted in Enrique Krauze, *Caudillos culturales en la Revolución Mexicana* (Mexico City: Siglo XXI, 1976), p. 157.

5. José Joaquín Blanco, *Se llamaba Vasconcelos,* p. 110.

6. Gabriela Mistral, introduction to *Lecturas para mujeres* (Mexico City: Departamento de Educación, 1924), p. 12.

7. Mistral, introduction to *Lecturas para mujeres*, p. 16. In an essay, "A la mujer mexicana," included in Gabriela Mistral, *Croquis mexicanos* (Mexico City: Costa-Amic, 1956? [undated]), she tells women not to turn their eyes toward "the crazy women of this century" (i.e., feminists); their role is to be collaborators, "the branch that holds up the hero who is like a red fruit" (pp. 40–41).

8. José Vasconcelos, *Ulíses criollo,* in *Obras completas,* vol. 1 (Mexico City: Libreros Mexicanos Unidos, 1957). Volume 1 of *Obras completas* includes the first three parts of his four-part autobiography, *Ulíses criollo, La tormenta, El desastre.* The fourth part, *El proconsulado,* is included in *Obras completas,* vol. 2, 1958.

9. Quetzalcóatl is the plumed serpent hero-god who left his people promising to return.

10. Vasconcelos, *Ulíses criollo,* p. 290.

11. Bertram D. Wolfe, *The Fabulous Life of Diego Rivera,* (New York: Stein and Day, 1969), p. 95. Renato Leduc's film *Frida* captures this same sense of size.

12. Diego praised Frida's painting in a conversation with Raquel Tibol, saying that "it was the first time in the history of art that a woman had expressed with absolutely naked and we might even say calmly ferocious sincerity those general and particular facts *particular to women*" (my emphasis). Diego's generous appraisal was thus somewhat double-edged. See Raquel Tibol, *Frida Kahlo: Una vida abierta* (Mexico City: Editorial Oasis, 1985), p. 96. As for Tina Modotti, who became a Communist militant, she was painted nude by Diego and photographed nude by Weston in interestingly different styles though in both of them the eyes are closed or shadowed. On the relation between Kahlo's painting and her personal life, Olivier Debroise, *Figuras en el trópico: Plástica Mexicana* (Mexico City: Oceano, 1984), pp. 166–176, takes a critical view of the painting as self-constitution. On the role of photography and the spectacle in sexual liberation, see Carlos Monsivais, *Escenas de pudor y liviandad* (Mexico City: Grijalbo, 1988).

13. On women's sexuality, see Jacques Lacan, "God and the Jouissance of the Woman," in *Feminine Sexuality: Jacques Lacan and the Ecole Freudienne,* Juliet Mitchell and Jacqueline Rose, eds, Jacqueline Rose, tr. (New York: Pantheon, 1982), pp. 137–148.

14. For a discussion of the National Palace murals in the context of Mexican painting, see Justino Fernández, *A Guide to Mexican Art,* Joshua C. Taylor, tr. (Chicago: University of Chicago Press, 1969), pp. 159–160.

15. The "recurring self-portraits" is a phrase used by Diego Rivera. See Tibol, *Frida Kahlo,* and Hayden Herrera, *Frida: A Biography of Frida Kahlo* (New York: Harper and Row, 1983), p. 260.

16. The paintings *Memory* (1937) and *Remembrance of an Open Wound* (1938) refer to Diego's affair with Frida's sister. See Herrera, *Frida,* pp. 189–191, where she attributes *A Few Small Nips* to Frida's bitterness. For self-mutilation, see particularly the painting *The Broken Column,* in which

her half-clothed figure faces the viewer, her body slit from waist to throat. Inside the body a crumbling Greek pillar is inserted. In *Without Hope* she is spewing out her internal organs onto a ladder over a bed. In *Tree of Hope* a clothed Frida bearing a flag and a surgical brace is sitting beside the operating table on which a half-naked Frida, back turned, shows the surgical stitches on her back.

17. *Moses* was commissioned by José Domingo Lavín in 1945, and is now owned by Marilyn O. Lubetkin. See Herrera, *Frida*, pp. 326–328; and Tibol, *Frida Kahlo*, pp. 58–62.

18. On the muralists, see Fernández, *A Guide to Mexican Art*, pp. 151–176.

19. See Otto Rank, *The Myth of the Birth of the Hero: A Psychological Interpretation of Mythology*, F. Robbins and Smith Ely Jelliffe, trs. (New York: Journal of Nervous and Mental Diseases Publishing Company, 1914); and Sigmund Freud, *Moses and Monotheism*, Katherine Jones, tr. (New York: Vintage Books, 1955). In one of the few feminist discussions of the text, Rosalind Coward, *Patriarchal Precedents: Sexuality and Social Relations* (London, Routledge and Kegan Paul, 1983), pp. 214–220, describes it as a "generally confused text," but does point out that the advance represented by monotheism for Freud is analogous to the recognition of paternity as a social institution. A similar point is made by Jonathan Culler in the chapter "Reading as a Woman," in *On Deconstruction: Theory and Criticism After Structuralism* (Ithaca, N.Y.: Cornell University Press, 1982), pp. 59–61.

20. Frida's letter describing the painting is reproduced in full in Tibol, *Frida Kahlo*, pp. 58–62.

21. Herrera, *Frida*, p. 320, quotes an amusing letter in which Frida tries to find something out about the "great" women of Mexican history because she was commissioned to do their portraits for the dining room of the National Palace. She never undertook the project, however.

22. For Lacan, the Other is that fictional construct which has the power to fill the lack. See "The Meaning of the Phallus," in *Feminine Sexuality*, p. 81. On Freud's "dream of symmetry," i.e., of sexual development in girls and boys, see Luce Irigaray, *Speculum of the Other Woman*, Gillian C. Gill, tr. (Ithaca, N.Y.: Cornell University Press, 1985), pp. 13–129.

23. The articles are collected in Antonieta Rivas Mercado, *La campaña de Vasconcelos*, Luis Mario Schneider, ed. (Mexico City: Oasis, 1985). Quotations from this work will be identified in the text by the short title *La campaña*; page numbers refer to this edition. The letters to Rodríguez Lozano are collected as Antonieta Rivas Mercado, *87 Cartas de amor y otros papeles*, 2d ed. (Mexico City: Universidad Veracruzana, 1981). Quotations from this collection are identified by the title *Cartas*; page numbers refer to this edition.

Rodríguez Lozano was a solitary figure, isolated by choice from the muralist movement, from which marginal position "he is able to judge and condemn a society, and an artistic world that he detests," notes

Debroise, *Figuras en el trópico,* p. 73. For the influence of a previous affair on Vasconcelos' "mysticism," see Enrique Krause, "Pasión y contemplación en Vasconcelos," *Vuelta* (May 1983), 8(78).

24. See Luis Mario Schneider, "Antonieta Rivas Mercado: Una mujer que puso condiciones al destino," introduction to Antonieta Rivas Mercado, *La campaña,* p. 10.

25. Antonieta Rivas Mercado, "Páginas arrancadas," in *Cartas,* pp. 129–135.

26. Schneider, "Antonieta Rivas Mercado," p. 16. The *Contemporáneos* group were poets and playwrights and took their name from the journal of that name. They resisted pressure to produce socially relevant writing, being generally more interested in inner experience.

27. The article was included in a special supplement on Mexico and published by *El Sol* (Madrid) in February of 1928. It is quoted by Schneider, "Antonieta Rivas Mercado," pp. 12–14.

28. Vasconcelos, *El proconsulado,* p. 121.

29. José Vasconcelos, *La flama: Los de arriba en la Revolución: Historia y tragedia* (Mexico City and Tlalpan: Editorial Continental, 1960). This is both a reworking and updating of the autobiography—much of it referring to himself in the third person—and an anthology of miscellaneous material—his opinions on historical characters and imaginary dialogues.

30. The campaign accounts, which appeared in Vasconcelos' journal *La antorcha* and were included in *La campaña,* were then quoted *in extenso* in Vasconcelos' autobiography.

31. Huitzilipochtili was the Aztec war god to whom defeated warriors were sacrificed. One of the chapters of *El proconsulado* has the title "Quetzalcóatl versus Huichilobos."

32. See Vasconcelos, *La flama,* p. 202. Mauricio Magdaleno, *Palabras perdidas,* 2d ed. (Mexico City: Porrúa, 1976), p. 146, describes Antonieta's participation in the campaign in rather sarcastic terms. But he also gives a good idea of the dangers and violence of the latter part of the campaign.

33. Vasconcelos, *El proconsulado,* p. 240.

34. Federico García Lorca, *Catorce cartas* (Madrid: 1987), p. 82.

35. Anita Brenner was the author of *Idols Behind Altars* (New York: Payson and Clarke, 1929) and a promoter of the muralists.

36. Vasconcelos, *La flama,* p. 214.

37. Vasconcelos, *El proconsulado,* p. 294.

38. The letter is reproduced by Vasconcelos in *El proconsulado,* pp. 301–307.

39. Antonieta Rivas Mercado, diary entry, quoted in Vasconcelos, *La flama,* pp. 243–246; also in *Cartas,* pp. 109–112.

40. The article was "La nueva psicología: Freud juzgado por James Oppenheim," *La antorcha* (April 1931), 1(1):20–25.

41. This is mentioned in her diary; *Cartas,* pp. 109–112. She also wrote

a note to Pani, which is included in the colophon to *Cartas* with a discussion of the suicide.

42. Vasconcelos, "Excursión imaginaria" (El purgatorio), *La flama,* pp. 256–263.
43. Vasconcelos, *El proconsulado,* pp. 474–475.
44. Vasconcelos, *El proconsulado,* p. 476.
45. The whole scene is described in a chapter entitled "En el reino de la sombra" (In the Kingdom of Shadows), *El proconsulado,* pp. 491–496.
46. Vasconcelos, *El proconsolado,* p. 494.
47. Vasconcelos, *La flama,* pp. 120–123.

6: ON THE IMPOSSIBILITY OF ANTIGONE AND THE INEVITABILITY OF LA MALINCHE

1. Nancy C. M. Hartsock, *Money, Sex and Power: Toward a Feminist Historical Materialism* (New York and London: Longman, 1983).
2. Mario Vargas Llosa, *The Real Life of Alejandro Mayta,* Alfred McAdam, tr. (New York: Farrar, Straus and Giroux, 1986).
3. Carlos Fuentes, *Where the Air Is Clear,* Sam Hilman, Jr. (New York: T. Obolensky, 1960).
4. Polinices was one of the sons of Oedipus who fought against Thebes. His brother Eteocles, who defended Thebes, is accorded honorable rites. Creon decrees that Polinices "is to have no grave, no burial, No mourning from anyone; it is forbidden./He is to be left unburied, left to be eaten/ By dogs and vultures, a horror for all to see"; Sophocles, *Antigone,* in *The Theban Plays* (London: Penguin Books, 1947). The pioneer discussion of the Polinices theme in contemporary Latin American literature is Pedro Lastra's essay on García Márquez' first novel, *La hojarasca:* "La tragedia como fundamento estructural, *La hojarasca,"* in *Relecturas hispanoamericanas* (Santiago de Chile: Editorial Universitaria, 1987).
5. See Jean Franco, "El pasquín y los diálogos de los muertos: Discursos diacrónicos en *Yo el Supremo,"* in Saúl Sosnowski, ed., *Augusto Roa Bastos y la producción americana* (Buenos Aires: La Flor, 1986), pp. 181–196.
6. George Steiner, *Antigones: How the Antigone Legend Has Endured in Western Literature, Art, and Thought* (Oxford: Clarenden Press, 1986), pp. 108–109. Lacan comments on Antigone in "L'Etique de la psychanalyse," but because this is an unpublished typescript it has not been much discussed. However, his interest in *Antigone* corresponds to the obsession with the death drive in his later writing. Jacques Derrida discusses Antigone in *Glas,* John P. Leavey, Jr. and Richard Rand, trs. (Lincoln, Neb. and London: University of Nebraska Press, 1986); see especially pp. 166–175.
7. Steiner, *Antigones,* p. 34 interprets Hegel's position thus: "the rites

of burial, with their literal re-enclosure of the dead in the place of earth and in the shadow-sequence of generations which are the foundation of the familial, are the particular task of woman. Where this task falls upon a sister, where a man has neither mother nor wife to bring him home to the guardian earth, burial takes on the highest degree of holiness."

8. Tzvetan Todorov, *La Conquête de l'Amérique: La Question de l'autre* (Paris: Seuil, 1982), pp. 106–107; Georges Baudot, "Malintzín, L'Irregulière," in *Femmes des Amériques*, Actes du Colloque International Toulouse (Toulouse: Université de Toulouse-Le Mirail, 1986), pp. 19–29. See also Rachel Phillips, "Marina/Malinche: Masks and Shadows," in Beth Miller, ed., *Women in Hispanic Literature: Icons and Fallen Idols* (Berkeley: University of California Press, 1983), pp. 97–114.

9. Octavio Paz, *The Labyrinth of Solitude*, Lysander Kemp, tr. (New York: Grove Press, 1961), p. 86.

10. I am aware that this community is mythic. For a discussion of the development of the myth, see Ruth Finnegan, *Oral Poetry: Its Nature, Significance and Social Context* (New York: Cambridge University Press, 1977), especially pp. 36–41.

11. Jean Franco, "The Utopia of a Tired Man," in *Social Text*, (Fall 1981), 4:52–78.

12. See especially Carlos Fuentes, *Terra Nostra*, Margaret Sayers Peden, tr. (New York: Farrar, Straus and Giroux, 1976) and Mario Vargas Llosa, *Historia de Mayta* (Barcelona: Seix Barral, 1984).

13. Teresa de Lauretis has a detailed discussion of the positioning of women in both classical narrative and film narrative; see "Desire in Narrative," pp. 102–157, in *Alice Doesn't: Feminism, Semiotics, Cinema* (Bloomington: Indiana University Press, 1984).

14. Elena Garro, *Los recuerdos del porvenir* (Mexico City: Joaquín Mortíz, 1963), was translated into English by Ruth L. C. Simms as *Recollections of Things to Come* (Austin: University of Texas Press, 1969). For an overview of Garro's writing, see Gabriela Mora, "A Thematic Exploration of the Works of Elena Garro," in Yvette E. Miller and Charles M. Tatum, eds., *Latin American Women Writers: Yesterday and Today*, in *Latin American Literary Review* (1977), pp. 91–97. According to Mora, the novel was written as early as 1950. See also Frank Dauster, "Elena Garro y sus recuerdos del porvenir," *Journal of Spanish Studies: Twentieth Century* (1980), 8:57–65.

15. Paz, *The Labyrinth of Solitude*, pp. 35–36.

16. Fredric Jameson, in *The Political Unconscious: Narrative as a Socially Symbolic Act* (Ithaca, N.Y.: Cornell University Press, 1981), p. 113, comments that Northrup Frye's typology of genres includes romance as one in which the protagonists are "marginalized," being either slaves or women, but he leaves it at that. The reason for women's identification with characters in popular romance has been discussed by many feminist critics. See for instance Tania Modleski, *Loving with a Vengeance: Mass Produced Fantasies for Women* (Hamden, Conn.: Archon Books, 1982).

17. Jean Meyer, *La Cristiada,* 2 vols., 1st ed. (Mexico City: Siglo XXI, 1974). The comment is made in the bibliography, 1:404.

18. General Obregón, in alliance with Venustiano Carranza, was on the victorious side in the revolutionary war, having turned against and defeated his former allies, Pancho Villa and Emiliano Zapata, the peasant leader of Morelos.

19. "Actant" refers to the deep structure of narrative which generates surface "actors" or characters, according to A. J. Greimas, *Sémantique structurelle* (Paris: Larousse, 1971).

20. Sandra M. Gilbert and Susan Gubar, *The Madwoman in the Attic: The Woman Writer and the Nineteenth-Century Literary Imagination* (New Haven: Yale University Press, 1979), p. 605.

21. See Carola García Calderón, *Revistas femeninas: La mujer como objeto de consumo* (Mexico City: El Caballito, 1980).

22. See Mora, "A Thematic Exploration of the Works of Elena Garro."

23. Rosario Castellanos, "Meditación en el umbral," included in the anthology of the same name, p. 73, and also included in *Poesía no eres tú: Obras poética 1948–1971* (Mexico City: Fondo de Cultura Económica, 1972). For a discussion of Castellanos and younger women poets, see Oscar Wong, "La mujer en la poesía mexicana," in Norma Klahn and Jesse Fernández, eds., *Lugar de encuentro: Ensayos críticos sobre poesía mexicana actual* (Mexico City: Katun, 1987). For a sympathetic and personal account of Castellanos's feminism, see Elena Poniatowska, prologue to *Meditación en el umbral: Antología poética* (Mexico City: F.C.E. 1983), in which she includes an autobiographical article by Castellanos which sums up the isolation of her childhood in Chiapas, the traumatic death of her brother, who was the favorite of the family, her illness from tuberculosis, her work among the Indians, her marriage at the age of thirty-three—a marriage which she says was monogomous on her part and polygamous on her husband's part—and the birth of three children, two of whom died. Though she was made Mexican ambassador to Israel, Castellanos was underrated by critics. She died tragically, electrocuted when lighting a lamp in her home in Tel Aviv in 1974. Elena Poniatowsksa dedicated another essay to her in ¡*Ay vida: no me mereces!* (Mexico City: Joaquín Mortíz, 1985), pp. 45–132. A discussion of her feminist views and her work is also to be found in Marta Robles, *La sombra fugitiva. Escritoras en la cultura nacional* (Mexico City: UNAM. 1987), 2:147–191. See also María Rosa Fiscal, *La imagen de la mujer en la narrative de Rosario Castellanos* (Mexico City: UNAM, 1980); and Maureen Ahern and Mary Seale Vásquez, Annotated Bibliography, in *Homenaje a Rosario Castellanos* (Valencia: Albatross, 1980), pp. 127–174. Castellanos briefly summarized the story of her literary apprenticeship and career in *Confrontaciones: Los narradores ante el público* (Mexico City: Joaquín Mortíz, 1966), pp. 89–98.

24. Rosario Castellanos, "Pasaporte," *Poesía no eres tú,* p. 335.

25. Georg Lukács, *The Historical Novel,* Hannah and Stanley Mitchell, trs. (London: Merlin Press, 1962). For Lukács, the protagonists of the historical novel were not necessarily world historical characters but rather "typical" characters who united specificity with a significant relationship to the historical forces of the period.

26. Joseph Sommers, "Literatura e historia: Las contradicciones ideológicas de la ficción indigenista," *Revista de Crítica Literaria,* Lima, (1989), pp. 9–39.

27. Rosario Castellanos, in a letter to Gastón García Cantú, quoted in Robles, *La sombra fugitiva,* 2:176.

28. Lázaro Cárdenas, who was president from 1934 to 1940, nationalized petroleum and carried out extensive land reforms, thus putting into effect one of the demands of the revolutionaries who had fought in the 1910–1917 revolution.

29. Most accounts of the Chiapas uprising are based on Vicente Piñeda, *Historia de las sublevaciones indígenas habidas en el estado de Chiapas* (Mexico City: Tipografía del Gobierno, 1888). See for instance Leticia Reina, *Las rebeliones campesinas en México 1819–1906,* 2d ed. (Mexico City: Siglo XXI, 1984), pp. 45–57. Contemporary documents quoted by Leticia Reina make clear the racial hostility behind accusations of Indian barbarism. For a revision of the official account which shows that the Indians were the victims rather than the perpetrators of the massacres and that the crucifixion was an invention, see Jan Rus, "Whose Caste War? Indians, Ladinos, and the Chiapas 'Caste War' of 1869," in Murdo J. Macleod and Robert Wasserstrom, eds., *Spaniards and Indians in Southeastern Mesoamerica: Essays on the History of Ethnic Relations* (Lincoln: University of Nebraska Press, 1983), pp. 127–168.

30. Ricardo Pozas, *Chamula,* 2 vols. (Mexico City: Instituto Nacional Indigenista, 1977).

31. Nelson Reed, *The Caste War of Yucatan* (Stanford: Stanford University Press, 1964).

32. Reed, *The Caste War of Yucatan,* pp. 139–140.

33. Robles, *La sombra fugitiva,* 2:174.

34. Throughout the remainder of this chapter, page numbers in the text refer to Rosario Castellanos, *Oficio de tinieblas* (Mexico City: Joaquín Mortíz, 1962). The novel has not been translated into English. Castellanos' first novel, *Balún Canán,* was translated by Irene Nicholson as *The Nine Guardians* (London: Gollancz, 1961).

35. For another perspective, see Stacey Schlau, "Conformity and Resistance to Enclosure: Female Voices in Rosario Castellanos' *Oficio de tinieblas* (The Dark Service)," *Latin American Literary Review* (Spring-Summer 1984), 12(24):45–57.

36. Fredric Jameson is responsible for the sweeping generalization that the Third World novel takes the form of national allegory. This can be debated, but it is true that realist novels generally deploy characters who

stand in for different forces within the nation. See Fredric Jameson, "Third World Literature in the Era of Multinational Capitalism," *Social Text* (Fall 1986), 15:65–88.

7: OEDIPUS MODERNIZED

1. See Carlos Monsivais, "Landscape, I've Got the Drop on You!" (On the Fiftieth Anniversary of Sound Film in Mexico), *Studies in Latin American Popular Culture* (1985), 4:236–246.

2. Teresa de Lauretis, *Alice Doesn't: Feminism, Semiotics, Cinema* (Bloomington: Indiana University Press, 1984).

3. García Riera, *Historia documental del cine mexicano: Época sonora* (Mexico City: Edición Era, 1963). The first three volumes cover the period from the origins of sound cinema up to the period in question.

4. Peter Stallybrass and Allon White, *The Politics and Poetics of Transgression* (Ithaca, N.Y.: Cornell University Press, 1986), p. 194.

5. See Jochen Schulte-Sasse, foreword to Peter Bürger, *Theory of the Avant-Garde*; Michael Shaw, tr. (Minneapolis: University of Minnesota Press, 1984), p. xxviii.

6. El Indio Fernández can definitely be described as an *auteur*. Although a womanizer, he liked women to be pure on the screen and to wear braids and little girl dresses. See Adela Fernández, *El Indio Fernández: Vida y mito* (Mexico CIty: Panorama Editorial, 1986).

7. See Anna Macías, *Against All Odds: The Feminist Movement in Mexico to 1940* (Westport, Conn.: Greenwood Press, 1982).

8. Benito Juárez is regarded as one of the founders of modern Mexico, but the film clearly revises the anticlerical policy that he helped to initiate.

9. A film that depends on portraiture is *Laura,* but more often it is a photograph rather than a painting that stands in for representation. A good example is *The Shining,* which plays on the idea of repetition and mechanical reproduction, which are also associated with death. The final shot tracks into Jack Nicholson in the foreground of a photograph taken twenty or thirty years before he was born. One of the most famous Mexican films, *María Candelaria* with Dolores del Rio, is a tragedy that begins with the painting of an indigenous woman in the nude.

10. Laura Mulvey, "Visual Pleasure and Narrative Cinema," *Screen* (Autumn 1975), 16(3):6–18. See also de Lauretis' discussion of the look in *Alice Doesn't,* pp. 138–157.

11. Quotations are from the script in English. See Luis Buñuel, *"The Exterminating Angel," "Nazarín" and "Los olvidados,"* Nicholas Fry, tr. (New York: Simon and Schuster, 1972).

12. See Francisco Aranda, *Luis Buñuel: A Critical Biography* (New York: Da Capo Press, 1976), p. 137.

13. Buñuel, in an interview with Bazin, said that although he regarded *Los olvidados* as a film with a social argument, it still bore traces of the

love of the "instinctive and irrational" (Aranda, *Luis Buñuel,* p. 138). There was clearly some sort of struggle between Buñuel's anarchistic views and those of the government, which in Mexico subsidized the film industry.

14. See Octavio Paz, "El poeta Buñuel," in *Las peras del olmo* (Barcelona: Seix Barral, 1971), pp. 183–187. Paz stresses the archetypal significance of both male and female characters.

15. Coatlicue is the Aztec goddess of fertility and death.

16. De Lauretis, *Alice Doesn't,* pp. 138–157.

17. Quotations in the remainder of this chapter that are followed by page numbers are from Oscar Lewis, *The Children of Sánchez: Autobiography of a Mexican Family* (New York: Vintage Books, 1963). For details of the controversy over the first Spanish translation, see the "nota preliminar" which prefaces *Los hijos de Sánchez* (Mexico City: Grijalbo, 1982). The first translation was published by Fondo de Cultura Económica in 1964, then withdrawn after criticism from official organizations. The head of Fondo de Cultura, Orfila, resigned over the censorship, which became a national scandal when Carlos Fuentes and other prominent writers joined the protest. On the other hand, Mexicans were offended at being made the object of a North American study of this kind, and a satire, "The Children of Jones," describing an American family, was purportedly circulated.

18. I have used the pseudonyms that Oscar Lewis employed. The father, whom he called "Jesús Sánchez," was killed by a hit-and-run driver on January 5, 1987. The identities of family members, which Oscar Lewis had tried to protect, had already been revealed by the son "Manuel," who had sold the story to a Mexican paper and was interviewed under his own name by Patrick Oster. In the newspaper article Consuelo is described as "the most educated member of the family." Manuel and the daughter Lewis called "Marta" both told Lewis that she was a first-class "bitch." She was out of touch with the family when her father died (*San José Mercury,* January 21, 1987). The name of the *vecindad,* the multifamily dwelling in which the children grew up, was also changed by Lewis from Casa Blanca to "Casa Grande." The Casa Blanca was entirely destroyed by the 1985 earthquake and is now razed. However, it is interesting that the neighborhood, which was badly damaged in the earthquake, showed a remarkable amount of initiative and mutual support during the crisis that followed.

19. Oscar Lewis, *A Death in the Sánchez Family* (New York: Vintage Books, 1963).

20. André Gunder Frank, *Capitalism and Underdevelopment in Latin America* (New York: Monthly Review Press, 1969) is particularly associated with dependency theory, whose validity has, in turn, been challenged. But in the historical context, dependency theory can be seen as the countertheory to "modernization."

21. This was the era of "development" theory.

22. Lewis' material is now held by the Library of the University of Illinois, Champaign-Urbana. It includes the tapes of the interviews, transcripts, and material written by Consuelo at Lewis' request. Much of the editing of the work was done by Ruth Lewis.

23. For instance, in Interview 1 (1957–1961), Lewis Archive, box no. 131, series no. 15/2/20, Lewis asks, "Do you remember when you lost money with Robert when he went to buy a record player or something and cheated you?" Lewis frequently asks this kind of question, which directs Consuelo toward the topic of dissidence within the family. In the same interview, Lewis asks if she has heard a rumor in the neighborhood that her father had tried to seduce one of her aunts. She is also asked to comment on what kind of character a man or woman needs to move from the lower to the lower middle class.

24. Oscar Lewis explains something of his method in the introduction to *The Children of Sánchez*, p. xix. He also says that the Sánchez family was one of a random sample of seventy-one families selected for study in the Casa Grande.

25. Consuelo had been asked to comment on her religious beliefs. The transcript is in box 131 of the archives. The material relating to Consuelo is very diverse. Apart from the original tapes, there are transcripts of the tapes, English translation, essays she wrote answering questions from Lewis, and an autobiographical essay, much of which was incorporated into the book.

26. Quoted by Lewis, *A Death in the Sánchez Family,* p. 34. In one of her essays on adolescent ideals and models, Consuelo says she wants to be useful to her family and if she is useful, it is thanks to Oscar and Ruth Lewis. She writes for them.

27. Quoted by Lewis, *A Death in the Sánchez Family,* p. 67.

28. Jean-François Lyotard, *The Postmodern Condition: A Report on Knowledge,* in *Theory and History of Literature,* 10:18–23 (Minneapolis: University of Minnesota Press, 1986).

29. See Kaja Silverman, "Suture," in *The Subject of Semiotics* (New York: Oxford University Press, 1983).

30. Subsequent quotations that are not followed by page numbers are from the miscellaneous material in the Lewis archive, box 131.

31. Lewis specifically asked Consuelo to comment on her sister.

32. Consuelo was specifically asked by the Lewises to respond to the question, "What kind of character is needed in a man or woman for them to rise from the lower classes to the lower middle class?" In an interview she speaks of a dream she didn't like in which she was by the side of a cascade but afraid to get wet. She is about to throw herself in when she wakes. This dream and others correspond to a recurrent metaphor of the *remolino* or whirlpool, which she also uses to describe moments of self-forgetfulness and which suggests her sense of losing identity. In another of the whirlpool dreams, she is surrounded by men in lines, some dressed

in red and others in white, who circle around her until they disappear and she is left alone on the street. In Lewis archive, box 131.

33. There are several of these mini-dramas, as well as some of Consuelo's own inner stream of consciousness, among the transcriptions in the archive. It is not clear whether it was her idea to present things in this way or whether Lewis himself suggested it.

34. In Lewis, *A Death in the Sánchez Family*, p. 36.

8: REWRITING THE FAMILY

1. Elena Poniatowska, *La noche de Tlatelolco* (Mexico City: Era, 1971), and *Hasta no verte, Jesús mío* (Mexico City: Era, 1969). For the latter I have given as the title in English the projected title of a translation that has not been published at the time of writing. Charles M. Tatum, in his article "Elena Poniatowska's *Hasta no verte, Jesús mío*," translates the title as "Until I See You, Dear Jesus," in Yvette E. Miller and Charles M. Tatum, eds., *Latin American Women Writers: Yesterday and Today,* in *Latin American Literary Review* (1977), pp. 49–58.

2. Octavio Paz, *El arco y la lira* (Mexico City: Fondo de Cultura Económica, 1956).

3. Carlos Fuentes, *Aura,* 2d ed. (Mexico City: Era, 1964); in English (same title), Lysander Kemp, tr. (New York: Farrar, Straus and Giroux, 1965).

4. Ricardo Pozas, *Juan Pérez Jolote,* 5th ed. (Mexico City: Fondo de Cultura Económica, 1965).

5. Elena Poniatowska, *Fuerte es el silencio* (Mexico City: Era, 1980).

6. Unpublished paper by Elena Poniatowska. It is interesting to contrast Poniatowska's method with a more conventional oral history project; see Griselda Vegas Muñoz, *Emilia, una mujer de Jiquilpan* (Mexico City: Centro de Estudios de la Revolución Mexicana "Lázaro Cárdenas" A.C., 1984).

7. Unpublished paper by Poniatowska.

8. According to Poniatowska, who got her data from the Secretaría de Gobernación, there were 160 spiritualist temples in the Federal District, although she claims that the devotees never totally break with Catholicism. She says the "Obra Espiritual was always obscure and often incomprehensible" to her and they didn't like being questioned. "They talked of Allan Kardec, of his father and protector Manuel Antonio Mesmer, and I thus discovered Franz Anton Mesmer, the founder of Mesmerism and the famous 'magnetic stick,' as well as the hypnosis experiments that Dr. Charcot practiced on schizophrenics in La Salpetrière." Poniatowska notes that there is difference between middle-class spiritualism and the *espiritualistas* of the lower classes. Luz de Oriente is one of the Mexican spirits who obeys Roque Rojas or Father Elías. Roque Rojas, "who be-

came Father Elías in 1866, is the founder of the *espiritualismo*." She then goes on to describe Jesusa's baptism into this church, after which she had a vision. Jesusa was later to leave the Church because people looked down on her. (Poniatowska, unpublished paper.)

9. See Jean Franco, "The Incorporation of Women: A Comparison of North American and Mexican Popular Narrative," in Tania Modleski, ed., *Studies in Entertainment: Critical Approaches to Mass Culture* (Bloomington: Indiana University Press, 1986).

10. María Luisa Puga, *Cuando el aire era azul* (Mexico City: Siglo XXI, 1980).

11. Margo Glantz, *Las genealogías* (Mexico City: Martín Casillas, 1981).

12. See Gilles Deleuze and Felix Guattari, "What is a Minor Literature?" in *Kafka: Towards a Minor Literature*, Dana Polan, tr. (Minneapolis: University of Minnesota Press, 1986).

13. Angeles Mastreta, *Arráncame la vida* (Mexico City: Océano, 1985).

14. Carmen Boullosa, *Mejor desaparece* (Mexico City: Océano, 1987).

15. Carmen Boullosa, in an interview, "*Mejor desaparece* es un mundo loco," *La Jornada* (Nov. 14, 1987), no. 148, p. 8.

16. See Moema Viezzer, ed., "*Si me permiten hablar*," *testimonio de Domitila, una mujer de las minas de Bolivia* (Mexico City: Siglo XXI, 1977).

17. Teresa de Barbieri, "La producción teórica feminista, *fem* (Feb.– March 1981), 4(17):7–11.

18. See special issue of *fem* dedicated to Alaide Foppa, (August–Sept. 1982), vol. 6, no. 24.

19. See Jean Franco, "Killing Priests, Nuns, Women, and Children," in Marshall Blonsky, ed., *On Signs* (Baltimore: Johns Hopkins University Press, 1985).

20. On new social movements, see Carlos Monsivais, *Entrada libre: Crónicas de la sociedad que se organiza* (Mexico City: 1988).

21. One tactic adopted by feminists to counteract these trends is the production of an alternative comic strip, *Esporádica*. I owe this information to Cynthia Steele, who closely monitors Mexican publications. There are also alternative video collectives such as Colectivo Cine Mujer, in Mexico City.

22. See especially Luisa Valenzuela, *La cola del lagarto* (Buenos Aires: 1983); in English, *The Lizard's Tail*, Gregory Rabassa, tr. (New York: Farrar, Straus and Giroux, 1983); Marta Traba, *Homérica Latina* (Bogotá: Carlos Valencia, 1979); Albalucía del Angel, *Estaba la pájara pinta, sentada en el verde limón* (Bogotá: Instituto de Cultura Colombiana, 1975); Magali García Ramos, *Felices Días Tío Sergio* (San Juan: Editorial Antillana, 1986); Rosario Ferré, *Maldito Amor* (Mexico City: Nueva Imagen, 1986): Cristina Peri Rossi, *La nave de los locos* (Barcelona: Seix Barral, 1984). No evaluation is intended here, nor is this list representative of writing by women. These are all novels, however, that parody the national allegory.

23. See Elena Poniatowska, "La literatura de las mujeres es parte de la literatura de los oprimidos," in a special issue of *fem* on literary criticism, (Feb.–March 1982), vol. 6, no. 21.

24. However, Cynthia Steele, in "Committed Feminism and Feminist Commitment in the Criticism of Latin American Literature" (unpublished paper), points out the dependence of women writers on domestic labor, and comments on the relationship of the upper-class writer to the domestic servant, which seems transposed into "testimonial" narratives such as those by Poniatowska.

INDEX